Further

of

WUTHERING

HEIGHTS

Selected Essays

Graeme Tytler

The manufacturer's authorised representative in the EU
for product safety is Authorised Rep Compliance Ltd,
71 Lower Baggot Street, Dublin D02 P593 Ireland (www.arccompliance.com)

Troubador Publishing Ltd
Unit E2 Airfield Business Park,
Harrison Road, Market Harborough,
Leicestershire. LE16 7UL
Tel: 0116 2792299
Email: books@troubador.co.uk
Web: www.troubador.co.uk

ISBN 978 1836283 454

British Library Cataloguing in Publication Data.
A catalogue record for this book is available from the British Library.

Printed and bound in Great Britain by 4edge Limited
Typeset in 11pt Aldine401 BT by Troubador Publishing Ltd, Leicester, UK

For Sachiko

Contents

Acknowledgements

I should like to thank most heartily the staff of Troubador Publishing — Alex Thompson, Carolina Santos, Beth Archer and Jonathan White in particular — for contributing so efficiently to the preparation of the second series of my selected essays on *Wuthering Heights*, all of which originally appeared in *Brontë Studies* under the able editorship of Amber Adams, Sarah Fanning and Claire O'Callaghan. I should also like to thank Sarah Laycock, curator at Brontë Parsonage Museum, for her help in providing the cover image. I am again most grateful to my wife Sachiko for the skills with which she brought to bear on the preliminary editing of all these essays from beginning to end; to her I most happily dedicate this book.

Preface

This book comprises the second series of my selected essays on *Wuthering Heights*, the first series having been published by Matador in 2018. A primary aim of these essays is to re-assert the idea that Catherine and Heathcliff, designated as they are all too often as transcendental creatures existing outside the confines of ordinary human society, are quite as human as any of the other characters portrayed in the novel. Some of these essays are intended to point up the author's ability to weave philosophy and metaphysics into her text; to enhance the realism of her narrative with descriptions of places and objects of local interest; to make ingenious use of her various methods of symbolism; and to present some of her minor characters with delightful comedy and humour. Of special function are the essays on Hindley Earnshaw and Joseph in particular, inasmuch as they suggest that both these characters are too complex to be satisfactorily explained by the caricatural images they are commonly known by. With these essays as well as the others included here, then, I hope I have confirmed what has doubtless been said time and again down the years, namely, that Emily Brontë deserves to be acclaimed for her multifarious gifts as a novelist as much as she is cherished for her world-famous love story.

An Appraisal of Catherine and Heathcliff's Love Relationship

Literary criticism on *Wuthering Heights* published in the last hundred years or so is conspicuous for the various ways in which Catherine and Heathcliff are bracketed together as if they were lovers practically second to none in the history of fiction.[1] Such a viewpoint has probably had much to do with their being designated now and again as transcendental figures who should not be judged by the moral standards of ordinary human society.[2] That evaluations of this kind may, however, have been largely the effect of impressionistic readings of the novel is an argument that might be legitimately put forward. Certainly the tendency to refer to Emily Brontë's masterpiece as a Gothic novel seems to have encouraged readers to ignore the fact that the narrative is deeply rooted in the world of reality, and that all the characters depicted therein are endowed with essentially human qualities

1

and dispositions. By therefore postulating that the author has her feet firmly on the ground, we may find certain critical assessments of Catherine and Heathcliff's love relationship somewhat unsatisfactory. That is why it is necessary to study it step by step in some detail, partly in conjunction with the heroine's relationship with Edgar, so that we may arrive at a rather more sober view of a bond that has all too readily been idealized over the years. I hope, then, to show that Emily's treatment of this famous love story is much more ambivalent than has been commonly assumed.

First of all, it is useful to remember that Catherine and Heathcliff's relationship is observed and recorded mainly by Nelly Dean, even if it is true that she is by no means privy to everything that goes on between the two of them, whether during their childhood or after Heathcliff's return from abroad. In any event, what emerges from Nelly's narrative is that Heathcliff remains consistently in love with Catherine both as a youngster and throughout his adulthood before, as well as after, Catherine's death, and until his own demise in April 1802.[3] Heathcliff's love of Catherine is perhaps nowhere more patent than when he is endeavouring to persuade Nelly to allow him to visit Catherine secretly at Thrushcross Grange now that he has been forbidden access there by Edgar. What is notable about Heathcliff's dialogue with Nelly is his claiming not only that he loves Catherine much more passionately than Edgar does, but that Catherine herself loves him infinitely more than she loves Edgar. This is borne out when, for example, he says to Nelly: 'You know as well as I do, that for every thought she spends on Linton, she spends a thousand on me!', and presently goes on to make the following assertion: 'If [Edgar] loved with all the powers of his puny being, he couldn't love as much in eighty years, as I could in a day', supplementing his disparagement of Edgar with these words: 'He is scarcely a degree dearer to her than her dog, or her horse — It is not in him to be loved like me, how can she love in him what he has not?'[4] We also note the

2

extent to which, amid these utterances, Heathcliff claims to know precisely what is going on in Catherine's mind. Examples of this are manifest when, in response to Nelly's reluctance to help him to fulfil his intention of visiting Catherine, he says: 'It is a foolish story to assert that Catherine could not bear to see me'; and, again, when he says: 'I guess, by her silence as much as any thing, what she feels'.[5] There can be little doubt that, presumptuous and even fallacious as they may be adjudged, all such sentiments have probably done much to encourage many readers, scholarly or otherwise, to look upon Heathcliff and Catherine as ideal lovers. Hence there is need at this point to examine how far Catherine's own feelings for Heathcliff may be said to correspond to those expressed by the latter in the foregoing.

To begin with, it is almost certain that Heathcliff's overweening confidence in Catherine's love for him is due principally to his having last seen her, when, previous to his showdown with Edgar in the Grange kitchen, she viciously insulted her husband for his fecklessness, at the same time as she spoke favourably of himself, especially for his manly virtues. Hardly less important for Heathcliff has surely been the enthusiasm with which Catherine has welcomed his unexpected arrival at the Grange after a three-year absence. And though Heathcliff does not witness every facet of Catherine's delight in his return, it is none the less difficult to escape our initial impression as readers that she seems by now to be much more on Heathcliff's side than on Edgar's. This we already gather when, in response to Edgar's suggestion that the visitor be entertained in the kitchen, Catherine insists on his being introduced into the parlour, telling Nelly to set two tables there, 'one for your master and Miss Isabella, being gentry; the other for Heathcliff and myself, being of the lower orders', and then, with further sardonic irony, addressing Edgar thus: 'Will that please you, dear? Or must I have a fire lighted elsewhere? If so, give directions'.[6] Catherine's joy in Heathcliff's return is further confirmed by her waking Nelly '[a]bout the middle of the night' because, as she says, 'I want some living creature to keep me company in my happiness!',[7] later going so far as to tell Nelly that '[t]he event of this evening has reconciled me to God and humanity!'[8] Noteworthy, too, are Catherine's complaints about Edgar's jealousy having been aroused by her complimentary remarks about Heathcliff — a jealousy quite obvious when she speaks of Edgar's 'melting into tears' because she said that Heathcliff is 'now worthy of any one's regard', and that it 'would honour the first gentleman in the country to be his friend'.[9] It is, moreover, in the same context that Catherine alludes to those problems of her marriage already known to the reader, as, for example, when she describes Edgar and Isabella as 'spoiled children' whom, she thinks, 'a smart chastisement might improve'.[10]

Although all such talk may have encouraged some readers to believe that Heathcliff has by now more or less replaced Edgar in Catherine's affections, it is still helpful to be reminded that, prior to the showdown in the Grange kitchen, Catherine has scolded Heathcliff there for making amorous advances to Isabella. Further, the fact that she has later gone on to encourage a possible marriage between Heathcliff and Isabella — a marriage which, as she says to Nelly, Edgar himself 'should approve' — would suggest that she was scarcely, if at all, jealous of this relationship.[11] Indeed, Catherine's apparent lack of jealousy in that respect is probably what seems to have incensed Heathcliff enough to induce him to complain about what he has long had on his mind, namely, that she has treated him 'infernally'.[12] Catherine's uncomprehending reaction to this complaint is such as to suggest that, unlike him, she did not regard their relationship before his flight from the Heights as an amorous one. This was already in part evident earlier when, anxious at the thought of Heathcliff's having overheard her saying that it would degrade her to marry him, she sought to console herself partly by asking Nelly: 'He does not know what being in love is?'.[13] But what is notable about Catherine's scolding of Heathcliff is that Edgar, informed as he has been by Nelly about what led up to it, puts an entirely negative construction upon it simply by declaring to Nelly that it is 'disgraceful' that Catherine 'should own [Heathcliff] for a friend, and force his company on me!'[14] Ironically enough, angered as she has been by his malicious insinuations about her relationship with Heathcliff, and by her (mistaken) assumption that he has eavesdropped on her altercation with the latter, Catherine will presently reproach Edgar for 'blind ingratitude' inasmuch as he is quite unaware that she was, as she assures him, 'defending you, and yours', and wishes, as she adds, that Heathcliff 'may flog you sick, for daring to think an evil thought of me!'[15] With these words in mind, we come to realize that, notwithstanding the favourable reference to Heathcliff, Catherine's resentment towards Edgar, an attitude she will further display through her vicious insults of his character, derives almost entirely from his being, as she believes, completely, even wilfully, oblivious to her loyalty to him. Such loyalty she has already hinted at when, having ordered Heathcliff to 'let Isabella alone',[16] she has added: 'I beg you will, unless you are tired of being received here, and wish Linton to draw the bolts against you!'[17] She will presently confirm this loyalty when she goes on to utter this warning: '[Q]uarrel with Edgar if you please, Heathcliff, and deceive his sister; you'll hit on exactly the most efficient method of revenging yourself on me'.[18]

Although Catherine subsequently draws a comparison between Edgar and Heathcliff as regards manliness, and that to the distinct advantage of the latter during the showdown shortly after Heathcliff's return, it would be erroneous to assume that she, therefore, loves Heathcliff more than she loves Edgar. On the contrary, it is almost certain that her vicious talk and behaviour in the Grange kitchen are but a continuance of her rage against Edgar for thinking that she has been a disloyal, not to say an unfaithful, wife to him. True, it may be tempting for the reader to think that Catherine's constant insistence on having Heathcliff as a friend is a sort of cover-up for her intention to enter into an affair with him. Such an intention is, doubtless, what Edgar suspects her of cherishing. Yet it is necessary at this juncture to recall that, just before telling Lockwood of Heathcliff's sudden return, Nelly has asserted her belief that, in spite of the early problems of their marriage, Catherine and Edgar 'were really in possession of deep and growing happiness'.[19] These words will be somewhat echoed later when Isabella counters Heathcliff's asseveration that '[I]t is not in [Edgar] to be loved like me' with this retort: 'Catherine and Edgar are as fond of each other as any two people can be!'[20], notwithstanding her having earlier told Catherine that she loved Heathcliff 'more than ever you loved Edgar'.[21] This assertion might confirm what the reader has perhaps already surmised, that is to say, that Catherine is essentially lukewarm in her love for Edgar. This interpretation may be said to be related to Nelly's having earlier stated that Catherine and Edgar's growing marital happiness 'ended when circumstances caused each to feel that the one's interest was not the chief consideration in the other's thoughts'.[22] The trouble with the word 'ended' is its suggesting that Catherine had therefore somehow become fully committed to Heathcliff.

There are, however, various contexts in Nelly's narrative to indicate the quite extraordinary extent to which Catherine remains committed to Edgar as his spouse. Thus, for example, it is noteworthy that despite her ironic response to Edgar's suggesting that the newly-returned Heathcliff be entertained in the kitchen rather than in the parlour, Catherine has nonetheless been concerned to involve Edgar fully in her delight at Heathcliff's return. This is obvious enough when, 'flinging her arms round his neck', she says: 'Oh, Edgar, Edgar! [...] Oh, Edgar, darling! Heathcliff's come back — he is!', at the same time as she 'tightened her embrace to a squeeze'.[23] Although such affectionate talk and questions on Catherine's part may have been understood by some readers as a kind of transference of her love for Heathcliff, they could be just as plausibly understood as genuine signs of her love for Edgar. This is further underlined by the fact that, when Heathcliff 'appeared at the door [of the parlour]', Catherine 'took both his hands, and led him to Linton; and then she seized Linton's reluctant fingers and crushed them into his'.[24] These gestures almost certainly form part of Catherine's attempt not only to encourage Edgar to be friends with Heathcliff, but, more importantly, to make him realize that she herself regards Heathcliff first and foremost as a friend. That this is sincerely meant will be later corroborated when, having expressed her anger with Edgar for his unjust accusations of her in respect of Heathcliff, she says to Nelly:

> Well, if I cannot keep Heathcliff for my friend — if Edgar will be mean and jealous — I'll try to break their hearts by breaking my own. That will be a prompt way of finishing all, when I am pushed to extremity! But it's a deed to be reserved for a forlorn hope — I'd not take Linton by surprise with it.[25]

As it happens, Catherine's relationship with the recently-returned Heathcliff seems to have clearly begun as a friendship, marked as it is at first, thanks to Edgar's sanction, by walks they take together, with or without Isabella's company, as well as by Heathcliff's visits to the Grange. Although Nelly knows nothing about the conversations that take place between Catherine and Heathcliff during their walks together, it may be assumed that such conversations turn on his current aims and ambitions rather than on the subject of love. This is in part suggested by the very grim impression that Catherine seems to have derived of Heathcliff's character through his talk in general. Indeed, this impression she will later seek to convey to Isabella in order to put her off her infatuation with him, and might even make some readers wonder how Catherine herself could be in love with such a man. Nevertheless, all goes well outwardly at the Grange and elsewhere, that is, until Catherine upbraids Heathcliff for wooing Isabella. Still, in spite of her scolding him for this misdemeanour, Catherine will later appear to be again very much on Heathcliff's side, at the same time as she is utterly contemptuous of Edgar. It is, moreover, probably the subsequent showdown between the two men, not to say her apparent inability to settle for one of them, that may be said to have caused the brain fever with which Catherine is afflicted soon afterwards. The earliest symptom of this illness is the black-out she undergoes in her bedroom, during which, as she tells Nelly, she thought she 'was enclosed in the oak-panelled bed at home' with 'some great grief which, just waking, [she] could not recollect —', namely, a grief that had arisen 'from the separation that Hindley had ordered between [her] and Heathcliff'.[26] Catherine presently supplements this reference to the Heathcliff of her childhood with a similar one when she says to Nelly:

> But supposing at twelve years old I had been wrenched from the Heights, and every early association, and my all in all, as Heathcliff was at that time, and been converted at a stroke into Mrs. Linton, the lady of Thrushcross Grange, and the wife of a stranger; an exile, and outcast, thenceforth, from what had been my world — You may fancy a glimpse of the abyss where I grovelled![27]

Significant, too, in this context are the visual and aural hallucinations she experiences during her delirium about her early years with Heathcliff, whereby, among their sundry outdoor activities together, and in characteristic domination of him at that time, she challenges him to defy the ghosts wandering over the graves of Gimmerton Kirk.[28]

If Catherine's foregoing memories of Heathcliff in childhood may have been understood by many readers to be indubitable testimonies to her love for him, not to mention her apparent regret about marrying Edgar, it is worth bearing in mind that she makes no spontaneous mention whatsoever of Heathcliff *qua* the newly-returned adult anywhere in the immediate aftermath of the showdown between Edgar and him. It is, of course, possible that, when having appeared in the parlour, where Catherine has taken temporary refuge after the showdown, Edgar has asked her if she 'intend[s] to continue [her] intimacy' with Heathcliff. Her following angry reaction to this question might suggest that she is again more on Heathcliff's side than on Edgar's: '[F]or mercy's sake, let us hear no more of it now! Your cold blood cannot be worked into a fever — your veins are full of ice-water — but mine are boiling, and the sight of such chillness makes them dance'.[29] On the other hand, those words might also imply that she is still embarrassed at the thought that Edgar suspects her of adulterous intentions. Again, when Edgar, seeing Catherine later in a delirious state in her bedroom, asks much the same question more pointedly thus: 'Am I nothing to you, any more? Do you love that wretch Heath—', her following angry response might be considered just as ambivalent as her earlier one:

> Hush, this moment! You mention that name and I end the matter, instantly, by a spring from the window! What you touch at present, you may have; but my soul will be on that hill-top before you lay hands on me again. I don't want you, Edgar; I'm past wanting you... Return to your books... I'm glad you possess a consolation, for all you had in me is gone.[30]

What is ironic about these sentiments, however, is that amid her apparent rejection of Edgar, Catherine is clearly evincing the same resentment she expressed earlier, namely, her resentment of Edgar's having neglected her while she was sequestered in her bedroom for three days. Moreover, when, just after opening her bedroom door, she tells Nelly, in a manner that betokens her attention-seeking nature, that she is dying 'since no one cares anything about [her]' before going on to murmur these words: 'No, I'll not die — he'd be glad — he does not love me at all — he would never miss me!', it is perfectly obvious that by 'he' she means Edgar, not Heathcliff.[31]

Catherine's annoyance at being neglected by Edgar may seem odd in view of the ways in which she has roundly insulted him recently. It is, moreover, her very insults that have probably prompted most readers to take it for granted that she does not love Edgar at all; indeed, that she only really loves Heathcliff. But, as we have seen, her rudeness to Edgar is surely due to his having adjudged her a disloyal wife and, possibly, to early symptoms of the brain fever she is soon to succumb to. Thus when she says to Edgar in the parlour, 'I require to be let alone! [...] I demand it! Don't you see I can scarcely stand? Edgar, you — you leave me!', such a request seems hardly intended as an insult, but, rather, as a desperate attempt to warn him that she is truly in a state of mental disorder.[32] It is, no doubt, easy enough to conclude from Catherine's ill-humoured language that she is fundamentally unhappy with her marriage, and increasingly so since Heathcliff's return. Yet it is necessary to point out that, far from meaning to end her marriage to Edgar, Catherine shows in a number of contexts how much she defers to him and is even somewhat in awe of him. Thus, for example, we are told that she 'deemed it judicious to moderate her expressions of pleasure in receiving [Heathcliff]'.[33] Sometimes, too, she seems afraid of Edgar's dominance of her, as, for example, when she tells Nelly: 'I couldn't explain to Edgar how certain I felt of having a fit, or going raging mad, if he persisted in teasing me!'[34] And, again, as if dreading to speak to him herself, she asks Nelly to say to Edgar: '[I]f you see him again to-night, that I'm in danger of being seriously ill — I wish it may prove true. He has startled and distressed me shockingly! I want to frighten him'.[35]

Nevertheless, amid her awareness of her precarious mental health at this time, Catherine shows how much she depends on Edgar's help and attention, and especially so while she is convalescing after her brain fever.[36] For example, after a bed has been set up for her in a room on the same floor as the parlour, we learn that she was 'strong enough to move from one to the other *leaning on Edgar's arm*' (emphasis added).[37] And though in her convalescence Catherine exhibits a petulant impatience with Edgar for 'trying to entice her attention to some subject which had formerly been her amusement', we have been previously informed that 'in her better moods [she] endured his efforts placidly, only showing their uselessness by now and then suppressing a wearied sigh, and *checking him at last with the saddest of smiles and kisses*' (emphasis added).[38] Such a detail clearly indicates the measure in which Catherine is still dogged by her mental ill-health at the same time as it gives no small hint of her affection for Edgar. This we have already gathered when, to Edgar's suggesting that she would be cured if she were 'a mile or two up those hills' where 'the air blows so sweetly', Catherine tenderly replies: 'I shall never be there, but once more! [...] and then you'll leave me, and I shall remain, for ever. Next spring you'll long again to have me under this roof, and you'll look back and think you were happy to-day'.[39] It seems appropriate, then, that amid these lyrical utterances between husband and wife, Nelly should speak of the importance of Catherine's being 'waited on'[40] at this time because she is expecting a child, thereby ironically reminding the reader that it was on the very night of Heathcliff's return that Catherine may be said to have confirmed her love for Edgar by going to his room and, presumably, conceiving the second Catherine.

It is, however, interesting to note that, delighted though she is with 'a handful of crocuses' which Edgar has put on her pillow one morning, the convalescent Catherine exclaims: 'These are the earliest flowers at the Heights! [...] They remind me of soft thaw winds, and warm sunshine'.[41] Such words are significant for having a certain connection with the hallucinations she has lately had about the Heights during her delirium and, more particularly, about her playful activities with Heathcliff during their childhood; indeed, it is through such references that Catherine amply makes plain that she has been at her very happiest while living at the Heights, not least on account of her close friendship with Heathcliff. Such is Catherine's loyalty to the latter at that time that, despite already being engaged to Edgar, she actually threatens to go with Heathcliff, should Hindley turn him out of the house.[42] Yet whereas it is abundantly clear from early on in their relationship that Heathcliff is in love with Catherine, it is doubtful that, for all her staunch support of him, whether before or after her betrothal to Edgar, she is ever equally enamoured of Heathcliff. We sense this not only when she has returned home after her five-week sojourn at the Grange, but also when, during an earlier consultation with Nelly, she defines the nature of her love for Heathcliff (as distinct from her love for Edgar) through her fanciful metaphors, her identification with him, and her references to him as a phenomenon occupying her mind, whereby she seems to lose sight of him as a separate flesh-and-blood being of a distinct individuality.[43] Again, the fact that Catherine only a short time later tells Nelly that she has 'forgotten'[44] what she has said about Heathcliff (and Edgar) cannot but underline the dubious, not to say nonsensical, quality of those utterances.[45] Further, when she admits to using her marriage to Edgar as a means of helping Heathcliff to rise socially, there is a certain ambiguity about some of her statements. This we sense when, for example, she says of Heathcliff: 'He'll be as much to me as he has been all his lifetime. Edgar must shake off his antipathy, and tolerate him, at least. He will when he learns my true feelings towards him'.[46] And even though Catherine vows that '[e]very Linton on the face of the earth might melt into nothing, before I could consent to forsake Heathcliff'[47], such words, like her other affirmative ones about Heathcliff, are by no means necessarily indications of erotic love on Catherine's part. Rather, it would appear they are tokens of the friendship she has long enjoyed with him, mainly in the form of hegemony over him, as well as foreshadowings of her concern to maintain that friendship after his return.

But over and above Catherine's more or less egotistical sentiments discussed above, and notwithstanding that they have been widely interpreted as veritable testimonies to her (erotic) love for Heathcliff, it is necessary to point out the extent to which she seems to be quite passive in both her love relationships; in other words, that she seems to be much more concerned to be loved than to love. Certainly, the peculiar nature of Catherine's talk about her love for her two men has little, if anything, of the passion with which, say, Isabella speaks of her love for Heathcliff.[48] We note, for example, that one reason why Catherine claims to love Edgar is, as she tells Nelly, 'because he loves me'.[49] That she is, moreover, perfectly confident of Edgar's love as her husband is quite evident when, on the night of Heathcliff's return, she somewhat frivolously answers Nelly's defence of Edgar and Isabella by saying: 'I tell you, I have such faith in Linton's love that I believe I might kill him, and he wouldn't wish to retaliate'.[50] The same frivolity may be felt when, in a garbled version of what Isabella has actually said to her, she informs Heathcliff thus: 'Isabella swears that the love Edgar has for me is nothing to that she entertains for you'.[51] Frivolous, too, is when, having just opened the door of her bedroom, where she has been cut off for three days, and then gathered from Nelly's refusal to inform Edgar that she will 'die of hunger'[52], Catherine utters the following egotistical words: 'How strange! I thought, though everybody hated and despised each other, *they could not avoid loving me* — and they have all turned to enemies in a few hours' (emphasis added).[53] A similar egotism may be noted even in some of her statements to Heathcliff. Thus, for example, when having just returned home after five weeks at the Grange,

Catherine is puzzled enough by Heathcliff's elusiveness to ask him if he has 'forgotten [her]?'[54] Again, when hardly able to believe that Heathcliff has returned from abroad as a physical reality, she tells him that he does not deserve the welcome he has just received, before adding: 'To be absent and silent for three years, and *never to think of me!*' (emphasis added),[55] the presumptuousness of which accusations seems but confirmed by Heathcliff's plausible reply: 'A little more than you have thought of me!'[56]

Heathcliff's answer is one of many illustrations of his continuous love for Catherine, adumbrating as it does that it will be indeed by dint of constantly thinking of her for some eighteen years after her death that his own life will end in partial insanity.[57] But as has been suggested above, we cannot be quite sure about the nature of Catherine's love for Heathcliff beyond the assumption that it seems to be much the same sort of affection that she cherished for him during their childhood. We surmise this even at their last tryst, which, though commonly understood as unmistakable evidence of their presentation as supreme lovers, should, despite their passionate talk and embraces, be considered hardly less memorable for the fact that Catherine remains throughout not only somewhat mentally unbalanced but also in a moribund condition. Further, it is not without significance that, early in their tryst, Catherine should say in reaction to Heathcliff's intense stare of her: 'What now? [...] You and Edgar have broken my heart, Heathcliff! And you both come to bewail the deed to me, as if you were the people to be pitied!'[58] Such words plainly suggest the dilemma she continues to be in, even at this crucial stage, between the two men in her life. Again, for those readers who look upon Catherine and Heathcliff as lovers second to none in the history of fiction, it might be averred that, even after the latter's return from abroad, there is practically nothing in the narrative to indicate that Catherine has at any time been unfaithful to Edgar or intended to terminate her marriage to him. Further, however much we may have doubts about the quality of Catherine's affection for Edgar, we should recall that, apart from showing how dependent she is on him for her security and well-being, it is almost certainly, if only implicitly, through Edgar, and not through Heathcliff, that she has discovered, albeit somewhat immaturely, what it is to be in love.[59] Similarly, those readers who are, or have been, convinced that Catherine and Heathcliff are ultimately united in death, might well be reminded that their conviction is perforce based on mere superstition in the form of the optical illusions attributed to Joseph and a shepherd boy as well as to other local inhabitants in the very last chapter.[60] Finally, it is hoped that those readers who look upon Heathcliff and Catherine as quasi-divine creatures exempt from the rules and codes of ordinary society may, by virtue of my discussions above, be persuaded to recognize that they are, especially with their sometimes glaring moral failings and shortcomings, after all just as human as all the other characters portrayed in Emily Brontë's wonderfully realistic novel.[61]

Brontë Studies, 47/3 (2022)

Notes

1 Among numerous critiques of this kind, see Halliwell Sutcliffe, 'The Spirit of the Moors', *Brontë Society Transactions*, 2 (1903), 174-190; J. C. Smith, 'Emily Brontë: A Reconsideration', *Essays and Studies*, 5 (1914), 109; Laura L. Hinkley, *The Brontës: Charlotte and Emily* (London: Hammond, Hammond & Co. Ltd, 1947), p. 248; Georges Bataille, *La Littérature et le Mal* (Paris: Gallimard, 1957), p. 12; Frederick R. Karl, *An Age of Fiction. The Nineteenth-Century British Novel* (New York: Farrar, Straus & Giroux, 1966), p. 81; Gordon Williams, 'The Problems of Passion in *Wuthering Heights*', *Trivium*, 7 (1972), 45; Lord David Cecil, 'Fresh Thoughts on the Brontës', *Brontë Society Transactions*, 16 (1973), 172; Jenny Oldfield, *Jane Eyre and Wuthering Heights: Study Guide* (London: Heinemann, 1976), p. 73; Raymond Williams, *The English Novel from Dickens to Lawrence* (London: Chatto & Windus, 1984), p. 64; Robert K. Wallace, *Emily Brontë and Beethoven: Romantic Equilibrium in Fiction and Music* (Athens, GA: University of Georgia Press, 1986), p. 152; Joanne E. Rea, 'A Note on Freudian Symbolism in *Wuthering Heights*', *Cahiers Victoriens et Edouardiens*, 25 (1987), 26; Emily Brontë, *Wuthering Heights,* introd. by Katherine Frank (London: J. M. Dent, 1991), p. xi; [Alistair McGowan], *BBC. The Big Read: Book of Books*, ed. by Mark Harrison and Hannah Beckerman (London: Dorling Kindersley, 2003), pp. 54-55.

2 See, for example, Emily Jane Brontë, *Wuthering Heights*, introd. by Alan Hodge (London: Hamish Hamilton, 1950), p. v; Dorothy Van Ghent, *The English Novel: Form and Function* (New York: Holt, Reinhart & Winston, 1953), p. 164; Georges Bataille, *La Littérature et le Mal* (Paris: Gallimard, 1957), p. 15; Arnold Kettle, 'Emily Brontë: *Wuthering Heights*', in *Wuthering Heights. Texts, Sources, Criticism*, ed. by Thomas Moser (New York, Chicago,

San Francisco and Atlanta: Harcourt Brace & World Inc., 1962), p. 193; Emily Brontë, *Wuthering Heights*, ed. by Philip Henderson & introd. by Margaret Lane (London: J. M. Dent, 1963), p. viii; C. Day Lewis, 'Emily Brontë and Freedom' in Emily Brontë, *Wuthering Heights*, ed. by William M. Sale, Jr. (New York: Norton, 1963), p. 367; Claire Rosenfeld, 'The Shadow Within: The Conscious and Unconscious Use of the Double', *Daedalus*, 92 (1963), 330; L. P. Hartley, 'Emily Brontë in Gondal and Gaaldine', *Brontë Society Transactions*, 14 (1965), 7; Wendy A. Craik, *The Brontë Novels* (London: Methuen, 1968), passim; John Hewish, *Emily Brontë: A Critical and Biographical Study* (London: Macmillan, 1969), p. 140; David Sonstroem, '*Wuthering Heights* and the Limits of Vision', *Publications of the Modern Language Association of America*, 86 (1971), 57; Mary Visick, 'The Genesis of *Wuthering Heights*', in *Emily Brontë: A Critical Anthology*, ed. by Jean-Pierre Petit (Harmondsworth: Penguin Books, 1973), p. 174; Emily Brontë, *Wuthering Heights*, ed. by Graham Handley (London: Macmillan Education Ltd., 1983), p. xiii; Frank Goodridge, *Emily Brontë: Wuthering Heights* (London: Edward Arnold, 1985), p. 28; Graham Holderness, *Wuthering Heights* (Milton Keynes and Philadelphia: Open University Press, 1985), p. 3; Muriel Spark and Derek Stanford, *Emily Brontë. Her Life and Works* (London: Arrow Books Ltd., 1985), p. 266; Cates Baldridge, 'Voyeuristic Rebellion: Lockwood's Dreams and the Reader of *Wuthering Heights*', *Studies in the Novel*, 20 (1988), 286; Victoria Moreland, '"It has devoured my existence": Emotion and Personality in *Wuthering Heights*', *Brontë Society Transactions*, 19 (1988), 263; Rod Mengham, *Wuthering Heights* (Harmondsworth: Penguin Books, 1989), p. 101; Emily Brontë, *Wuthering Heights*, introd. by Katherine Frank (New York: Knopf Doubleday, 1991), p. xvi; Linda H. Peterson, *Emily Brontë: Wuthering Heights* (Boston, MA: Bedford Books, 1992), p. 10; Robert Barnard, 'What Does

Wuthering Heights Mean?', *Brontë Society Transactions*, 23 (1998), 112; Stevie Davies, *Emily Brontë* (Plymouth: Northcote House Publishers Ltd., 1998), p. 39; *Emily Brontë. Wuthering Heights. A Reader's Guide to Essential Criticism*, ed. by Patsy Stoneman (Cambridge: Icon Books Ltd., 2000), p. 55; Q. D. Leavis, 'A Fresh Approach to *Wuthering Heights*', in *Emily Brontë*, ed. by Patsy Stoneman, p. 58; Emily Brontë, *Wuthering Heights*, ed. by Ian Jack and introd. by Helen Small (Oxford: Oxford University Press, 2009), p. ix.

3   For Heathcliff's love of Catherine in his boyhood, see especially Emily Brontë. 1847. *Wuthering Heights*, ed. by Ian Jack and Patsy Stoneman (Oxford: Oxford University Press, 1998), pp. 44, 60, 61, 69, 70.

4   Brontë, pp. 131-32.

5   Ibid., p. 135; see also Brontë, pp. 42, 43, 146.

6   Brontë, 84.

7   Ibid., p. 86.

8   Ibid., p. 88.

9   Ibid., p. 87.

10 Ibid.

11 Brontë, p. 99.

12 Ibid.

13 Brontë, p. 72.

14 Ibid., p. 101.

15 Ibid., p. 102.

16 Ibid., p. 99.

17 Ibid.

18 Brontë, p. 100.

19 Ibid., p. 81; Catherine and Edgar's marital happiness is also somewhat hinted at when, about to announce Heathcliff's unexpected arrival at the Grange, Nelly is hesitant to do so because she notices the couple looking at 'the valley of Gimmerton' out of an open window in the Grange parlour thus: 'Both the room, and its occupants, and the scene they gazed on, looked wondrously peaceful. I shrank reluctantly from performing my errand' (Brontë, p. 83).

20 Brontë, p. 132.

21 Ibid., p. 90.

22 Ibid., p. 81.

23 Ibid., pp. 83-84.

24 Ibid., p. 84.

25 Ibid., p. 104.

26 Ibid., p. 110.

27 Ibid., p. 111. These words are, of course, an ironic reminder that, during her consultation with Nelly in Chapter 9, Catherine said this: 'I've no more business to marry Edgar Linton than I have to be in heaven' (Brontë, p. 71).

28 See Brontë, pp. 111-112.

29 Ibid., p. 104.

30 Ibid., p. 113.

31 Ibid., p. 106.

32 Ibid., pp. 104-05.

33 Ibid., p. 88.

34 Ibid., p. 110.

35 Ibid., p. 103. In this connection, it is interesting to recall Edgar's effective control of Catherine when he forbids her to go down to greet the newly-arrived Heathcliff and orders Nelly to do so instead. See Brontë, pp. 84-86.

36 Catherine will surely also have been aware of Edgar's tireless care for her during her second delirium. See Brontë, pp. 116, 118.

37 Brontë, p. 119.

38 Ibid., p. 138.

39 Ibid., p. 118.

40 Ibid., p. 119.

41 Ibid., p. 118.

42 See ibid., p. 77.

43 See ibid., pp. 72-73. Catherine's tendency to regard Heathcliff in the form of a mental image is shown even at this last tryst when, noticing him standing away from her on the hearth, she says: 'Oh, you see, Nelly! he would not relent a moment, to keep me out of the grave! *That* is how I'm loved! Well, never mind! That is not *my* Heathcliff. I shall love mine yet; and take him with me — he's in my soul' (Brontë, p. 141). For useful discussions on Catherine's inability to see Heathcliff as an identity separate from her own, see Bernard J. Paris, '"Hush, hush! He's a human being": A Psychological Approval to Heathcliff', *Women and Literature*, 2 (1981), 101-117; and Elizabeth R. Napier, 'The Problem of Boundaries in *Wuthering Heights*', *Philological Quarterly*, 63 (1984), 103-104.

44 Brontë, p. 74.

45 Nelly herself refers to such talk as 'nonsense' (Brontë, p. 73).

46 Brontë, p. 72.

47 Ibid., p. 72.

48 See ibid., pp. 89-92, 106.

49 Ibid., p. 69.

50 Ibid., p. 87.

51 Ibid., p. 93.

52 Brontë, p. 107.

53 Ibid.

54 Brontë, p. 47.

55 Ibid., p. 85.

56 Brontë, p. 85.

57 For an account of Heathcliff's partial insanity, see Graeme Tytler, 'Heathcliff's Monomania: an Anachronism in *Wuthering Heights*', *Brontë Society Transactions*, 20.6 (1992), 331-43. Heathcliff's monomania seems to have been caused chiefly by the fact that Catherine did not mention his name on her deathbed. See Brontë, p. 147.

58 Brontë, pp. 139-40.

59 For a similar viewpoint, see Vincent Buckley, 'Passion and Control in *Wuthering Heights*', *Southern Review* (University of Adelaide), 1 (1964), 17.

60 See Brontë, p. 299.

61 As regards such failings and shortcomings, it is enough to point

not only to Catherine's unkindness to Isabella as well as her tendency to tell lies, but also to Heathcliff's cruelty to Isabella, Linton Heathcliff and the second Catherine.

The Presentation of
the First Catherine in
Wuthering Heights

A survey of literary criticism published on *Wuthering Heights* during the past several decades shows the extraordinary extent to which the first Catherine has been loved and admired by a good many Brontë scholars over the years. Some of these scholars have gone so far as to deem Catherine a kind of transcendental figure and even to declare her the moral centre of the novel.[1] Whether or not other Brontë scholars and general readers would agree with such assessments or, for that matter, with negative opinions of Catherine, would, of course, depend on the evidence available to support the arguments put forward. All this may, then, help to explain why it seems eminently worthwhile to consider assessments or opinions of Catherine partly in the light of a detailed examination of her presentation in the novel both during her lifetime and in the years following her death, such as I intend to carry out here. This endeavour necessarily entails taking account of the author's portrayal of the secondary narrator, namely, Nelly Dean, whose narrative is usefully enhanced by incorporating not only the comments made about Catherine by some of the other characters portrayed, but also the utterances of Catherine herself. It is thus that I hope to suggest that Catherine should be understood as a normal human being, if also as a rather unusual kind of fictional heroine.

It is interesting to note first of all that, notwithstanding her complimentary remarks about Catherine's beauty and vitality in girlhood such as might be seen befitting a budding heroine, Nelly nevertheless harbours a fundamentally critical attitude towards her throughout the first half of her narrative.[2] As she admits to Lockwood: 'I own I did not like her, after her infancy was past' (Brontë 1998, 58). And though Nelly is quite supportive of her and Heathcliff while they are being subjected to Hindley's tyranny, she seems to justify her dislike of Catherine by, for example, giving accounts of her domineering over her fellow youngsters, of her inveterate naughtiness to her father and other members of her household, of her frivolous laughter when being upbraided for her misdemeanours, of her tendency to resort to tears in order to have her own way, and so on.[3] Much more serious in Nelly's eyes, it seems, is Catherine's behaviour after she has become acquainted with the Linton family, notably on the occasion Edgar Linton has come to Wuthering Heights for his rendezvous with her. Thus it is during this meeting that Nelly both witnesses and suffers from Catherine's wilful behaviour, manifest as it is through her physical violence and her blatant lies.[4] All this is enough to prompt Edgar to walk out on his relationship with her once and for all, and for Nelly herself to encourage him, albeit in vain, to do so by calling out to him thus: 'Miss is dreadfully wayward, sir! [...] As bad as any marred child — you'd better be riding home, or else she will be sick, only to grieve us' (Brontë 1998, 64). It is, no doubt, owing partly to Nelly's advice which has an opposite effect, and partly to Catherine's self-pitying tears that Edgar rescinds his decision to leave.

The fact that this curious episode ends with the couple becoming betrothed is somewhat ironic, and all the more so when Catherine consults Nelly as to whether or not she has been right to accept Edgar's proposal of marriage. Catherine's dependency on Nelly for advice in this respect is perhaps understandable enough in so far as it is sought by someone aged only fifteen who has no one else in her household to turn to for such help. So dependent on Nelly has Catherine become that, even at the age of eighteen, she insists, quite against the housekeeper's wishes, on her accompanying her to Thrushcross Grange on her marriage to Edgar. That Catherine's reliance on Nelly as an indispensable confidante is sometimes excessive may be seen when, having rather roughly woken her up in the middle of the night amid her joy at Heathcliff's unexpected return to the neighbourhood earlier that day, she says this to the housekeeper: 'I cannot rest, Ellen. […] And I want some living creature to keep me company in my happiness!' (Brontë 1998, 86). It is, nevertheless, by complaining to Nelly about Edgar's tearful resentment of her praise for the newly-returned Heathcliff that Catherine clearly benefits from this nocturnal visit inasmuch as Nelly's staunch defence of Edgar (and Isabella) encourages her to be reconciled with him, and supposedly enough so for their child to be conceived that very night. Catherine's dependency on Nelly is especially conspicuous after the showdown that takes place between Edgar and Heathcliff in the Thrushcross Grange kitchen in Volume 1 Chapter 11. This we see more particularly when she complains about Edgar and asks Nelly to warn him against alienating her. By this time, however, Nelly has reached a point where she has come to regard this request as unreasonable, and continues to regard as such other similar ones from her mistress, notably when the latter has opened the door of her bedroom after three days of sequestration therein.

Catherine's extreme dependence on Nelly for help and advice betokens certain limitations in her mentality as well as her immaturity. This is not to say that Catherine lacks intelligence; on the contrary, already as a child of twelve or thirteen she appears to have been quite well-educated; and there are moments when she is quick-witted, with a gift for repartee. Her diary, which Lockwood reads in the oak-panelled room, is interesting for some of its perceptive comments. As an eighteen-year-old Catherine displays good sense, for example, in her comments about Hindley as a widower, especially when pointing out the severe risk he takes in accommodating Heathcliff at Wuthering Heights.[5] Nevertheless, it is curious to note the occasions when her intelligence is clouded by her chronic emotionalism. A striking example may be seen in her relationship with Isabella. First of all, there can be little doubt that Catherine's warning Isabella against amorous involvement with Heathcliff proves to have been sheer good sense. Yet it is simply because Isabella has called her a dog in the manger for depriving her of Heathcliff's company on their walk across the moors that, out of a spirit of vengeance, she decides to humiliate her sister-in-law by carelessly informing Heathcliff of her passionate love for him, thereby forcibly bringing about the most tragic event in the novel, namely, Isabella's unhappy marriage to him and her subsequent estrangement from Edgar. Certainly, but for Catherine's careless talk, it is very unlikely that Heathcliff would have taken advantage of Isabella to his own ends.

What is of some interest about the foregoing episode is Isabella's accusing Catherine of wanting, as she says to her, 'no one to be loved but yourself' (Brontë 1998, 90). This statement may be somewhat confirmed when, in the same context, Catherine informs Heathcliff about the passionate nature of Isabella's love for him, doing so with this garbled version of the latter's actual words: 'Isabella means that the love Edgar has for me is nothing to that she entertains for you' (Brontë 1998, 93). The passivity inherent in this utterance will be further confirmed when, amid her second delirium, Catherine, having presumed that Nelly does not like her, facetiously adds: 'How strange! I thought, though everybody hated and despised each other, they could not avoid loving me' (Brontë 1998, 107).[6] Moreover, although she is a faithful wife throughout her marriage, Catherine is strangely passive in her relationship with Edgar, overweeningly confident as she always is of his love for her, while seldom openly reciprocating that love. Indeed, at no time in her life is Catherine conspicuous for showing love, respect or tenderness to family, acquaintances or even servants. Further, we are told of her tendency to be uncomprehending of other people's feelings, as is manifest, for example, in her inability to understand her father's irritability during his final illness; Heathcliff's angry reaction to the laughter she directs at him for his scruffy appearance on her return from her five-week sojourn at Thrushcross Grange; and, most curiously, Heathcliff's accusation of her for treating him 'infernally' (Brontë 1998, 99) shortly before he took flight from Wuthering Heights.[7]

Perhaps the most glaring example of Catherine's failure to understand other people may be seen in her total unawareness of Heathcliff's amorous feelings for her. This is made quite plain when, wondering if he has overheard her consultation with Nelly about Edgar's marriage proposal, she says this to the housekeeper: 'He does not know what being in love is?' (Brontë 1998, 72) — an assumption that Nelly dismisses in much the same matter-of-fact manner with which she questions some of Catherine's reasons for marrying Edgar.[8] The same manner is markedly obvious in Nelly's reaction to Catherine's intention of using her marriage as a means of helping Heathcliff to climb the social scale. Even the somewhat pseudo-philosophical utterances Catherine resorts to towards the end of this context in order to justify her concern for Heathcliff's future, not to mention the distinction she metaphorically draws between her love for Edgar and her love for Heathcliff as well as her words: 'I *am* Heathcliff! He's always, always in my mind' (Brontë 1998, 73) — all these are roundly rejected by Nelly as follows: 'If I can make any sense of your nonsense, Miss, [...] it only goes to convince me that you are ignorant of the duties you undertake in marrying; or else, that you are a wicked, unprincipled girl' (Brontë 1998, 73). Even Catherine's talk during her last tryst with Heathcliff is dismissed as 'ravings' (Brontë 1998, 143) by Nelly, whose exasperation with her mistress's mentality has by now reached a point where, despite suddenly noticing the latter's ominous-looking physical posture, she says this to herself: 'She's fainted or dead, [...] so much the better. Far better that she should be dead, than lingering a burden and a misery-maker to all about her' (Brontë 1998, 143). In this connection, it is noteworthy that such words should have in some sense been foreshadowed in the previous chapter by Lockwood's following warning to himself in his diary: '[L]et me beware of the fascination that lurks in Catherine Heathcliff's brilliant eyes. I should be in a curious taking if I surrendered my heart to that young person, and the daughter turned out a second edition of the mother!' (Brontë 1998, 136).[9]

Nelly's exasperation with Catherine's talk and behaviour towards the end of Volume 2 Chapter 2 doubtless has much to do with the housekeeper's earlier references to the latter's having been a difficult patient, not only when, laid up with measles in childhood, she (like Hindley) 'harassed me terribly' (Brontë 1998, 33), but also when, during her first delirium, she was 'as wearisome and headstrong as a patient could be' (Brontë 1998, 78). Such exasperation with Catherine is again evident during the early symptoms of her second delirium. Thus it is while Catherine is reproving Edgar for his neglect of her during her three-day sequestration in her bedroom that Nelly tells Lockwood of her inability to 'get rid of the notion that [Catherine] acted a part of her disorder', even though, in spite of her defence of

Edgar for being 'among his books since he has no other society', she presently admits that 'should not have spoken so, if [she] had known her true condition' (Brontë 1998, 107). Through such words we are made aware, perhaps for the first time, of Nelly's tendency to show sympathy for Catherine from the time she has been diagnosed with 'a brain fever' (Brontë 1998, 118). This tendency is particularly apparent in Nelly's warm-hearted way of mentioning Edgar's care of Catherine during that illness: 'No mother could have nursed an only child more devotedly than Edgar tended her' (Brontë 1998, 118). It is, moreover, in much the same spirit that Nelly does her best to discourage Heathcliff from visiting Catherine illicitly at Thrushcross Grange, first by blaming her, 'as she deserves, for bringing [the illness] all on herself' (Brontë 1998, 130) and then by reproving Heathcliff for dashing Catherine's 'hope of a perfect recovery' (Brontë 1998, 121). Nelly's concern for Catherine's well-being is corroborated by her further attempts to discourage Heathcliff's determination to visit Catherine with these words: 'The commonest occurrence startles her painfully. [...] She's all nerves, and she couldn't bear the surprise, I'm positive' (Brontë 1998, 135). And though Nelly feels guilty about promising Heathcliff to help fulfil his intention later, she tries to excuse herself by suggesting the advantage to Catherine's health of this illicit visit to her. As she says to Lockwood: 'I thought, too, it might create a favourable crisis in Catherine's mental illness' (Brontë 1998, 136). Through this and similar sentences, then, we see, as seldom before, Catherine becoming something of a sympathetic figure in Nelly's eyes.

It is, however, after Catherine has died that Nelly's sympathy for her seems to be practically at a maximum. This we first recognize when, conscious that Heathcliff already knows, she tearfully says this to him: 'Yes, she's dead! [...] Gone to heaven, I hope, where we may, everyone, join her, if we take due warning, and leave our evil ways to follow good!' (Brontë 1998, 147). And though Heathcliff asks if at any time Catherine mentioned his name on her deathbed, Nelly ignores his question as she says this to his dismay and anger: 'Her senses never returned — she recognised nobody from the time you left her. [...] She lies with a sweet smile on her face; and her latest ideas wandered back to pleasant early days. Her life closed in a gentle dream — may she wake as kindly in the other world!' (Brontë 1998, 147). It is, nevertheless, noteworthy that, having told Lockwood that she is 'seldom otherwise than happy while watching in the chamber of death' (Brontë 1998, 145), she momentarily returns to the fundamental attitude she held towards Catherine during her lifetime: 'To be sure one might have doubted, after the wayward and impatient existence she had led, whether she merited a haven of peace at last. One might doubt in seasons of cold reflection, but not then, in the presence of her corpse. It asserted its own tranquillity, which seemed a pledge of equal quiet to its former inhabitant.' (Brontë 1998, 146).

Especially striking about Nelly's description of Catherine in death is her recourse to physiognomy, namely, the moral or psychological interpretation of the human appearance. Already before her final tryst with Heathcliff is to take place, Catherine's face has assumed the look of someone noticeably moribund as she sits at her bedroom window: 'The flash of her eyes had been succeeded by a dreamy and melancholy softness: they no longer gave the impression of looking at the objects around her; they appeared always to gaze beyond, and far beyond — you would have said out of this world —' (Brontë 1998, 137-138). Such a description is a far cry from those overwrought facial expressions that Nelly has observed earlier in Catherine, especially during the early stages of her second delirium.[10] Moreover, it will appear from Nelly's following description of her on the morning of her death that Catherine has been morally rehabilitated:

> Her brow smooth, her lids closed, her lips wearing the expression
> of a smile, no angel in heaven could be more beautiful than she
> appeared; and I partook of the infinite calm in which she lay.

My mind was never in a holier frame than while I gazed on that untroubled image of Divine rest. I instinctively echoed the words she had uttered, a few hours before. 'Incomparably beyond and above us all! Whether still on earth or now in Heaven, her spirit is at home with God!' (Brontë 1998, 145)[11]

This description of Catherine turns out to be the first of several physiognomic references to her facial features in the latter half of the narrative. And here it is useful to recall that in her brief account of Catherine's physicality as a youngster in Volume 1 Chapter 5, Nelly relates that she had 'the bonniest eye' (Brontë 1998, 36). For it is especially after her death that Catherine's eyes constitute a kind of leitmotif of no little dramatic interest. It is, moreover, chiefly as a family characteristic that Catherine's eyes play their part in her presentation. Thus Isabella's love for Catherine is conspicuously attested for the first time just after she has arrived at Wuthering Heights as Heathcliff's unhappy bride, when, having entered the kitchen, she notices, as if quite nostalgically, an infant Hareton standing by the fire, 'a ruffianly child, strong in limb and dirty in garb, with a look of Catherine in his eyes and about his mouth', just as she will presently notice that the eyes of Hareton's pathetic-looking father are 'like a ghostly Catherine's, with all their beauty annihilated' (Brontë 1998, 121). And whereas this detail seems to bespeak Isabella's poignant awareness of her sister-in-law's mental illness at that time, it is while attending to Hindley's severe injuries as inflicted on him by Heathcliff that she confirms her affection for the now-departed Catherine when, in response to Heathcliff's ordering her out of 'the house', she defiantly retorts:

I beg your pardon. [...] But I loved Catherine too; and her brother requires attendance which, for her sake, I shall supply. Now that she's dead, I see her in Hindley; Hindley has exactly her eyes, if you had not tried to gouge them out, and made them black and red, and her — (Brontë 1998, 160)

Noteworthy in the same context is Isabella's saying this to Hindley in defence of Catherine: 'At the Grange, every one knows your sister would have been living now, had it not been for Mr. Heathcliff.[12] [...] When I recollect how happy we were — how happy Catherine was before he came — I'm fit to curse the day' (Brontë 1998, 160). Isabella presently goes further in her idealization of Catherine when, in further response to Heathcliff's ordering her out of 'the house', she defiantly retorts: '[I]f poor Catherine had trusted you, and assumed the ridiculous, contemptible, degrading title of Mrs. Heathcliff, she would soon have presented a similar picture! *She* wouldn't have borne your abominable behaviour quietly; her detestation and disgust must have found voice' (Brontë 1998, 160). If all such complimentary comments on the late Catherine may seem odd for coming from someone who was so often bullied by her, they are none the less notable as expressions of Isabella's tendency to romanticize the past, at the same time as they bespeak her exceptional capacity to continue loving those closely related to her, even if, like Catherine, they have treated her badly, or, like Edgar, turned against her.[13] Yet, as with Isabella, much the same sort of romanticism can also be felt in Edgar's own attitude to the departed Catherine, knowing as we do that she was by no means an easy wife to live with. Certainly, Edgar is remarkable for his devotion to her as her widower through his assiduous visits to her grave. Catherine's posthumous significance for Edgar is by then also confirmed partly by his naming his daughter after her and partly by the fact that Cathy's birthday is never celebrated because, as Nelly avers, 'it is also the anniversary of my late mistress's death' (Brontë 1998, 187). Significant, too, on that head is the moment when, as he lies dying, Edgar says this to Cathy: 'I am going to her, and you, darling child, shall come to us' (Brontë 1998, 251).[14]

Catherine's posthumous power over Heathcliff is, by contrast, that of a continuous and relentlessly painful presence. This has already been adumbrated during their last tryst when, affected enough by her rambling utterances, Heathcliff at one point addresses her thus: 'Do you reflect that all those words will be branded in my memory, and eating deeper eternally, after you have left me?' (Brontë 1998, 140). We also note how, despite knowing that Catherine has just died, Heathcliff continues to regard her as if she were still alive, not only by reproving a tearful Nelly with these words: 'Damn you all! she wants none of *your* tears!' (Brontë 1998, 146) but by going on to slander Catherine herself for not mentioning his name on her deathbed. Thus, having accused her of being 'a liar to the end' and blamed her for caring 'nothing of [his] sufferings', he proceeds to say this to her:

> And I pray one prayer — I repeat it till my tongue stiffens — Catherine Earnshaw, may you not rest, as long as I am living! You said I killed you — haunt me then! [...] Be with me always — take any form — drive me mad! only *do* not leave me in this abyss, where I cannot find you! (Brontë 1998, 147-148)

Such words will, of course, be a major contributory factor for the mental illness, namely, monomania, to which Heathcliff will gradually succumb, and of which he is eventually to die.[15]

Catherine's power over Heathcliff after her death is, however, by no means confined to the words she said to him during their last tryst. This may be adjudged by a number of references to his awareness of her physical appearance, particularly through the physical resemblance borne to her by members of her family. The earliest example thereof is hinted at on the occasion when, to Cathy's strenuous attempt to wrest from his hand the front door key with which he has locked her and Nelly in Wuthering Heights in order to secure them for the illicit marriage to his son, Heathcliff is observed reacting as follows: 'He looked up, seized with a sort of surprise at her boldness, or, possibly, reminded by her voice and glance, of the person from whom she inherited it' (Brontë 1998, 239). A later example is suggested when, having unexpectedly come to Thrushcross Grange to take Cathy back to her husband, he shortly afterwards says this to Nelly about Catherine's portrait: 'I shall have that at home. Not because I need it, but —' (Brontë 1998, 255). The hesitancy at the end of the second sentence, as one realizes retrospectively, seems to indicate that Catherine's haunting of Heathcliff is utterly physiognomical. And though Heathcliff appears to have retained a distinct memory of Catherine's looks, her haunting of him is continually sustained by his acute consciousness that those related to her by blood — Hindley, Hareton and Cathy — bear a speaking likeness to her.

It is, first of all, interesting to note the earliest references to Heathcliff's sensitivity to the Earnshaw family physiognomy in Volume 2 Chapter 17. Thus, having 'gazed' at Hareton, who has just come out of Wuthering Heights but is reluctant to speak on account of his vicious conflict with Cathy shortly beforehand, Heathcliff is overheard by Lockwood saying this to himself about the young man: 'It will be odd, if I thwart myself! […] But, when I look for his father in his face, I find *her* every day more! How the devil is he so like? I can hardly bear to see him' (Brontë 1998, 269). It is, nevertheless, when Heathcliff subsequently gives Nelly one reason for wanting her to return to Wuthering Heights as his housekeeper is that he is tired of seeing Cathy, as if he were constantly disturbed by her resemblance to her mother. Indeed, this very resemblance is a principal cause of Heathcliff's vexed relations with Cathy, and at no time more so than in his conflict with her in Volume 2 Chapter 19, when, seemingly 'ready to tear [her] to pieces', but then, having 'gazed intently in her face', he 'drew his hand over his eyes' (Brontë 1998, 285). Later that day, when Cathy and Hareton are described sitting together in 'the house' and poring over a book as 'pupil and teacher' (Brontë 1998, 286), shortly before Heathcliff has suddenly returned from outside and noticed the two cousins by the fire, Nelly reveals her own sensitive awareness of the Earnshaw physiognomy with the following description to Lockwood:

> [Cathy and Hareton] lifted their eyes together, to encounter Mr Heathcliff — perhaps you have never remarked that their eyes are precisely similar, and they are those of Catherine Earnshaw. The present Catherine has no other likeness to her, except a breadth of forehead and a certain arch of the nostril that makes her appear rather haughty, whether she will or not. With Hareton the resemblance is carried farther: it is singular, at all times — then, it was particularly striking: because his senses were alert, and his mental faculties wakened to unwonted activity. (Brontë 1998, 286-87)

The passage above forms a kind of prelude to Heathcliff's admitting for the first time to Nelly how distressing for him has been the physicality of Cathy and Hareton. And while acknowledging that Hareton's 'startling likeness to Catherine connected him fearfully with her', he goes on to qualify that statement with the following words:

> That, however, which you may suppose the most potent to arrest my imagination, is actually the least — for what is not connected with her to me? and what does not recall her? I cannot look down to this floor, but her features are shaped on the flags! In every cloud, in every tree — filling the air at night, and caught by glimpses in every object by day, I am surrounded with her image! The most ordinary faces of men and women — my own features — mock me with a resemblance. The entire world is a dreadful collection of memoranda that she did exist, and that I have lost her! (Brontë 1998, 288)

Betokening as they do an apex in Heathcliff's mental illness, those words suggest the measure in which Catherine's presentation has by now reached a point where, quite unusually, she may be considered to have become the heroic figure she scarcely was, if ever, during her lifetime.[16] And it is surely owing to Heathcliff's having a short while earlier renounced his intention to complete his vengeance on Cathy and Hareton, alluding to them as he does as 'representatives' of his 'old enemies' (Brontë 1998, 287), that even after his own death, Catherine continues to maintain her heroic presence through those two young people who, bearing the closest physical resemblance to her, achieve no little heroic status themselves towards the end of the novel.

My discussion on the presentation of the first Catherine, then, has been based almost entirely on Nelly Dean's narrative and on the statements and utterances of some of the other characters, including Lockwood himself. And notwithstanding the unfavourable comments made about Catherine during her lifetime, it is interesting to note how the sympathy felt for her both during her final mental illness and in the years following her death contributes to her eventually becoming something of a fictional heroine. In this connection, it is not without interest to see how well the author suggests the important part played by the vagaries of memory with respect to the shifts in, the contrasts between, and the intensification of, attitudes towards Catherine on the part of Nelly Dean, Heathcliff, Edgar and Isabella in particular. Indeed, it is partly through these characters that we come to realize that, whatever has been said by some Brontë scholars about Catherine being something of a supernatural creature exempt from all social criteria, Emily Brontë appears to have been none the less intent on presenting her heroine not only as someone with intrinsically human qualities of mind and body, but as someone to be seen from a number of equally human perspectives.

Brontë Studies, 48/3 (2023)

References

Brontë, Emily. 1998. *Wuthering Heights*. Edited by Ian Jack and Patsy Stoneman. Oxford: Oxford University Press.

Brontë, Emily Jane. 1950. *Wuthering Heights*. Introduction by Alan Hodge. London: Hamish Hamilton.

Gilbert, Sandra M. and Guber, Susan. 1979. *The Madwoman in the Attic: The Woman Writer and the Nineteenth-Century Literary Imagination*. New York and London: Yale University Press.

Kavanagh, James H. 1985. *Emily Brontë*. Oxford: Basil Blackwell.

Mengham, Rod. 1989. *Wuthering Heights*. Harmondsworth: Penguin Books.

Tytler, Graeme. 1982. *Physiognomy in the European Novel: Faces & Fortunes*. Princeton, NJ: Princeton University Press.

———. 1992. "Heathcliff's Monomania: An Anachronism in *Wuthering Heights*." *Brontë Society Transactions* 20.6: 331-343.

———. 1994. "Physiognomy in *Wuthering Heights*." *Brontë Society Transactions* 21.4: 137-148.

———. 2022. "An Appraisal of Catherine and Heathcliff's Love Relationship." *Brontë Studies* 47.3: 202-213.

Van Ghent, Dorothy. 1953. *The English Novel: Form and Function*. New York: Holt, Reinhart & Winston.

Visick, Mary. 1973. "The Genesis of *Wuthering Heights.*" *Emily Brontë: A Critical Anthology.* Edited by Jean-Pierre Petit. Harmondsworth: Penguin Books.

Notes

1   See, among numerous examples, Emily Jane Brontë (1950, v); Sandra M. Gilbert and Susan Guber (1979, 223-285); James H. Kavanagh (1985, passim); Rod Mengham (1989, 101); Dorothy Van Ghent (1953, 164); Mary Visick (1973, 174).

2   For Nelly's criticisms of Catherine, see especially Brontë (1998, 33, 58, 62, 63, 73, 78, 81, 118, 130, 143, 162).

3   For details, see especially Brontë (1998, 36, 37, 43, 47, 63, 71, 85, 87, 92, 102).

4   For Catherine's tendency to lie or prevaricate, see Brontë (1998, 60, 61, 77, 93).

5   See Brontë (1998, 87, 88).

6   For other examples of Catherine's passivity in love, see Brontë (1998, 87, 93).

7   See Brontë (1998, 36, 47, 48).

8   See Brontë (1998, 68-71). For a more detailed discussion on Catherine and Heathcliff's relationship, see Tytler (2022).

9   This sentiment has been virtually adumbrated when, in his admiration for Edgar's portrait, Lockwood records these words in his diary: 'I marvelled much how he, with a mind to correspond with his person, could fancy my idea of Catherine Earnshaw' (Brontë 1998, 58).

10 For references to Catherine's distorted facial features when in illness or in a state of anxiety, see especially Brontë (1998, 62, 70, 72, 108).

11 Emily Brontë may have been influenced by Johann Kaspar Lavater's *Essays on Physiognomy* for her treatment of the facial appearance in death. See Tytler (1982, 245-249). For a discussion on the treatment of physiognomy in the novel, see Tytler (1994).

12 Edgar will later echo this sentiment inasmuch as Nelly recalls that it was 'his constant bitter reflection' to say that Catherine 'might have been living yet, if it had not been for [Heathcliff]!' (Brontë 1998, 196). Isabella's assertion has already been foreshadowed by Nelly's own assessment of Catherine and Edgar's marriage when, just before telling Lockwood of Heathcliff's return to Gimmerton, she says: 'I believe I may assert that they were really in possession of deep and growing happiness' (Brontë 1998, 81).

13 For Catherine's tendency to domineer over Isabella, see Brontë (1998, 52, 87, 89, 90, 92, 93, 94).

14 That Edgar's loyalty to Catherine after her death is utterly unthinkable for her at the time of her second delirium is ironically evident when, picturing her funeral, she facetiously imagines him 'standing solemnly by to see it over; then offering prayers of thanks to God for restoring peace to his house, and going back to his *books!*' (Brontë 1998, 102).

15 For a detailed discussion on Heathcliff's mental illness, see Tytler (1992).

16 Heathcliff is practically the only character in the novel to see Catherine now and then in a heroic light during her lifetime, whether it be through his admiration for her stoicism as well as for her beauty or through his presumptuously affirmative readings of her mind. For details see especially Brontë (1998, 42, 46, 135).

The Presentation of Hindley Earnshaw in *Wuthering Heights*

Hindley Earnshaw has been described by one scholar as 'the villain of *Wuthering Heights*',[1] a judgement that might well be vindicated by the fact that there are more negative references to him than to any other character in the novel. Certainly, Hindley is for the most part shown in the narrative as a rather unsavoury type of person in respect of speech and behaviour, and enough so for us to wonder to what extent he can be said to be a worthy figure of discussion. And yet it is only by examining his presentation in some detail that we may come to realize that, far from simply being a mere caricature of villainy as which he might be all too readily dismissed, Hindley is portrayed with remarkably ingenious complexity. This has partly to do with his being presented not from the viewpoint of one omniscient narrator alone, but from several narratorial or personal viewpoints and attitudes, whereby we are able not only to judge Hindley fairly objectively, but also to note how, through their close association with him, some of the characters reveal unfamiliar or unexpected aspects of themselves.[2]

From a perusal of the first eight chapters of the novel, it is easy to see that Hindley's early years have been dogged by sheer bad luck. First of all, we learn that, as well as having been brought up by a seemingly ineffectual, if well-meaning, mother, Hindley has a vexed relationship as a youngster with his rather staid and humourless father, principally, it seems, after the latter has returned from Liverpool with a foundling who is immediately made part of his family and soon afterwards named Heathcliff. Again, one can hardly help feeling sorry for the fourteen-year-old Hindley when he 'blubbered aloud' (*WH*, p. 32) on discovering that the 'fiddle' he has asked his father to bring back as a present for him has been completely destroyed on the return journey — an occurrence that seems symbolic of the disruptive influence that Heathcliff is to exert on Hindley as well as on the Earnshaw household in general. Later on, it is probably on account of his resentful violence towards Heathcliff that Hindley is sent off to 'college' (*WH*, p. 35), i.e. boarding school, for three years, eventually to return home on the death of his father and take over the mastership of the Heights. The fact that Hindley is accompanied by a wife might be thought justified compensation for the disappointments of his boyhood; and though Frances is for the most part supportive of Hindley, to the extent of colluding with him against Heathcliff and Catherine, their exclusive, not to say separatistic, bond as a happily married couple is soon brought to an end by Frances' untimely death from consumption shortly after she has given birth to Hareton. Even before her demise, while Hindley is hoping against hope amid his obstinate refusal to accept Mr Kenneth's dire prognosis, it is difficult not to feel the deepest sympathy for him.[3]

Hindley's subsequent behaviour, though not altogether unpredictable in the light of what we have been told about him hitherto, is a striking illustration of Emily Brontë's possibly first-hand knowledge and understanding of those in an unbearable state of bereavement. As Nelly recalls: 'he grew desperate; his sorrow was of that kind that will not lament; he neither wept nor prayed — he cursed and defied — execrated God and man, and gave himself up to reckless dissipation' (*WH*, p. 57). If such speech and behaviour might induce us to sympathize fully with Hindley, sympathy is unlikely to be felt where it is a matter of his relations with members of his household. Thus his tyrannical attitude towards his servants is intensified to the point of motivating all of them but Nelly and Joseph to leave his service.[4] Moreover, despite having been delighted at the birth of his son, Hindley is evidently too distraught by the loss of Frances to be bothered with his upbringing, leaving the child as he does in the care of Nelly, who recalls that, 'provided he saw [Hareton] healthy, and never heard him cry, [Hindley] was contented, as far as regarded him' (*WH*, p. 57). Nevertheless, we later note, amid his inebriate talk and demeanour in Chapter 9, that Hindley, not unlike his own father, looks upon himself as a traditional patriarch inasmuch as he expects the son with whom he has been scarcely concerned since his widowhood to display unconditional love for him. There can be few episodes more realistic in nineteenth-century fiction than the one in which Hindley utters vicious language and exhibits unruly behaviour towards an infant too afraid or too loath to demonstrate the love demanded of him. That this episode should end in Hareton's being accidentally dropped by Hindley over a bannister, but saved from certain death by Heathcliff, is an ironic foreshadowing of the fact that it will be the latter whom the boy will look up to as a kind of father, and whom, as Nelly later discovers, he much prefers to his own father.

By now, most readers would surely be harbouring much the same hostility towards Hindley as Heathcliff has so far done, and as Catherine herself will do, especially after he has become master of the Heights. This is manifest when, for example, she gives Nelly one reason for marrying Edgar as being a means of enabling her to 'aid Heathcliff to rise, and place him out of my brother's power' (*WH*, p. 72). That Hindley himself has at best an essentially mercenary attitude towards Catherine at this juncture is evident on her second return home from Thrushcross Grange, where she has been treated for her first bout of delirium. Thus he is now prepared to put up with his sister's 'caprices', primarily because, as Nelly tells Lockwood, he 'wished earnestly to see her bring honour to the family by an alliance with the Lintons', and that 'as long as she let him alone, she might trample us like slaves for ought he cared!' (*WH*, pp. 78-79). Such words amply indicate how tenuous Hindley's association is with Catherine, and why her occasional comments on him are almost always negative. A typical example may be noted when she is asked by Nelly what she thinks of the newly-returned Heathcliff's going to the Heights. Thus, having explained that her brother at first invited Heathcliff to join him and his 'companions' at cards, and then again in the evening, since the guest was 'plentifully supplied' with money, Catherine goes on to make this derogatory utterance: 'Hindley is too reckless to select his acquaintance prudently; he doesn't trouble himself to reflect on the causes he might have for mistrusting one whom he has basely injured' (*WH*, p. 87). Similarly, after informing Nelly that Heathcliff 'means to offer liberal payment for permission to lodge at the Heights', Catherine proceeds to envisage Hindley's response as follows: 'doubtless my brother's covetousness will prompt him to accept the terms; he was always greedy, though what he grasps with one hand, he flings away with the other' (*WH*, p. 88). At the same time, Catherine's claims that she 'stand[s] between [Hindley] and bodily harm' (*WH*, p. 88) is surely made less out of a sense of sisterly affection than out of a sense of family duty. And though such a sentiment betokens a certain feeling of responsibility for her brother's welfare, it is through Catherine's scathing comments, as much as through Heathcliff's, that we are apprised of the sundry defects and deficiencies of Hindley's character, as if he were indeed the villain of the novel, and there was nothing to be said in his defence.

Although Hindley's relations with members of his family are, as we have seen, for the most part unpleasant enough for them to keep their distance from him as much as he wishes them out of his way, it is interesting to reflect that, detached as he is from the household he is master of while entertaining various card-playing companions at the Heights, he nevertheless inspires a certain loyalty and even sympathy from some characters unrelated to him by blood, Joseph being a notable case in point. It is true that, during Hindley's boyhood, Joseph evinces much the same hostile attitude towards him as does Mr Earnshaw, going so far as to encourage the latter to regard his son as a 'reprobate' (*WH*, p. 36). And even when Hindley is master of the Heights, we are told that Joseph, together with the local curate, 'reprimanded his carelessness when [Catherine and Heathcliff] absented themselves' (*WH*, p. 40) from church on Sundays. Later, during the storm that breaks out on the night of Heathcliff's disappearance, Joseph, having prayed to God to 'spare the righteous, though he smote the ungodly', is quick to condemn Hindley for his blasphemous response to Nelly's shaking 'the handle of his den' in order to ascertain 'if he were yet living'. As Nelly says to Lockwood: 'He replied audibly enough, in a fashion which made my companion vociferate more clamorously than before, that a wide distinction might be drawn between saints like himself and sinners like his master' (*WH*, p. 75).

But if Joseph is not afraid to criticize Hindley, whether overtly or covertly, for defying Christian ethics, as we gather most memorably from his description of his dissipated mode of life at the Heights since Heathcliff has begun to lodge there, he nevertheless remains fundamentally submissive to him as master of his household, and that in spite of the fact that, on the very day of Hindley's return to the Heights, and contrary to his late father's practice of allowing his servants to join his family in the evening, he and Nelly, in spite of being the only retainers that have not left his service, are instructed that they 'must thenceforth quarter [themselves] in the back-kitchen, and leave the house for him' (*WH*, p. 39). Joseph's unmistakable loyalty to Hindley — a loyalty underpinned by the old servant's frequent references to him as 'maister' — is earliest evident when, having noticed the damage Heathcliff's horse has done, as he says, to 'two rigs uh corn, un' plottered through, raight o'er intuh t' meadow!' he goes on to say, 'Hahsomdiver, t' maister 'ull play t' divil to-morn, and he'll do weel. He's patience itsseln wi' sich careless, offald craters — patience itsseln he is! But he'll nut be soa allus — yah's see, all on ye! Yah munn't drive him aht uf his heead fur nowt!' (*WH*, p. 74). Again, on the morning after the storm in Chapter 9, when Hindley has asked a shivering Catherine what took her 'into the rain', Joseph butts in with these words: 'Running after t'lads, as usuald! [...] If Aw wur yah, maister, Aw'd just slam t'boards i' their faces all on 'em, gentle and simple!' (*WH*, p. 77), before proceeding to sneak on Catherine, Nelly and Edgar Linton for their untoward behaviour while his master is absent from the Heights.[5]

Nor should we forget how very humane, not to say loveable, Joseph comes across through his anxious concern for Hindley in the wake of his fight with Heathcliff; an attitude we see confirmed by his determination to go to Edgar Linton as the local magistrate on the supposition that they had been 'murthering on' (*WH*, p. 157) his master, being eventually dissuaded from doing so only by Isabella's honest account of the fight. Joseph's devotion to Hindley is especially conspicuous when, convinced that he was 'alive still', he 'hastened to administer a dose of spirits', by which 'his master presently regained motion and consciousness' (*WH*, p. 158). Similarly, having acknowledged that the cause of Hindley's death, as Heathcliff tells

Nelly, was by continuous heavy drinking several hours beforehand, he goes on to say that it would have been better had Heathcliff 'goan hisseln fur t'doctor' instead of himself, adding: 'Aw sud uh taen tent uh t'maister better nur him — un' he warn't deead when Aw left, nowt uh t'soart!' (*WH*, p. 165). Such is Joseph's loyalty to all the Earnshaw heads of his household that, given his tendency to confuse people with one another, we may wonder whether it is not Hindley, rather than Hareton, that he has in mind when, having snidely reacted to Nelly's offering Lockwood 'a drink of our old ale' (*WH*, p. 275) on his sudden re-appearance at the Heights and mocked her for having 'fellies at her time of life', he goes on to say this: 'And then, to get them jocks out uh t' Maister's cellar!', adding that he 'fair shaamed to bide still and see it' (*WH*, p. 275).[6]

While Joseph's devotion to Hindley may be understood largely as a matter of principle for someone who has served the Earnshaw family for a good sixty years, Nelly Dean's devotion to Hindley, such as it is, is almost certainly due to her memories of her comradeship with him in childhood, for, as she tells Lockwood early in her narrative: '[M]y mother had nursed Mr. Hindley Earnshaw, [...] and I got used to playing with the [Earnshaw] children' (*WH*, p. 30). Her familiarity with him as a foster brother and childhood friend is suggested partly by the humour with which, in Chapter 9, she reacts to a drunken Hindley's threat to kill her with a kitchen knife, as if she were long familiar with such antics from earlier years: 'But I don't like the carving knife, Mr. Hindley, [...] it has been cutting red herrings — I'd rather be shot, if you please' (*WH*, p. 65). It is no doubt owing to this familiarity that, though now subordinate to him in social status, Nelly is quick to condemn Hindley for his violent behaviour towards a very young Hareton, going so far as to accuse him outright of being 'worse than heathen' for carelessly dropping the child over the bannister, and then to vilify him further by exclaiming: 'You shall not meddle with him! [...] He hates you

— they all hate you — that's the truth! A happy family you have; and a pretty state you're come to!' (*WH*, pp. 66-67). In the next moment, however, she shows sincere distress over Hindley's dire alcoholism, as is evident when, observing him pour some brandy into a tumbler, she entreats him thus: 'Nay don't! [...] Mr. Hindley, do take warning. Have mercy on this unfortunate boy, if you care nothing for yourself!' (*WH*, p. 67). Sensing as he seems to do Nelly's evident concern for his welfare, Hindley replies with self-deprecatory words, especially about his inadequacies as Hareton's father, as if he were now intent on eliciting her pity.[7] Nevertheless, he presently re-asserts his authority, as Nelly thus recalls: 'He drank the spirits, and impatiently bade [me and Heathcliff] go; terminating his command with a sequel of horrid imprecations, too bad to repeat, or remember' (*WH*, p. 67).

Yet it is noteworthy how, in her almost inveterate tendency to switch her allegiance from one character to another, Nelly fluctuates in her attitude to Hindley, even during his boyhood. For example, having instantly aligned herself with him in his hatred of the recently-arrived foundling, she recalls how, on finding Heathcliff far less trouble to nurse than Hindley and Catherine while all three were laid up with measles, she was pleasantly affected by Mr Kenneth's commending her for helping Heathcliff to recover: 'I was vain of his commendations, and softened towards the being by whose means I earned them, and thus Hindley lost his last ally' (*WH*, p. 33). This perhaps explains Nelly's readiness on Christmas Day to encourage Heathcliff to think better of himself both physically and mentally, and even to regard himself as superior to Hindley: 'Were I in your place, I would frame high notions of my birth; and the thoughts of what I was should give me courage and dignity to support the oppressions of *a little farmer*!' (*WH*, p. 50; italics mine). This, in turn, accounts for her defending Heathcliff shortly before the Christmas dinner against Hindley's ordering Joseph to 'keep the fellow out of the room' because '[h]e'll be cramming his fingers in the tarts, and stealing the fruit, if left alone with them a minute' (*WH*, p. 51). Indeed, it seems that Nelly is by now more on Heathcliff's side than on Hindley's, as we note, for example, when on the night the former has returned home alone from his illicit Sunday evening visit to the Grange with Catherine, she lets him in, despite Hindley's having 'in a passion told [his staff] to bolt the doors, and [sworn] nobody should let them in that night' (*WH*, p. 40). As we are eventually to see, that reference marks one of several occasions when, as the Heights housekeeper, Nelly shows herself disloyal to Hindley, mainly by uttering negative things to him or about him, even though on that occasion she is at least loyal enough as his subordinate to warn Heathcliff with these words: 'You are incurable, Heathcliff, and Mr Hindley will have to proceed to extremities, see if he won't' (*WH*, pp. 44-45).[8]

It is, nevertheless, curious to think that, while she is housekeeper at the Grange and therefore quite out of touch with Hindley except through hearsay, Nelly becomes strangely concerned about him in ways hardly imaginable while she was under his harsh jurisdiction at the Heights. Thus we may refer to the fact that, despite feeling conscience-stricken to 'see how all was at the farm', primarily in order to warn Hindley 'how people talked regarding his ways', but then recollecting 'his confirmed bad habits, and, hopeless of benefiting him', she generally 'flinched from re-entering the dismal house, doubting if [she] could bear to be taken at [her] word' (*WH*, p. 96). Shortly afterwards, however, while on her way to Gimmerton one day, Nelly comes to the guide-post near the Heights, where, as she tells Lockwood, 'I cannot say why, but all at once, a gush of child's sensations flowed into my heart. Hindley and I held it a favourite spot twenty years before' (*WH*, p. 96). It is by then 'stooping down' at a hole near the bottom of the guide-post, which is 'still full of snail-shells and pebbles', that Nelly has a visual hallucination of her 'early playmate seated on the withered turf' in such a way as to feel compelled to exclaim: 'Poor Hindley!' (*WH*, p. 96). Believing that the child (who, of course, turns out to be Hareton) 'lifted its face and stared straight into [hers]', Nelly relates that 'immediately, I felt an irresistible yearning to be at the Heights', adding: 'Superstition urged me to comply with this impulse — supposing he should be dead! I thought — or should die soon! — supposing it were a sign of death!' (*WH*, p. 96). It is in the same superstitious mood that Nelly presently addresses the boy with a distinct touch of nostalgia: 'Hareton, it's Nelly — Nelly, thy nurse' (*WH*, p. 97), unaware as she is that she is by now a perfect stranger to him. The rest of Nelly's visit is memorable for its distinctly comic moments, first, through Hareton's throwing a flint at Nelly in response to her heartfelt greeting, and, secondly, when, having just seen Heathcliff, instead of Hindley, as she had hoped, appear 'on the door stones' of the Heights, she 'turned directly and ran down the road as hard as ever [she] could race, making no halt till [she] gained the guide post, and feeling as scared as if [she] had raised a goblin' (*WH*, p. 98). What is particularly significant about this episode is that it represents a striking example of Nelly's tendency to become extraordinarily sentimental about someone to whom she has been attached in earlier years, and with whom she has now and then even been at loggerheads, but from whom she has through force of circumstance later been separated.

Such sentimentality is nowhere more manifest than in Nelly's account of her reaction to Mr Kenneth's news of Hindley's death: 'I confess this blow was greater to me than the shock of Mrs Linton's death: ancient associations lingered round my heart; I sat down in the porch and wept as for a blood relation' (*WH*, p. 164). Through such words we sense that Hindley has been as much rehabilitated in Nelly's eyes as Catherine was after her passing.[9] Again, nowhere in her narrative does Nelly better prove her fundamental commitment to Hindley than when, in the wake of Kenneth's announcement, she asks herself: 'Had he had fair play?' — an idea that she finds so 'tiresomely pertinacious' as to resolve on 'requesting leave to go to Wuthering Heights, and assist in the last duties to the dead' (*WH*, p. 164); or, later, when in the face of Heathcliff's having contemptuously suggested that, since Hindley had in effect committed suicide by excessive drinking, he deserved no formal burial, she nevertheless 'insisted on the funeral being respectable' (*WH*, p. 165). And though it must be said that, some seventeen years after his death, Nelly compares Hindley's behaviour in bereavement unfavourably with Edgar's in Chapter 17, thereby once again showing a characteristic shift of her allegiance from one person to another, there can be little doubt that the author has made use of her presentation of Hindley as a means of revealing something of the history of Nelly's inner being as well as of her outward existence.[10]

Just as Nelly's sentimental memories of, and her carking concern for, her foster brother might induce us to hold a much less negative attitude towards Hindley than we have done in many an earlier episode, so Isabella's relations with the latter will eventually arouse in us a scarcely dissimilar attitude. At the same time, it is through such relations that we realize how extraordinarily, not to say unexpectedly, she develops into the self-assured young woman she has shown very little sign of being before her elopement. It is true that, not unlike the characters discussed above for their association with Hindley, Isabella finds her re-acquaintance with him initially quite unpleasant, partly because, shortly after she has arrived at the Heights as Heathcliff's hapless bride, he is at first too gloomy to act on her request to be taken to a bedroom. Moreover, Isabella must have by then felt uneasy about Hindley from a purely visual angle, at least to judge by the fact that, after going round to a side entrance, she finds the door opened to her, as she writes to Nelly, 'by a tall, gaunt man, without neckerchief, and otherwise extremely slovenly; his features were lost in masses of shaggy hair that hung on his shoulders; and *his* eyes, too, were like a ghostly Catherine's, with all their beauty annihilated' (*WH*, p. 121). By spotting the resemblance between Hindley and his late sister as sensitively as she has earlier spotted that between a very young Hareton and the latter in the Heights kitchen, Isabella displays an evident gift for physiognomy, her description of Hindley being one of only two in the entire narrative to convey some idea of his outward appearance, albeit a description suggesting that he is physically and mentally at the very lowest point in his life.[11] This description somehow points forward to that moment when, presuming that Isabella will be sharing Heathcliff's bedroom, he tells her to 'turn [her] lock, and draw [her] bolt' because, as he warns her, 'every night' he goes up there, intent on murdering Heathcliff. And though Isabella is briefly fascinated by the curious pistol with a knife attached by which Hindley plans to execute his heinous deed, and that to the extent of imagining '[h]ow powerful' she would feel in 'possessing such an instrument' (*WH*, p. 123), she is wise enough to endeavour to dissuade him from his criminal intention, albeit in vain. It is, then, hardly surprising that, in her letter to Nelly, she should judge Hindley to be 'on the verge of madness', adding that she 'shuddered to be near him, and thought on the servant's ill-bred moroseness as comparatively agreeable' (*WH*, p. 124), little realising at the time, however, that the old servant is about to treat her with utmost disrespect and mockery.[12]

Although, from her oral account to Nelly in Chapter 17, we learn that Isabella soon afterwards sets up a daily routine for herself at the Heights, thereby achieving a measure of independence in a markedly hostile household, we may also wonder whether her presence there has not had a certain calming influence on Hindley, as is suggested, for example, by early references she makes about him on the night before her flight from the Heights. Thus she tells Nelly that he 'does not interfere with [her] arrangements', and that he is 'quieter, now, than he used to be, if no one provokes him; more sullen and depressed, and less furious' (*WH*, p. 154). And though she goes on to corroborate this statement with Joseph's having confidently affirmed that Hindley is 'an altered man', that 'the Lord has touched his heart, and he is saved "so as by fire"', she is nevertheless 'puzzled to detect signs of the favourable change', adding that 'it is not [her] business' (*WH*, p. 154), as if to imply that, closely observant as she has been of Hindley's moods and behaviour on the opposite side of the hearth at which they are both usually sitting, she remains quite detached from, not to say wholly indifferent to, him. There are, however, moments when Hindley appears intent on pulling himself together, as Isabella notes when she says that, in order to attend Catherine's funeral, he 'kept himself sober for the purpose — tolerably sober; not going to bed mad at six o'clock and getting up drunk at twelve'. But because, as she later recalls, Hindley consequently 'rose, in suicidal low spirits, as fit for the church as for a dance', he 'sat down by the fire, and swallowed gin or brandy by tumblerfuls' (*WH*, p. 153). Such a tergiversation on his part seems to form a kind of prelude to the fact that, though having agreed with Hindley to keep Heathcliff locked out of the Heights after the latter has just returned from a nocturnal visit to Catherine's grave, Isabella, unexpectedly taken aback by Hindley's renewed resolution to kill Heathcliff, bravely resists both his attempt to make her his accomplice and the machismo with which he assures her that, through his intended deed, she will presently be 'a free woman' (*WH*, p. 155). As it happens, and despite her longing for his death, Isabella once again shows her intrinsically moral nature by actually warning Heathcliff not to enter the premises for fear of Hindley's nefarious threat.

It is, however, only after seeing Hindley faint from excessive pain and loss of blood as a consequence of Heathcliff's flinging himself on the latter's aforementioned weapon that Isabella can be said to have at last become truly concerned for the welfare of someone she has despaired of distracting from his insane resolution.

Indeed, having observed Heathcliff further assaulting an already unconscious Hindley while holding her with one hand, Isabella somehow manages to hurry off to seek the help of Joseph, whose intentions to get Edgar Linton as local magistrate to inquire into this untoward incident, as we noted above, is averted, thanks to her truthfully, if reluctantly, convincing him that her husband was not 'the aggressor' (*WH*, p. 158). In her oral account to Nelly in Chapter 17, Isabella betrays much the same conspicuously amoral streak by which, for example, she complacently observed the two men on the morning after their fight while herself 'eating heartily' (*WH*, p. 158), that is to say, by avowing her determination to avenge herself on Heathcliff through playing some part in bringing about his death. At the same time, we note how compassionate she is towards Hindley in the short interval before she takes flight from the Heights. Such compassion is already noticeable when, after giving him the glass of water he has asked for and then heard about the injuries he is still smarting under, she goes on to describe to him the inordinate violence to which, in his unconsciousness, his body was subjected by Heathcliff, and not without adding: 'And his mouth watered to tear you with his teeth; because he's only half a man — not so much' (*WH*, p. 159).

If some readers might adjudge Heathcliff's vicious treatment of Hindley as justified revenge for all the atrocities inflicted on him during his boyhood by the latter, for Isabella the utter gratuitousness of the brutality she has just witnessed is quite enough to bring about a radical change in her attitude towards someone whom she once admired for his manliness.[13] This is especially evident when, in answer to Hindley's pathetically wishing for God-given strength to 'strangle' Heathcliff, she responds 'aloud' by blaming the latter not only for Catherine's death, but also for disrupting the happiness of the Linton family. Notable, too, is the defiance with which Isabella reacts to Heathcliff's then ordering her out of his sight: 'I beg your pardon [...] But I loved Catherine too; and her brother requires attendance which, for her sake, I shall supply. Now that she's dead, I see her in Hindley; Hindley has exactly her eyes, if you had not tried to gouge them out, and made them black and red, and her —' (*WH*, p. 160).[14] It is, however, when she has ended her vituperation of Heathcliff by sardonically averring that Catherine, too, would, no more than herself, have borne being married to him, that he is angered enough to throw a dinner knife at her and injure her 'beneath [her] ear' (*WH*, p. 160), though not without her retaliating with a similar implement before making her escape through the Heights kitchen. Yet just as we find ourselves now admiring Isabella for displaying immense physical and moral courage as well as for expressing quite tender feelings towards Hindley, so we find ourselves presently admiring Hindley himself for somehow managing, despite great physical weakness, to prevent Heathcliff from possibly killing his fleeing wife. As Isabella recalls: 'The last glimpse I caught of [Heathcliff] was a furious rush on his part, checked by the embrace of his host; and both fell locked together on the hearth' (*WH*, p. 161). And it is perhaps through this quite heroic act that the author is suggesting that, despite his many failures and failings, Hindley has in some sense been somewhat rehabilitated.

Although the interpretation just put forward above might seem unduly generous towards someone remembered most of all for his violence, cruelty, swearing, blasphemy, dissipation, pig-headedness, machismo, separatism, misanthropy, vindictiveness, bitterness, and self-pity, to say nothing of his incompetence as head of his household and the alcoholism by which he will die at the age of twenty-seven, there can be no question that Emily Brontë's presentation of Hindley exemplifies her remarkable understanding of human beings and their relationships.[15] This we note especially through the sundry ways in which through different narrators or speakers Hindley relates to, and is regarded by, both members of his household and other local residents, including Mr Kenneth, at the same time as we are continually impelled to modify our attitude towards Hindley anywhere from utter dismay to heartfelt sympathy.[16] Further, it is through this intricate web of relationships and viewpoints that the author has succeeded in casting unwonted light on some of the characters most closely involved with Hindley, principal among them being Nelly Dean, Joseph and Isabella. That is surely why we come to realize that, remembered as she all too often tends to be for her famous love story alone, Emily Brontë deserves to be no less remembered as a very perspicacious observer of many different kinds of human nature and human conduct. This may explain why one might be tempted to speculate whether Hindley's valiant deed on Isabella's behalf has not in some way been subtly foreshadowed when, as a fourteen-year-old lad he asked his father for the gift of a violin; in other words, whether by dint of this quite noble request, Emily Brontë is not thereby hinting that Hindley already promises to grow up into the normal, well-balanced young man that, owing to a combination of adverse circumstances and a deeply problematic relationship with his father during his early adolescence, he is sadly destined never to be.[17]

Brontë Studies, 47/1 (2022)

Notes

1   See Millicent Collard, *Wuthering Heights — The Revelation. A Psychological Study of Emily Brontë* (London & New York: Regency Press Ltd, 1960), p. 13. Although Hindley Earnshaw is mentioned now and again in various critiques of *Wuthering Heights*, references to him are usually subordinate to the particular topic being discussed. And whereas some such references are of factual or biographic interest, a good many are essentially unfavourable, as may be noted in the following select publications: Vereen M. Bell, '*Wuthering Heights* and the Unforgivable Sin', *Nineteenth-Century Fiction* 17.2 (1962), 188-91; John Hagan, 'Control of Sympathy in *Wuthering Heights*', *Nineteenth-Century Fiction* 21.4 (1967), 305-23; N. M. Jacobs, 'Gender and Layered Narrative in *Wuthering Heights* and *The Tenant of Wildfell Hall*', *The Journal of Narrative Technique* 16.3 (1986), 204-19; Steven Vine, 'The Wuther of the Other in *Wuthering Heights*', *Nineteenth-Century Literature* 49.3 (1994), 339-59; Eric P. Levy, 'The Psychology of Loneliness in *Wuthering Heights*', *Studies in the Novel* 28.2 (1996), 158-77; Laura Inman, '"The Awful Event" in *Wuthering Heights*', *Brontë Studies* 33.3 (2008), 192-202. To my knowledge, there has been no monograph entirely devoted to Hindley other than one recently published, namely, Pam Lock, 'Hindley's "Reckless Dissipation": Making Drunkenness Public in Emily Brontë's *Wuthering Heights*', *Brontë Studies* 44.1 (2019), 68-81. For useful comments on Hindley's character and behaviour, see Melissa Fegan, *Wuthering Heights: Character Studies* (London & New York: Continuum, 2008), passim.

2   For references to, or quotations from, the text, see Emily Brontë, *Wuthering Heights*, eds. Ian Jack and Patsy Stoneman (Oxford: Oxford University Press, 1998), hereafter *WH*.

3   See *WH*, p. 57.

4   So unpleasant is the atmosphere in the Heights at this time that, as Nelly recalls, '[t]he curate dropped calling, and nobody decent came near us, at last; unless Edgar Linton's visits to Miss Cathy might be an exception' (*WH*. p. 58).

5   See *WH*, p. 77.

6   A notable example of Joseph's confusing identities may be seen when he sardonically reproaches Isabella by addressing her as 'Miss Cathy' for angrily flinging down the tray containing her porridge and leaving 'brocken pots' (*WH*, p. 127) on the ground. For other examples of Joseph's loyalty to Hindley, see *WH*, pp. 17, 127.

7   See *WH*, p. 67.

8   For another example of Nelly's disloyalty to Hindley as her master, see *WH*, p. 53.

9   For Catherine's rehabilitation in Nelly's eyes, see *WH*, pp. 145-6.

10 For a discussion on Nelly's comparison between Hindley and Edgar as bereaved husbands, see Graeme Tytler, '"He's more myself than I am": The Problem of Comparisons in *Wuthering Heights*', *Brontë Studies* 42.2 (2017), 109-17.

11 Isabella is also especially observant of Hindley's habit of restlessly pacing up and down 'the house'. See *WH*, pp. 122-4. For the resemblance she has noted between Hareton and Catherine,

see *WH*, p. 121. An earlier description of Hindley's physicality concerns his having 'altered considerably in the three years of his absence', that is to say, 'grown sparer, and lost his colour' (*WH*, p. 39) on his return as the new master of the Heights.

12 See *WH*, pp. 124-7.

13 See *WH*, p. 158.

14 This description of Hindley's eyes is ironically linked with the moment when Lockwood overhears Heathcliff muttering these sentiments as he gazes after a distraught-looking Hareton breaking away on the causeway, just after the latter has left 'the house' in the wake of having burnt Cathy's books. 'It will be odd, if I thwart myself! [...] But, when I look for his father in his face, I find *her* every day more! How the devil is he so like? I can hardly bear to see him' (*WH*, p. 269). This in turn is linked with that moment when Heathcliff confirms the enormity of his partial insanity by telling Nelly of the painful effect on him of Hareton's 'startling likeness to Catherine' (*WH*, p. 288). In this connection, see Graeme Tytler, 'Physiognomy in *Wuthering Heights*', *Brontë Society Transactions* 21.4 (1994), 137-48.

15 Especially interesting is the way in which the author has somewhat evoked Hindley's social status as a yeoman farmer through his idiosyncratic manner of speaking. For notable examples thereof, see *WH,* pp. 51, 52, 65-7, 77.

16 For Mr Kenneth's mixed feelings for, and memories of, Hindley, see *WH*, pp. 163-4.

17 One might also point out that in a novel about a household

with its assortment of characters, Hindley epitomises *Wuthering Heights*, in so far as, being both son and heir and then master thereof, he can be said to embody that domicile and its tragic fate during his short life of twenty-seven years.

The Presentation of Nelly Dean as a Servant in *Wuthering Heights*

L iterary criticism on *Wuthering Heights* is remarkable for the many different perspectives from which Nelly Dean's presentation has been discussed over the years. Prominent among them are assessments of her character and personality, with references being made, on the one hand, to her good sense, her sobriety, her kindness and her humanity, and, on the other, to her sundry mental and moral limitations. Of particular interest has been Nelly's function as the secondary narrator of the novel, whereby some scholars have gone so far as to designate her as a spokeswoman for the reader, and even for the author herself. But whatever the opinions expressed by Brontë scholars during the past several decades about Nelly's character or about her function as the secondary narrator, their critical discussions cannot but benefit by the extent to which they have also taken into account her role as a servant.[1] The importance of this idea is manifested by the fact that, notwithstanding her general efficiency as a housekeeper, there can be no question but that her domestic virtues have been adversely offset by a particularly well-known grievous error on her part, namely, her having contributed not a little to Catherine's untimely death. That is why her somewhat triumphant survival at the end of the narrative is bound to raise the question as to whether *Wuthering Heights* is not after all the amoral novel that some scholars have claimed it to be (Tytler 2010). On the other hand, if we carefully examine Nelly's seemingly honest account of events, especially where they concern her own shortcomings, we might be induced to look upon it as something of a confession, at the end of which she hopes to be given, so to speak, some sort of absolution by a complete outsider, namely, Lockwood, knowing at the same time that he is so far the only person in her life with whom she can afford to be entirely confidential about her past. It is with this consideration in mind that I shall now survey Nelly's domestic career in some detail.[2]

As is evident from biographies of the Brontë sisters as well as from their works of fiction, domestic service in forms ranging from manual jobs to positions as governesses or schoolmistresses was what a good many women not born into well-to-do families had to settle for as a means of earning a living in the eighteenth and nineteenth centuries. *Wuthering Heights* is conspicuous for showing the part played by female servants in everyday life and, indeed, by male servants, the most prominent of them being Joseph, who has served the Earnshaw household for some sixty years by the end of the narrative. How far economic or social factors originally determined his decision to become a servant in the first place the reader is unable to ascertain. His persistent use of dialectal speech may be assumed to be one main reason why he appears not to have cherished any higher professional ambition, and that in spite of possessing a seemingly wide knowledge of theology by which he might have become a permanent preacher for the Dissenters. At the same time, it is clear that Joseph's pride as a long-standing retainer capable of manifold tasks is such as to suggest that he regards his job as nothing less than a vocation. That the same can scarcely be said of most of the other servants portrayed in the novel is apparent enough from the fact that, quite apart from being given to gossip and disloyalty to their masters or mistresses, they are seldom mentioned fulfilling any specific task assigned to them (Brontë 1998, 8, 15, 161, 217, 218, 223). Further, servants tend to leave their jobs comparatively early, sometimes for reasons not specified. It is true that the unnamed housekeeper taken on by Heathcliff after Hindley's death remains for some fifteen years before leaving the Heights. Her replacement, Zillah, however, gives up the same post after barely two years. Noteworthy in this connection is Nelly's telling Lockwood of the adverse influence exerted by Hindley's heavy hand on his staff shortly after Frances' passing: 'The servants could not bear his tyrannical and evil conduct long: Joseph and I were the only two that would stay' (Brontë 1998, 57). And whereas Joseph's reason for not leaving his job seems to stem largely from his unshakeable loyalty to the Earnshaws as a matter of principle, Nelly's reason for staying on derives both from her reluctance to 'leave her charge', namely, an infant Hareton, and from her having been Hindley's 'foster sister', who, as she adds, 'excused his behaviour more readily than a stranger would' (Brontë 1998, 58).

The fact that Nelly had by then been reduced in status as a servant inasmuch as, on his return to the Heights as the new master thereof, Hindley ordered her and Joseph to 'quarter [themselves] in the back-kitchen, and leave the house for him' (Brontë 1998, 39), makes one wonder whether her reason for staying on is not actually due to her awareness of a lack of professional opportunities available to her. That Nelly originally becomes a servant more by chance than by intention is suggested when she relates that, since her mother had nursed Hindley as an infant, she 'got used to playing with the children' and that she 'ran errands too, and helped to make hay, and hung about the farm ready for anything that anybody would set [her] to' (Brontë 1998, 30). And though Nelly will be 'sent out of the house' by Mr Earnshaw for removing his foundling (Heathcliff) from the children's bedroom, her return to the Heights 'a few days afterwards' because she 'did not consider [her] banishment perpetual' (Brontë 1998, 32) underlines her awareness, through her readiness to help the household voluntarily in several different ways, of how indispensable she has by then become to Mr Earnshaw. Her early return to the Heights is also notable for being the first of several initiatives she will take beyond her official remit as a servant (Brontë 1998, 114, 234, 292). Nelly's emergence as a full-fledged retainer is evident enough from her references to her domestic tasks throughout her narrative, many of them being those she may well have taught herself to carry out, if not observed being once carried out by some of her elders. Thus she tells Lockwood of preparing or supervising meals, cooking or baking, sweeping hearths, dusting or wiping utensils or furniture, ironing linen, dressing or undressing children and adults, nursing adults and youngsters in sickness, and so on, with some of these references to her domestic work playing a useful part in the plot throughout.[3] Nelly's pride in her domestic duties is especially exemplified when she is admiring the splendid neatness of the Heights kitchen on Christmas Eve, or when, during a period of tension involving Edgar, Catherine, Isabella and Heathcliff at the Grange, she recalls that she 'went about [her] household duties, convinced that the Grange had but one sensible soul in its walls, and that lodged in [her] body' (Brontë 1998, 106). The importance that Nelly attaches to her job is even more apparent when, referring to her three-week illness in Chapter 24, she speaks of being 'incapacitated for attending to my duties – a calamity never experienced prior to that period, and never, I am thankful to say, since' (Brontë 1998, 214). Nevertheless, as well as wondering whether Nelly is not somewhat exaggerating the amount of housework she has had to do in the past, perhaps in order to impress Lockwood, we may think that she sometimes gives undue priority to her domestic services over more important matters. Certainly, nowhere does Nelly's houseproud nature manifest itself more blatantly or more inappropriately than when, on arriving at the Heights in answer to Isabella's letter of distress, her first concern is with the 'dreary, dismal scene' as presented by the formerly cheerful house, whereby she goes so far as to say this in addition: 'I must confess that, if I had been in the young lady's place, I would, at least, have swept the hearth, and wiped the tables with a duster' (Brontë 1998, 129).

It is noteworthy that during the first part of her domestic career, which begins as that of a youngster willing to do any job required at the Heights and ends with the death of Mr Earnshaw, Nelly appears to have been subordinate to Joseph, whose duties include the running of the farm, ensuring the security of the household, and seeing to the religious indoctrination of the children as well as to punishing them for their misdemeanours. Joseph's position as head servant under Mr Earnshaw is somewhat confirmed when, on the night of the latter's death, he tells Nelly to 'put on [her] cloak and run to Gimmerton for the doctor and the parson'; a journey which she undertakes 'through wind and rain' (Brontë 1998, 38). After Frances Earnshaw's death, however, we sense that Nelly enjoys more or less equal status with Joseph, at least to judge by their disagreements and quarrels with each other (Brontë 1998, 73, 75, 178, 208).[4] It is not until Nelly has become the Grange housekeeper that she can be truly said to match Joseph in rank in so far as she finds herself in charge of servants both male and female. This we gather, for example, when, in order to facilitate Heathcliff's entry into the Grange for his tryst with Catherine, she tells 'a man servant' to 'run over to the village' to buy a few oranges, 'to be paid for on the morrow' (Brontë 1998, 137); or when, in order to assuage Isabella's annoyance at the continual crying of baby Cathy at the beginning of Chapter 17, she 'rang the bell, and committed [the infant] to a servant's care' (Brontë 1998, 152); or when, on Edgar's return to the Grange from the South, she 'hastened before to prepare the servants' (Brontë 1998, 177); or, again, when, so as to enable Edgar to change his will, she 'despatched a man to fetch the attorney', at the same time as she sends 'four more, provided with serviceable weapons' to fetch Cathy from the Heights, only later to upbraid 'the stupid fellows', as she refers to them, for allowing themselves to be persuaded by Heathcliff that the girl is 'too ill to quit her room' (Brontë 1998, 250). Nelly's authority over the servants at the Grange is also conspicuous when she scolds them for untoward behaviour, whether it be by ordering the maid called Mary to 'hold [her] noise' (Brontë 1998, 116) just as the latter seems about to announce Isabella's elopement with Heathcliff; or, later, when, mistaking Isabella's laughing entry into the Grange parlour after her escape from the Heights for that of 'one of the maids', she exclaims: 'Have done! How dare you show your giddiness here? What would Mr Linton say if he heard you?' (Brontë 1998, 150, 249, 250).

It is clear from the words just quoted above that, within only a short time as the Grange housekeeper, Nelly has achieved the highest rank as a domestic, and one seldom enjoyed by servants portrayed in nineteenth-century fiction. One reason for this is almost certainly her extraordinary function, both hitherto and later on, as a confidante to practically all the main characters. At the Heights, for example, occupied as it is by comparatively few superiors, it is not unusual for any of those superiors when in conflict with, or ostracised by, others of similar social status, to fall back on an intelligent servant like Nelly for comfort or advice. And as Brontë's novel plainly conveys, Nelly's role as confidante is facilitated by the extent to which the main characters – Catherine, Heathcliff, Isabella and Cathy in particular –

turn to her spontaneously for help far beyond the parameters of her domestic duties. Yet it is easy to forget that, amid her advice or her reproaches to her social superiors, delivered as they are in motherly or sisterly fashion, Nelly remains nonetheless a servant, and that even when she is daunted on occasion to intrude upon the conversations of her social superiors or even to give them gratuitous counsel. Indeed, it is because she *is* a servant that her masters and mistresses or those of similar status are disposed to consult her on matters which they are too afraid to talk about with their social equals, or for which they need help in order to carry out certain untoward machinations. And it is quite possible that Nelly's usefulness in those respects is in some measure based on the author's relations with Tabitha Aykroyd, the Brontë family's beloved housekeeper at Haworth parsonage (Gérin 1978).[5] Yet despite these and other initiatives she takes without specific permission from those in authority over her, Nelly is sometimes nothing loath to remind Lockwood of some of the ways in which she has been under orders and been obedient to them. One example may be noted when, to a Catherine eager to go down and fetch a newly-returned Heathcliff upstairs to the Grange parlour, Edgar reacts preventively by instructing Nelly thus: '*You* bid him step up', just before saying this to his wife: 'and, Catherine, try to be glad, without being absurd! The whole household need not witness the sight of your welcoming a runaway servant as a brother' (Brontë 1998, 84).

It is likely that Edgar's words quoted above are doubtless a reminder to Nelly that she is intrinsically subservient to him as her master. Indeed, there are moments when Nelly conveys the idea of herself as but a common or garden wage-earning servant. A striking example may be noted when, in the wake of Catherine's opening her bedroom door after three days of sequestration, Edgar accuses Nelly of encouraging him to harass his wife as well as of failing to inform him about the latter's physical deterioration during those three days. Interpreting this accusation as being due to her having told Edgar of Catherine's scolding of Heathcliff for making amorous overtures to Isabella, Nelly asserts that she 'didn't know that, to humour [Catherine], [she] should wink at Mr Heathcliff'. She even goes on to defend herself sardonically as follows: 'I performed the duty of a faithful servant in telling you, and I have got a faithful servant's wages! Well, it will teach me to be careful next time. Next time you may gather intelligence for yourself!' (Brontë 1998, 113). Such defiant words, uttered as they are by someone who knows how little her master can do without her services, suggest how cleverly, not to say hypocritically, Nelly falls back on her menial position in order to justify herself in the face of such criticism. There are also occasions when Nelly uses her position in quite mercenary ways for purely tactical reasons. For example, when in response to Cathy's telling Linton Heathcliff that she has been forbidden by her father to enter the Heights – and that, just before she is trapped in that building – Heathcliff has by then asked Nelly to 'take [his son] in', adding that he will 'follow [her] advice concerning the doctor, without delay', Nelly replies: 'You'll do well, […] but I must remain with my mistress. To mind your son is not my business' (Brontë 1998, 237). Again, one may refer to that comical moment when, in order to persuade Linton Heathcliff next day to inform her of Cathy's whereabouts, she not only reminds him of the sundry journeys which the latter once regularly made to the Heights for his sake, and for which she had, ironically enough, reported her young mistress to Edgar, but endeavours, albeit unsuccessfully, to make him feel remorse for his callous treatment of his new wife by vouchsafing the following self-deprecatory sentiment: 'I shed tears, Master Heathcliff, you see – an elderly woman, and a servant merely' (Brontë 1998, 248, 166, 262).[6]

Yet notwithstanding Nelly's shifting views of herself as a retainer from pompous pride to abject humility, it is chiefly as Edgar's housekeeper and Cathy's nanny that she forcibly comes across as an unwontedly complex type of servant. Thus whereas, on the one hand, Nelly undoubtedly runs the Grange household efficiently and keeps her subordinates on their toes and in line, we note, on the other hand, that she is by no means wholly reliable in her guardianship of Cathy. It is true that Nelly's mention of Cathy's first twelve years of childhood as 'the happiest of [her] life' (Brontë 1998, 167) suggests that that was a period when she was a competent nursemaid in full control of her young mistress. It is, therefore, little wonder that, rather like a mother who does not want her child to grow up, Nelly is anxious, even beyond those twelve years of happiness, that Cathy should continue to remain content with her sheltered way of life. This is at first quite evident from Nelly's attempt to discourage the girl's interest in Penistone Craggs as much as it is from her efforts to distract her from her melancholy moods or restlessness, and sometimes not without unfortunate consequences. One memorable example occurs when, during Edgar's three-week absence, she finds herself, as she says, 'too busy' to amuse Cathy or to distract her from 'an interval of impatient, fretful weariness' (Brontë 1998, 169), Nelly sends her off on expeditions round the Grange grounds on horseback, only to find on one occasion that her young mistress has broken bounds, not only by visiting Penistone Craggs, but also by discovering the existence of Wuthering Heights. Further, it is at the Heights on that occasion that Cathy appears for the first time to have openly defied Nelly's authority both by flatly refusing to return immediately to the Grange with her and – much to the amusement of Hareton Earnshaw and the unnamed housekeeper of the Heights – by successfully evading her attempts to put her hat back on her head in preparation for their departure (Brontë 1998, 171–172). But it is more particularly after her first reunion with Linton Heathcliff in Chapter 22 that Cathy becomes more and more defiant of Nelly's orders and requests, mindful as she is by then that she has been deceived by her as well as by her father as to Linton's whereabouts since his sudden departure on the day after his arrival at the Grange. At this point Nelly still wields over Cathy the power delegated to her as her nursemaid, notably when, for instance, she reports her to her father for her illicit visits to the Heights or, later, when she puts an end to her correspondence with Linton Heathcliff. At the same time, it is surprising to see how often Nelly fails to take advantage of the official responsibilities enjoined on her as Cathy's guardian, and the most likely reason being she is aware enough of Edgar's reclusiveness to take liberties which, under a more vigilant master, she might have scarcely dared to take (Brontë 1998, 130, 136, 238, 244).[7]

Noteworthy in this connection is the measure by which Nelly's disloyalty to Edgar is further exemplified in Chapter 21. We find, to begin with, that, because charmed by Heathcliff at her first meeting with him on the moors, Cathy overrides Nelly's militant attempts to prevent her from entering the Heights and thus becoming reunited with Linton Heathcliff. But despite Edgar's later tactfully disallowing her to have anything more to do with Heathcliff's household, Cathy is nevertheless determined to send Linton a note saying that she cannot see him at the Heights next day as she has promised to do. And though Nelly adamantly refuses to allow the note to be sent, it is partly due to the importance she attaches to keeping her promises that Cathy manages not only to have the note 'forwarded to its destination by a milk-fetcher' (Brontë 1998, 198), but, as Nelly will later discover to her dismay, to conduct a regular correspondence with Linton. And whereas Nelly succeeds in stopping the correspondence once and for all, it is curious to see how, in spite of her denial of Heathcliff's account of the suffering endured by his son through no longer receiving letters from his cousin, Nelly is affected enough by Cathy's tearful anxiety over Linton's apparent mental distress to agree to accompany her on a visit to the Heights next day. Thus we see how, instead of loyally backing Edgar's request that Cathy cease all communication with Heathcliff's household, Nelly shows that, as well as being intent on ingratiating herself with her young mistress, she is primarily concerned out of sheer pride to be proved right in her disbelief of what Heathcliff has told Cathy about his son's dire state of health (Brontë 1998, 207).

It is, nevertheless, interesting to see how often Nelly continues to be upstaged by Cathy after the latter's second reunion with Linton Heathcliff (Brontë 1998, 150, 151).[8] Further, we have by then noted Cathy's tendency to ignore Nelly's scrupulous concern to observe the time limits usually set by Edgar for their excursions. But it is both during Cathy's more or less vexed conversations with Linton and after her reconciliation with him that Nelly proves how diminished her authority over her young mistress has become. Especially notable in this context is Cathy's resistance to Nelly's endeavours to put an end to her relations with Linton. Thus to Nelly's determination to ensure this by having Thrushcross park door's lock mended, Cathy retorts: 'I can get over the wall [...] The Grange is not a prison, Ellen, and you are not my jailer' (Brontë 1998, 213). Significant, too, in the same context is the fact that, just after assuring Nelly that her 'intimacy' with Linton 'has been revived', and then to Nelly's saying that 'it must not be continued', Cathy, as Nelly recalls, 'set off at a gallop, leaving [her] to toil in the rear' (Brontë 1998, 214). How often do we not also find Nelly using the verb 'follow' as applied to herself in her movements with Cathy, as if not only to emphasise her subservience to Cathy, but also to symbolise the latter's moments of superiority over her both socially and morally speaking (Brontë 1998, 188, 202, 249).

Induced as we might be at this juncture to review Nelly's domestic career up to this point, we realise that she has by now run the gamut from the highest status as the Grange housekeeper to practically the lowest status as a menial servant. At the same time, we might also wonder whether, owing to economic circumstances or not, Nelly does not see herself fated to be a retainer for life. This we have already sensed when, reluctant to leave the Heights and accompany Catherine to the Grange on the latter's marriage to Edgar, but nonetheless compelled by Hindley to do so, as he 'wanted no women in the house'. Nelly concludes that she 'had but one choice left', that is, 'to do as [she] was ordered' (Brontë 1998, 79).[9] Apart from confirming her apparent inability to emulate those fellow servants who leave the Heights or the Grange for some reason or other and who supposedly find similar employment or some other mode of life elsewhere, Nelly's submissiveness here may be due not so much to inertia as to her realization that, celibate as she appears to be by nature and content enough to live her life vicariously through those whom she serves, there are many benefits to be accrued from her position, not the least of them being the fact that, as may be noted here and there in the narrative, she is able to get away with all sorts of amoral and even immoral deeds, conscious as she is how heavily she is generally depended on for her services. That may well explain why, for example, Edgar does not dismiss Nelly for illicitly allowing Heathcliff into the Grange and thereby indirectly causing Catherine's untimely death.

No doubt, it is the premature birth of Cathy that ultimately deters Edgar from taking such a drastic action, which, in more favourable circumstances, he would probably have scarcely hesitated to do. This has already been suggested when he warns Nelly that she will have to 'quit [his] service' the next time she brings him 'a tale' (Brontë 1998, 113) about Catherine. But if Nelly's various disloyalties to Edgar should be deemed quite serious shortcomings on her part, some of them may nonetheless be adjudged to have been motivated in good part by her concern for Cathy's well-being, just as her earlier disloyalties to Hindley stem largely from a warm-hearted concern for young Heathcliff's welfare.[10] And though Nelly perhaps sets too much store by her domestic duties and may even have exaggerated the amount of work she has done, especially as housekeeper at the Grange, and that with a sense of self-importance such as partly explains her occasionally martinet-like treatment of her fellow servants, she nevertheless deserves commendation for some of the services she renders to her masters and mistresses. Even Nelly's futile endeavours to put an end to Cathy's relations with Linton Heathcliff may in hindsight be thought to have been vindicated, considering how disastrous the marriage of the cousins turns out to have been from beginning to end. Much more important for an evaluation of Nelly's services, however, are those she provides as a sick nurse, whether they be on behalf of Heathcliff and the two Earnshaw children while they were afflicted with measles or, more particularly, the complicated ones she offers Catherine during her two bouts of delirium, and that despite her marked failure to safeguard her mistress's convalescence enough to prevent her premature death.

Perhaps the most important and most memorable of all Nelly's services, however, are her care and education of Hareton during the first five years of his life, and the motherliness with which, whether through advising, scolding, threatening or consoling, she acts as nursemaid and guardian to Cathy. It is with this background in mind that the reader may come to understand why, when informing Lockwood that Cathy and Hareton are to be married on New Year's Day 1803, Nelly should apprise him that 'on their wedding day – there won't be a happier woman than [herself] in England!' (Brontë 1998, 281, 291, 292).[11] We also gather from Nelly's final words not only that she can look forward to what promises to be the most delightful phase of her work as a servant, but that she has in some sense reached the apex of her domestic career. This we realize when, though mindful of all her failures to keep Cathy fully in control during her adolescence, we are given to understand how much the latter has now come to depend on her. For when Lockwood asks Nelly about whom to pay the rent he thinks he still owes as tenant of the Grange,

Nelly replies: 'Oh! then it is with Mrs Heathcliff you must settle [...]
or rather with me. She has not learnt to manage her affairs yet, and
I act for her; there's nobody else' (Brontë 1998, 274). And perhaps
it is with such words that Nelly may be hoping, as it were, to clinch
the absolution she seems to have been seeking through her warts-
and-all account of her life as a servant. Some readers, however, might
think that, notwithstanding her sundry domestic achievements,
she hardly deserves such absolution. Thus they might aver being
perturbed by the mixture of vanity and sentimentality with which
she has endeavoured to ingratiate herself with Heathcliff and even
with Cathy, and that at the expense of the implicit trust placed in
her by her kindhearted master, Edgar Linton. They might also point
out that, in spite of being fully conscious of the difference between
right and wrong, Nelly not only tends to excuse her disloyalties as
somehow unavoidable, but abysmally fails to stick to the important
resolutions she has made with a view to preventing things from later
getting disastrously out of hand. That is why on coming to the end
of the novel, and still mindful of her good points *qua* servant, we
might nevertheless wonder whether, confronted once again by the
same problematic dilemmas as before while continuing to enjoy the
liberties available to her as a housekeeper, Nelly would not yield to
the temptations of expediency rather than to the demands of morality
(Brontë 1998, 136, 189).[12]

Brontë Studies, 48/1-2 (2023)

References

Brontë, Emily. 1998. *Wuthering Heights*, Edited by Ian Jack and Patsy Stoneman. Oxford: Oxford University Press.

Fraser, John. 1965. "The Name of Action: Nelly Dean and *Wuthering Heights*." *Nineteen-Century Fiction* 20 (3): 223-236.

Gérin, Winifrid. 1978. *Emily Brontë: A Biography*. Oxford, New York & Melbourne: Oxford University Press.

Hafley, James. 1958. "The Vilain in *Wuthering Heights*." *Nineteen-Century Fiction* 13 (3): 199-215.

Meier, T. K. 2013. "*Wuthering Heights* and the Violation of Class." *Brontë Studies* 38 (4): 309-312.

Sternlieb, Lisa. 2002. *The Female Narrator in the British Novel: Hidden Agendas*, Chapter 2, "Nelly Dean: Changing Tactics": 39-51. London: Palgrave Macmillan.

Tytler, Graeme. 2010. "*Wuthering Heights*: An Amoral Novel?" *Brontë Studies* 35 (3): 194-207.

Tytler, Graeme. 2008. "Masters and Servants in *Wuthering Heights*." *Brontë Studies* 33 (1): 44-53.

Notes

1   For some useful articles on Nelly Dean as servant, see especially Hafley 1958, Fraser 1965, Sternlieb 2002, Tytler 2008, Meier 2013.

2   For the sake of convenience, the elder Catherine will be referred to as 'Catherine', the younger as 'Cathy'.

3   For references to Nelly's domestic duties, see especially Brontë 1998, 33, 39, 41, 46, 48, 49, 52, 56, 57, 60, 62, 72, 73, 86, 92, 104, 144, 150, 161, 167, 169, 183, 197, 199, 201, 202, 275, 276, 277, 279, 280, 286, 292, 294.

4   Nevertheless, there are occasions when Nelly depends on Joseph's help; see especially Brontë 1998, 78, 293.

5   For information about Tabitha Aykroyd, see especially Winifrid Gérin 1978, 29, 60, 225.

6   Relevant here is Nelly's mercenary attitude to her profession through her references to wages in other contexts.

7   It is interesting to note how often Nelly seeks to mitigate some of her disloyalties to Edgar with vain self-justifying excuses.

8   Noteworthy in this connection is the way in which Nelly has already been similarly upstaged by Isabella in Chapter 17.

9   We sense much the same diffidence in Chapter 30 when, despite thinking of getting a cottage and having Cathy live with her, she tells Lockwood that 'Mr Heathcliff would as soon permit that,

as he would set up Hareton in an independent house; and I can see no remedy, at present, unless she could marry again; and that scheme, it does not come within my province to arrange' (Brontë 1998, 264).

10 For Nelly's disloyalties to Hindley, see especially Brontë 1998, 41, 50, 51, 53.

11 In this connection, Heathcliff deserves some credit for giving his blessing, as it were, to Cathy and Hareton's love relationship a few days before his death.

12 We see, especially in Chapters 14 and 21, Nelly making vows on behalf of Edgar that she fails to keep.

The Presentation of Joseph in *Wuthering Heights*

The frequency of references to Joseph in *Wuthering Heights* is enough to suggest that he plays much more than the rather minor role usually assigned to servants in nineteenth-century English fiction.[1] There is, however, a tendency among Brontë scholars to look upon Joseph as a somewhat caricatural figure, that is to say, as someone memorable almost entirely for his religious fanaticism, his cantankerousness and his dialectal speech.[2] Yet to limit oneself to such views of Joseph is to do scarce justice to the skill with which Emily Brontë has portrayed him and made him integral to a novel which, though remembered chiefly for its famous love story, is none the less concerned, among other things, to inform us about people living and working on a farm in late eighteenth-century rural Yorkshire. What is especially interesting about Joseph is that, while he is in absolutely no doubt about his role in life as being that of a servant earning a servant's wage, his relations with his sundry masters and mistresses, as well as with his other social superiors, are somehow so complex as to induce us to wonder whether, in spite of the humble position which he seems so grimly committed to occupy, he might not in the end be thought not only to deserve our respect, but in some measure even to have won our affection. That such thinking may be seen as a little out of the ordinary, not to say questionable, is what I hope in part to counter through my discussion on his presentation.

Let us first of all consider some of the reasons for Joseph's comparatively poor image among scholars and readers alike. One probable such reason may be found in Nelly Dean's generalizations about Joseph's character, as, for example, when she describes him as 'the wearisomest, self-righteous pharisee that ever ransacked a Bible to rake the promises to himself and fling the curses on his neighbours' (*WH*, p. 35); or when she explains why he was the only servant, apart from herself, not to leave the Heights shortly after Hindley had been widowed, 'Joseph remained to hector over tenants and labourers; and because it was his vocation to be where he had plenty of wickedness to reprove' (*WH*, p. 58). Nelly's patent dislike of Joseph, as already implicit in such statements, may be further surmised when, for example, she speaks of the 'evil tongue' (*WH*, p. 77) with which he tells Hindley about Catherine's outdoor frolics with Heathcliff and about related matters; or when she alludes to the tensions existing between herself and Joseph while they are working or sitting at leisure in the kitchen or having meals together.[3] Hostility towards Joseph is also markedly noticeable towards the end of the account that young Heathcliff gives Nelly about his illicit visit to Thrushcross Grange, as it is also in Catherine's diary, which Lockwood peruses in the oak-panelled closet.[4] Further, there is much in Isabella's epistolary and oral reports about her sojourn at the Heights as Heathcliff's hapless bride to indicate how much she hates Joseph for his rudeness, for his lecturing to her and for his ability to make her cry.[5] Interestingly enough, Isabella's reference in this context to Joseph as 'that odious old man' (*WH*, p. 154) will be practically echoed when, informing Nelly of the *schadenfreude* exhibited by Joseph in the wake of Hareton's having turned her and Linton Heathcliff out of 'the house', Cathy refers to him as 'that odious Joseph' (*WH*, p. 221). Again, it is while Cathy is quarrelling with Joseph in Chapter 2 that Lockwood, having mistakenly presumed that the old servant's verbal attack on her is aimed at himself, relates that, because 'sufficiently enraged', he 'stepped towards *the aged rascal* with an intention of kicking him out of the door' (*WH*, p. 11; italics mine). And probably it is Joseph's having set the dogs on him for stealing his lantern that may explain why, at the end of his disappointing third visit to the Heights, Lockwood hopes, albeit in vain, to depart by way of the kitchen in order not only to catch a glimpse of Cathy, but also to 'annoy old Joseph' (*WH*, p. 270).[6]

The fact that the term 'old' and synonyms thereof are quite often used with respect to Joseph, whether with hostile or dispassionate intent, is a reminder of Lockwood's very first impression of him as 'an elderly, nay, an old man: very old, perhaps, though hale and sinewy' (*WH*, p. 2) — a designation which foreshadows that moment when Joseph prefaces his complaint to Heathcliff about his uprooted currant bushes with a threat to leave the Heights, where, as he says, he has 'sarved fur sixty year' (*WH*, p. 283).[7] Accordingly, if, as we may suppose, Joseph's animosity towards people so much younger than himself, especially those whom he treats as outsiders, seems based on his apparent pride in his long period of domestic service, another reason for such animosity surely has to do with his having, for example, exerted a strong religious influence on Mr Earnshaw, and that principally through being, as Nelly has observed, 'relentless in worrying him about his soul's concerns' (*WH*, p. 36). Such influence is, of course, very much that of a hard-line Dissenter given to prayer and Bible-reading, to invoking the Deity, even while rebuking someone for their untoward talk or behaviour, and to a puritanical repudiation of all forms of secular recreation.[8] Joseph's power at the Heights is further enhanced by his being delegated not only to instruct Mr Earnshaw's children in religious matters, but even to punish them for their misdemeanours — a privilege just as evident when, under Hindley's mastership, Joseph supervises the meals partaken of by Nelly, Catherine and Heathcliff.[9] It is, then, little wonder that, having acted so often on his advice, Mr Earnshaw should, only moments after his death, be regarded by his loyal servant as already 'a saint in Heaven' (*WH*, p. 38). Such an assumption is utterly characteristic of someone who, even while possessing a 'store of theology' (*WH*, p. 266), as Cathy puts it, seems to have curiously naïve ideas about God and the devil. This is evident enough when, having caught sight of Heathcliff's corpse, he confidently asserts that '[t]h' divil's harried off his soul' (*WH*, p. 298). That there is also something quite eccentric, even ridiculous, about Joseph's religious practices is nowhere better exemplified than when, according to Isabella, instead of mopping up Hindley's blood, as ordered by Heathcliff, he 'joined his hands, and began a prayer which excited [her] laughter from its odd phraseology' (*WH*, p. 157).[10]

Although Joseph's talk and behaviour as a staunch yet deeply superstitious Dissenter seem to be reasons for his unpopularity with those characters who are portrayed as more or less rational creatures, including those who, like Nelly Dean, wear their Christianity lightly, it is almost certainly his very uncompromising religiosity that helps to explain why he is so consistently loyal and devoted to the various Earnshaws he has served under since the early 1740s. Indeed, the idea that Joseph's dependability as a retainer seems to be largely the effect of his religious extremism may well account for the strong moral influence he exerts on Mr Earnshaw as his head servant, just as it probably accounts for his apparent need to have not only a master to look up to, but also one to care about. This may be seen especially in contexts where he is mindful of a particular master being inconvenienced for one reason or another. In this connection, it is interesting to note that Joseph's attachment to Mr Earnshaw is just as pronounced even after the latter's death, when, tearing down the curtain that Catherine has made out of her and Heathcliff's pinafores in 'the house', he boxes the girl's ears and upbraids her for her irreligious conduct, not least because, as he adds elliptically, '[t]' maister nobbut just buried' (*WH*, p. 17). Again, Joseph's complaint about Heathcliff's having knocked down two hayricks and left the gate open on the night he has ridden away from the Heights is supplemented by the following complimentary reference to Hindley: 'Hahsomdiver, t' maister 'ull play t' divil to-morn, and he'll do weel. He's patience itsseln wi' sich careless, offald craters — patience itsseln he is! Bud he'll nut be soa allus — yah's see, all on ye! Yah munn't drive him aht uf his heead fur nowt!' (*WH*, p. 74). Similarly, part of his scolding of Isabella for flinging down the tray containing her bowl of porridge entails his anticipation of the effect it will have on Hindley: 'Hahsiver, t' maister sall just tum'le o'er them brocken pots; un' then we's hear summut; we's hear hah it's tuh be' (*WH*, p. 127). Joseph's loyalty to Hindley is again noticeable in his awareness of the trouble he has to put up with from youngsters. Indeed, as Nelly recalls, Joseph had been 'in the habit of accusing Catherine Earnshaw and Heathcliff, when children, of putting the master past his patience, and compelling him to seek solace in drink, by what he termed their "offalld ways"' (*WH*, p. 174).[11]

Yet quite apart from showing respect for his masters in ways suggested in the foregoing, Joseph shows his deference to them when appealing to them for help. The earliest example of this occurs on the occasion when, having had the lantern by which he has been milking cows snatched from him by Lockwood, Joseph shouts this to Heathcliff: 'Maister, maister, he's staling t'lantern!' (*WH*, p. 13). The fact that immediately after uttering those words Joseph sets the dogs on to Lockwood might suggest that his appeal to Heathcliff was not so much a cry for help as an expression of deference. Another example is recorded several years earlier in Catherine's diary when, on discovering in the wake of the three-hour religious service he has held in an attic that Catherine and Heathcliff have flung or kicked into a dog-kennel the theological books he has lent them, Joseph cries out: 'Maister Hindley! [...] Maister, coom hither!' (*WH*, p. 17). Interestingly enough, Joseph follows up that appeal with a muttered criticism of Hindley for not being as strict with the children as Mr Earnshaw used to be: 'It's fair flaysome ut yah let 'em goa on this gait. Ech! th' owd man ud uh laced 'em properly — bud he's goan! ' (*WH*, p. 17). Certainly one wonders whether Hindley's immediately afterwards hurling the two youngsters into the back-kitchen is sufficient punishment in Joseph's eyes. No doubt, it is the memory of Mr Earnshaw's strictness that later prompts Joseph to give a somewhat laid-back Hindley much the same sort of advice as he used to give to his father. Thus, for example, when having remarked that Catherine looks 'as dismal as a drowned whelp' (*WH*, p. 76) on the morning he is as yet ignorant of Heathcliff's departure from the Heights the previous evening, Hindley asks her what 'took [her] into the rain', Joseph butts in by prefacing his malicious and somewhat prurient gossip about the recent antics of Catherine, Heathcliff, Edgar and even Nelly herself with the following counsel: 'If Aw wur yah, maister, Aw'd just slam t'boards i' their faces all on 'em, gentle and simple!' (*WH*, p. 77).

The fact that, in his concern that Hindley as master of the Heights should assert his authority and not be unduly inconvenienced, Joseph is hardly, if at all, critical of him for, say, his eccentric tyranny, his dissolute way of life with Heathcliff as his lodger or even his addiction to drink, very likely has to do with Hindley's being an Earnshaw. By contrast, it is noteworthy that, though outwardly obedient to Heathcliff, as is plainly illustrated when, dressed in his Sunday best, he is aggressively determined to obey the latter's order to fetch his son from the Grange, albeit in vain, Joseph seems to be actuated in his aggressiveness towards Edgar Linton by fear of Heathcliff rather than by the kind of the loyalty he has invariably shown to the Earnshaws, and that irrespective of their failings or shortcomings. Moreover, though Joseph has been on familiar terms with, say, Mr Earnshaw, it is quite apparent that he enjoys no such familiarity with Heathcliff. This is clearly suggested when, just after Linton Heathcliff has rejected the porridge that Joseph has brought him shortly after his arrival at the Heights, Nelly makes this observation: 'I saw the old man servant shared largely in his master's scorn of the child, though he was compelled to retain the sentiment in his heart, because Heathcliff plainly meant his underlings to hold him in honour' (*WH*, p. 184). That Joseph, however, scarcely holds Linton Heathcliff 'in honour' is ironically underlined at the beginning of Chapter 23, when, presumably on the strength of Heathcliff's week-long absence from the Heights, he flatly refuses to obey the boy's request to bring him coal for his fire.[12] Joseph's disobedience in this respect is, of course, disobedience to Heathcliff himself, manifestations of which, together with those references to his fear and hatred of the latter, point forward to that moment when he will rejoice at the death of Heathcliff, thankful that 'the lawful master and the ancient stock were restored to their rights' (*WH*, p. 298). For Joseph, 'the lawful master' is now Hareton Earnshaw, and has been so in his eyes ever since the death of his father Hindley. Indeed, so strongly has Joseph by then been imbued with this idea that, according to Nelly, he 'would, had he dared, have fostered hate between him and the present owner of the Heights' (*WH*, p. 174), namely, Heathcliff, and that not least because he holds the latter largely responsible for Hareton's undisciplined upbringing. And though there is something very touching about Joseph's constant care and support of Hareton as a child and, more particularly, about the way in which his dread of losing this favourite of his to Cathy is intense enough to stir up his inveterate misogyny, the reader may nevertheless consider whether Joseph's attachment to Hareton is not after all but an expression of the unswerving loyalty with which he has served the Earnshaw family for so many years.[13]

It is, however, worth mentioning that, whereas under Mr Earnshaw's mastership Joseph comes across as a domineering figure and, at his worst, as a harsh disciplinarian, notably through his treatment of Catherine and Heathcliff as youngsters, it is not until he is under a widowed Hindley and, later, under Heathcliff as his masters that he is seen to be surly in manner and rude in speech, especially towards outsiders. Thus Lockwood's reference to the hostile look and tone of voice with which Joseph greets him as he relieves him of his horse on his very first visit to the Heights is an ironic foreshadowing of the similar manner in which the old servant had received the newly arrived Isabella at the same place some seventeen years earlier. That Joseph's initial unfriendliness to Lockwood seems to betoken an intrinsic discontent on his part to serve under Heathcliff is somewhat confirmed when, as Lockwood recalls, he is so dilatory about fetching a bottle of wine from the cellar that Heathcliff is compelled to '[dive] down to him' (*WH*, p. 4) to fetch it himself. Nor, as Lockwood is careful to add, does the noise caused by his fight with the dogs induce Heathcliff and Joseph to ascend the cellar steps 'one second faster than usual' (*WH*, p. 4). And though there is something seemingly gratuitous about Joseph's unfriendly reception of Lockwood and Isabella, it is as if he perhaps already sensed that they were each in their way potential troublemakers, which is actually what they both turn out to be — Lockwood chiefly through his theft of Joseph's lantern, and Isabella chiefly through her bungled cooking of the porridge and her flinging down her tray and leaving broken crockery scattered on the stairway.[14] It is, moreover, through our awareness of such childish behaviour in his presence that Joseph, by virtue of his pointed responses and reactions, gives the impression of being a comparatively sensible human being.

Joseph's cantankerous attitude towards outsiders may also be understood in part as the expression of someone who knows full well that but for him the efficient running of the Heights and its farm would be practically impossible. There are even occasions when Joseph finds it necessary to act the master of the household, as, for example, on the night of Mr Earnshaw's death, when as well as instructing Catherine and Heathcliff to say their bedtime prayers without his help, he orders Nelly to run 'through wind and rain' (*WH*, p. 38) to fetch the doctor and the parson. There is, moreover, much in the narrative to suggest that despite those moments when, as we saw above, he is slow to carry out an order or declines to obey one, Joseph is a hard-working servant and as such is almost always available to those who need his services. Thus as well as the context in which to Isabella's asking, shortly after her arrival at the Heights as Heathcliff's bride, where she is to sleep, Hindley replies: 'Joseph will show you Heathcliff's chamber [...] open that door — he's in there' (*WH*, p. 123), or that in which Nelly, on entering the Heights with Cathy, overhears Linton Heathcliff 'calling to Joseph to bring him dry shoes' (*WH*, p. 190), there are references to Joseph 'loading lime on the farther side of Pennistow Crag' (*WH*, p. 60); telling Heathcliff 'some tale concerning a lame horse' (*WH*, p. 182); conversing with Heathcliff about 'some farming business' (*WH*, p. 294); going to Gimmerton fair with some cattle on Easter Monday and, later, overlaying his Bible with 'dirty bank-notes from his pocket-book, the produce of the day's transactions' (*WH*, p. 280); and so on. One example of Joseph's diligence as a servant is, however, perhaps nowhere more ironically underlined than when, some two days before Heathcliff's death, Nelly tells of being bewildered by the latter's strange talk and demeanour, and that 'in the afternoon, while Joseph and Hareton were at their work' (*WH*, p. 297).[15]

References to Joseph in various narratives, however casual they may appear to be, are sometimes of interest for particular structural reasons. For example, Isabella's acute sense of loneliness at the Heights late one night seems much aggravated by her feeling it at a time when, as she says, 'Hareton and Joseph were probably fast asleep' (*WH*, p. 154), as if by adding that detail she were somehow aware of the ironic contrast between her abnormal situation and the normality of Joseph's way of life as a servant. Joseph's presence is also an important factor for Linton Heathcliff's general discomfiture at the Heights, foreshadowed as it is when on arriving there with him in the early morning, Nelly recalls their being greeted thus: '[Heathcliff] got up and strode to the door: Hareton and Joseph followed in gaping curiosity. Poor Linton ran a frightened eye over the faces of the three' (*WH*, p. 182). That detail is something of a portent for the troubles the boy is to experience in his father's household, and that in part not only, say, because 'Joseph's 'bacca pipe is poison' (*WH*, p. 186), as the unnamed housekeeper informs Nelly, but because, as Heathcliff admits to Cathy in his attempt to get her to resume her relations with Linton, he has 'little patience with Linton — and Hareton and Joseph have less', adding, 'I'll own that he's with a harsh set' (*WH*, p. 206). Again, Zillah mentions Joseph three times in her long account to Nelly about Cathy's conduct both before and after Linton's death, one memorable example being the way in which she confirms her ridiculous respectability when relating that the first thing the girl did on her return to the Heights after her father's funeral was to 'run upstairs without even wishing good-evening to me and Joseph' (*WH*, p. 259).[16]

No less interesting for structural purposes than references to Joseph's presence at the Heights are those that have to do with his temporary absences, some of which are important enough for us to suppose that without them certain deeds or incidents are unlikely to have happened. Consider, for instance, the occasion when, having found Cathy at the Heights after a long and frantic search for her, Nelly is assured by the unnamed housekeeper that 'both [Heathcliff] and Joseph are off, and [...] won't return this hour or more' (*WH*, p. 170). Indeed, had Joseph alone been on the premises, his presence would have almost certainly shortened, if not altogether prevented, the subsequent conflict between Cathy and Hareton. Again, Cathy's illicit visit to Linton Heathcliff one evening clearly suits Zillah in so far as, thanks partly to Joseph's being 'out at a prayer-meeting', she can tell Cathy that she and Linton 'might do what [they] liked' (*WH*, p. 218). But a much more important reason for Joseph's being, like Zillah, 'off on a journey of pleasure' (*WH*, p. 238) is suggested by Heathcliff on the afternoon he traps Nelly and Cathy in the Heights in order to have the latter married to his son the following day. Indeed, it is likely that Nelly's and Cathy's loud lamentations would hardly have gone unheeded had Joseph been there to hear them. That Joseph is a sort of guarantor of law and order at the Heights is evident enough when, on the afternoon young Catherine is nervously expecting Edgar's visit, she tells Heathcliff not to stop working, as he has decided to do, because, as she warns him, 'Joseph will tell'. It is only because, as we saw earlier, Joseph at the time happens to be 'loading lime on the farther side of Pennistow Crag', and that 'it will take him till dark' that Heathcliff is confident enough to conclude that 'he'll never know' (*WH*, p. 60), the implication being, of course, that, were Joseph to 'know', he would scarcely hesitate to report Heathcliff to Hindley. On the other hand, Joseph's very moral integrity as a servant is precisely what makes him an utterly dependable person to turn to in an emergency.[17] Thus we see Isabella, than whom practically no other character in the novel suffers greater rudeness or worse insults from Joseph, resorting to him for help on the occasion Hindley is being violently assaulted by Heathcliff for trying to kill him. And it is only through Isabella's recapitulation of what actually happened that Joseph is eventually persuaded not to report Heathcliff to Edgar as local magistrate for attempted murder, as he had intended to do.[18] Also worth mentioning here is Isabella's telling Nelly that 'in [her] flight through the kitchen' in order to escape from the Heights, she 'bid Joseph speed to his master' (*WH*, p. 161), namely Hindley, who, because locked at that point in combat with Heathcliff on the hearth, has thereby managed to prevent her being caught up by the latter. Even Nelly herself, though often enough at odds with Joseph and very ill-disposed towards him, has moments when she counts on him for help, as we see when, for example, she finds herself unable to cope with Heathcliff's weird talk and behaviour one morning towards the end of his life, and, more particularly, when she is too afraid to handle Heathcliff's corpse on the morning she finds him dead on his bed.[19]

Unavoidable and ineluctable as Joseph's presence so often is for good or ill, it is hardly surprising that some of the characters should be sensitively aware of his physical appearance, noting aspects of it with the kind of attention that is otherwise seldom bestowed on servants portrayed in fiction. Certainly, through their descriptions of Joseph's face, facial expressions, voice, laughter, gestures, postures, gait, and so on, some characters convey a vivid impression of his extreme old age as well as his odiousness, memorable among such descriptions being Lockwood's of '[v]inegar-faced Joseph' (*WH*, p. 6), Isabella's of Joseph's 'lantern jaws' (*WH*, p. 121) and Nelly's observing a moment or two before Joseph complains about the uprooting of his currant bushes that his jaws 'worked like those of a cow chewing its cud' (*WH*, p. 283).[20] And just as Joseph's peculiar uniqueness of character is rendered by such physiognomic details, so it is corroborated by the extent to which his speech exerts a curious influence on those whom he addresses. Indeed, despite having served under several masters presumably speaking a more or less standard English as well as his apparent ability to read and understand various theological texts, the fact that Joseph has rigidly stuck to his dialectal speech, and that irrespective of whether or not he is fully understood by his interlocutors, is an attestation of his stubborn individuality.[21] Certainly, his pride in his Yorkshire dialect is nowhere more manifest than when, for example, he mocks Isabella's upper-class accent or mimics her pronunciation of such words as 'parlour' and 'bedroom'.[22] No doubt, it is the very originality of Joseph's language that may also explain why some characters are inclined to repeat, usually verbatim, some of the words or phrases he has uttered. Thus, for instance, Nelly recalls Joseph going to 'a neighbour's' on the night the Heights is to be entertained by the Gimmerton band, in order to be 'removed from the sound of our "devil's psalmody," *as it pleased him to call it*' (*WH*, p. 53; italics mine); Isabella tells Nelly how, locked out of the Heights, Heathcliff ordered her to let him in, adding, as she recalls, 'or I'll make you repent, he "girned," *as Joseph calls it*' (*WH*, p. 156; italics mine); and Cathy informs Nelly how, in a bid to prevent her visiting Linton upstairs, shortly after she and the latter have been evicted from 'the house' by Hareton, Joseph 'locked the door' and 'declared I should do "no sich stuff," and asked me whether I were "bahn to be as mad as him"' (*WH*, p. 222).[23]

Although some readers might readily sympathise with Cathy through the words just quoted, other readers might be rather on Joseph's side for simply showing a strong sense of responsibility as head servant during his master's absence. To be sure, there is an unmistakable gruffness about Joseph's utterance here to put us in mind of those unpleasant aspects of his character that we have noted above. Nevertheless, neither they nor indeed Joseph's generally narrow-minded outlook on life should deter us from judging him first and foremost as the worthy servant he has so often proved to be. Certainly, it is clear that by dint of continual hard work he has played an indispensable part in the running of a farming household, which, but for his sedulous vigilance, might well have long since gone under.[24] At the same time, there is much about Joseph to offset the usually austere image of him that has been harboured over the years, and enough so even to inspire in us a certain affection for him. Thus we may recall those occasions when he shows a very human side through his painful jealousy of Hareton's relationship with Cathy; when he is mischievously insubordinate to his social superiors or reluctant to obey some of their orders; or when he comes across as something of a *grand seigneur* on the morning Nelly Dean finds him in the Heights kitchen 'sitting in a sort of elysium alone, beside a roaring fire; a quart of ale on the table near him, bristling with large pieces of toasted oat cake; and his black, short pipe in his mouth' (*WH*, p. 208).[25] Finally, those readers who are possibly grateful to Joseph for suggesting through his optical illusions on rainy nights that Heathcliff and Catherine are united in death, might also do well to acknowledge that amid her hallucinations about her childhood in Chapter 12, at one stage of which she can see lights shining in the Heights, Catherine seems tenderly to honour, not to say apotheosize, someone whom, notwithstanding their having been so often at loggerheads with each other in past years, she still remembers as an utterly reliable servant: 'Look! […] that's my room, with the candle in it, and the trees swaying before it … and the other candle is in Joseph's garret … Joseph sits up late, doesn't he? He's waiting till I come home that he may lock the gate … Well, he'll wait a while yet' (*WH*, p. 111).[26]

Notes

1   For quotations from the novel, see Emily Brontë, *Wuthering Heights*, ed. by Ian Jack and Patsy Stoneman (Oxford: Oxford University Press, 1998); henceforth *WH*. For the sake of convenience, the first Catherine will be referred to as Catherine, the second as Cathy. For references to Joseph other than those given in the main body and notes, see *Wuthering Heights,* pp. 12, 14, 24, 30, 34, 41, 48, 51, 70, 72, 76, 78, 87, 154, 164, 240, 254, 260, 269, 277.

2   Among numerous studies, most of which contain more or less passing comments on Joseph, see especially Arnold Shapiro, '*Wuthering Heights* as a Victorian Novel', *Studies in the Novel*, 1 (1969), 284-296; David Sonstroem, '*Wuthering Heights* and the Limits of Vision', *Publications of the Modern Language Association of America*, 86 (1971), 51-62; Margaret Homans, 'Repression and Sublimation of Nature in *Wuthering Heights*', *Publications of the Modern Language Association of America*, 93 (1978), 9-19; Beth Newman, 'The Situation of the Looker-on: Gender, Narrative and Gaze in *Wuthering Heights*', *Publications of the Modern Language Association of America*, 105 (1990), 1029-41. For a recent detailed discussion on Joseph, see Melissa Fegan, *Wuthering Heights. Character Studies* (Continuum: London & New York, 2008), pp. 43-46.

3   See *Wuthering Heights*, pp. 49, 73, 274.

4   See *Wuthering Heights*, pp. 16-7, 42.

5   See *Wuthering Heights*, pp. 153-4.

6   No doubt, Lockwood is still also mindful of his conflicts with Joseph in his first nightmare. See *Wuthering Heights*, pp. 18-24.

7 For synonymous nominal and adjectival designations of Joseph as 'old', see *Wuthering Heights*, pp. 73, 120, 127, 158, 184, 298, 299.

8 See *Wuthering Heights*, pp. 2, 48, 124, 127, 157, 218, 274.

9 See *Wuthering Heights*, pp. 73-4.

10 For other examples of Joseph's eccentric religious outlook, see *Wuthering Heights*, pp. 11, 17, 75, 76, 150, 274.

11 Joseph's devotion to Hindley is touchingly exemplified when, on the day Nelly has come to the Heights about the latter's funeral, he tells her that he might well have been able to save his master's life had Heathcliff gone to fetch the doctor instead of himself. See *Wuthering Heights*, p. 165. Joseph's strong sense of family is also evidenced when, for example, he sees a character's bad behaviour as inherited from one or other of their parents, as he does in the case of Cathy and Linton Heathcliff, or when to Isabella, who has angrily dropped the tray containing her porridge, he twice exclaims, 'Weel done, Miss Cathy!' (*WH*, p. 127). See also *Wuthering Heights*, pp. 11, 221.

12 See *Wuthering Heights*, p. 208.

13 For instances of Joseph's misogyny, see *Wuthering Heights*, pp. 13, 77, 124, 279, 280, 284.

14 See *Wuthering Heights*, pp. 124-5, 127.

15 For other references to Joseph as servant, or guardian of the Heights, see *Wuthering Heights*, pp. 51, 72, 127, 161, 259, 261, 300.

16 For Zillah's two other references to Joseph in this context, see *Wuthering Heights*, pp. 200, 208.

17 Joseph's moral disposition is especially confirmed when, after repeating his account of the dissipated way of life at the Heights since Heathcliff went to live there as Hindley's lodger, Nelly in an attempt to put Isabella off her infatuation with Heathcliff adds these words: 'Now, Miss Linton, Joseph is an old rascal, but no liar' (*WH*, p. 92). Nor without obvious relevance here is Heathcliff's reference to the effects of Catherine's relentless haunting of him in the oak-panelled closet: 'I've often groaned aloud, till that old rascal Joseph no doubt believed that my conscience was playing the fiend inside of me' (*WH*, p. 257) — words that Nelly somewhat endorses when, bothered by Heathcliff's weird speech and behaviour after his long confession to her in Chapter 33, she tells of being 'inclined to believe, as [Heathcliff] said Joseph did, that conscience had turned his heart to an earthly hell —' (*WH*, p. 289).

18 See *Wuthering Heights*, pp. 157-8.

19 See *Wuthering Heights*, pp. 293, 298.

20 For physical descriptions of Joseph, see *Wuthering Heights*, pp. 2, 6, 12, 17, 19, 24, 77, 120, 121, 124, 126, 150, 152, 157, 178, 179, 208, 221, 283, 298. All such descriptions seem to be so many testimonies to the influence exerted by physiognomic theory on the writing of *Wuthering Heights*. See Graeme Tytler, 'Physiognomy in *Wuthering Heights*', *Brontë Society Transactions*, 121.4 (1994), 137-148.

21 Joseph's language is also interesting for two other reasons:

first, his frequent use of negative words or phrases as somehow symbolic of his fundamental misanthropy; and, secondly, his tendency to repeat his phrases or sentences, as if the author were thereby evoking one of the central themes of her novel, namely, the phenomenon of the recurrence of certain events or situations in the narrative. For Joseph's use of negatives and repetitions, see *Wuthering Heights*, pp. 6, 11, 13, 17, 73, 74, 77, 91, 121, 125, 126, 127, 165, 172, 179, 189, 208, 221, 274, 280.

22 See *Wuthering Heights*, pp. 125-6.

23 For other examples of Joseph's language being singled out by the characters, see *Wuthering Heights*, pp. 17, 37, 74, 125, 154, 259, 277, 280, 299. For studies on Joseph's dialect, see especially J. Waddington-Feather, 'Emily Brontë's Use of Dialect in *Wuthering Heights*', *Brontë Society Transactions*, 15 (1966), 12-19, and K. M. Petyt, *Emily Brontë and the Haworth Dialect: A Study of the Dialect Speech in Wuthering Heights* (Leeds: Yorkshire Dialect Society, 1970).

24 Joseph's importance for the maintenance and survival of Wuthering Heights seems to be symbolically clinched when to Lockwood's asking Nelly who will look after the place after Cathy and Hareton's marriage on New Year's Day 1803, Nelly replies: 'Why, Joseph will take care of the house, and, perhaps, a lad to keep him company. They will live in the kitchen, and the rest will be shut up' (*WH*, p. 300).

25 See *Wuthering Heights*, pp. 6, 74, 121.

26 For Joseph's optical illusions, see *Wuthering Heights*, p. 299. For references to Catherine's conflicts with Joseph, see *Wuthering Heights*, pp. 74, 77, 78.

The Presentation of
Two Housekeepers in
Wuthering Heights

As a novel that for a good many readers past and present has been memorable above all for its tragic love story, *Wuthering Heights* might therefore not be so readily adjudged equally memorable for the presentation of some of its minor characters. Yet notwithstanding the primacy of the tale of Heathcliff and Catherine, it is worth keeping in mind that the author is just as intent on giving us a picture of everyday life in a Yorkshire rural community made up of a number of individuals of different social backgrounds and professional functions, conspicuous among them being various retainers ranging from a senior figure such as Joseph to the odd manservant or maidservant in both households. Of particular interest in this respect are four women portrayed as housekeepers: Nelly Dean, the unnamed housekeeper of Thrushcross Grange, Zillah and the unnamed housekeeper of

Wuthering Heights, the last two of whom will be the main focus of attention in this paper.[1]

The first housekeeper to be discussed here is the woman taken on at the Heights by Heathcliff after the death of Hindley in 1784. Heathcliff's reason for employing a female housekeeper is both his awareness of the squalid state of the Heights since Nelly left for the Grange a year earlier and his apparent recognition that women are best fitted to maintain an orderly household.[2] This housekeeper is first referred to on the afternoon Nelly has arrived at the Heights after her frantic search for Cathy in Chapter 18. Thus Nelly relates that the front door was opened to her by '[a] woman, whom [she] knew, and who formerly lived in Gimmerton', and yet a woman who, though known to Nelly, is, curiously enough, not once mentioned by name either here or, for that matter, anywhere else in the narrative. Nevertheless, she already shows that she is well acquainted with Nelly, as may be gathered from her first words to the latter: 'Ah, [...] you are come a seeking your little mistress! don't be frightened. She's here safe — but I'm glad it isn't the master' (*WH*, p. 170). At the same time, the housekeeper's relief at finding she has not opened the door to Heathcliff evokes an important motif, namely, the awe in which Heathcliff is held by all his servants. In the warmth with which she then invites Nelly to '[s]tep in and rest you a bit' (*WH*, p. 170), the housekeeper behaves as if she were as good as mistress of the Heights. This is plain enough when she presently joins with Hareton in laughing at Cathy's scampering about the house[3] in defiance of Nelly's efforts to make her return to the Grange immediately. Moreover, the housekeeper actively sides with Cathy after she has heard Nelly remonstrating with the latter, saying: 'Nay, [...] don't be hard on the bonny lass, Mrs Dean. We made her stop — she'd fain have ridden forwards, afeard you should be uneasy' (*WH*, p. 171). But if with such words the housekeeper comes across as an essentially sympathetic person, it is nevertheless noteworthy that, once she has been ordered by Cathy to 'bring the pony' and 'let [her] dog free' because Hareton has refused to do so, she stands up to her, saying: 'Softly, Miss, [...] You'll lose nothing, by being civil. Though Mr Hareton, there, be not the master's son, he's your cousin; and *I was never hired to serve you*' (*WH*, p. 173; italics mine). As well as fulfilling a useful function in the plot, such words are partly interesting for indicating that, amiable as the housekeeper has hitherto been in this episode, there has come a point where, because offended by Cathy, she has seen fit to fall back on the idea that her relationship with her social superiors is ultimately but a purely mercenary one.

The second time the unnamed housekeeper is mentioned is shortly after Nelly has brought Linton Heathcliff to the Heights in Chapter 20. On this occasion Nelly describes her 'clearing and wiping down the table' (*WH*, p. 182) just after 'the family' have finished breakfast — a chore which at the time will surely have reminded Nelly of similar ones she herself had done at the Heights before 1783. Then, when Linton has refused to eat the porridge brought to him by Joseph, the housekeeper is instructed to prepare 'boiled milk or tea' (*WH*, p. 185), as recommended by Nelly. That Linton's fastidiousness about food on his very first day at the Heights may have been reason enough for the housekeeper already to dislike the boy is quite apparent when, at her third meeting with Nelly, she refers disparagingly to his pernickety eating habits. Much more important, however, is the fact that the housekeeper has no sympathy whatever for Linton's symptoms of ill-health, seeming to regard him as little more than a malingerer. This we sense when she tells Nelly that Linton 'lay in bed all day; for he was constantly getting coughs, and colds, and aches, and pains of some sort' (*WH*, p. 186). With such a rapid enumeration of terms, the housekeeper hardly seems to take Linton's ailments seriously, indeed minimizes their significance. And when she adds, 'I never knew such a faint-hearted creature [...]

nor one so careful of hisseln' (*WH*, p. 186), she clearly regards the boy as a sort of 'spoilt brat' instead of seeing him as someone who in a loveless household is trying to cope with the symptoms of what will eventually prove to be a fatal disease. Such is the housekeeper's evident irritation at this stage of her account that the reader may scarcely wonder at the violence she vicariously betrays through her next utterance: 'I believe the master would relish Earnshaw's thrashing him to a mummy, if he were not his son: and, I'm certain he would be fit to turn him out of doors, if he knew half the nursing he gives hisseln' (*WH*, pp. 186-87). Furthermore, by the end of her report, the housekeeper has made it abundantly clear that she is in full sympathy with Heathcliff's hostility towards his son.

Not the least interesting effect of the housekeeper's account is the way in which it brings about a change in Nelly's own attitude to Linton. Thus Nelly concludes that 'utter lack of sympathy had rendered young Heathcliff selfish and disagreeable, if he were not so originally' (*WH*, p. 187). It is, therefore, scarcely surprising that, not unlike the unnamed housekeeper, Nelly herself regards Linton as a 'spoilt brat' rather than as someone who has by then become a genuine invalid. And though Nelly acknowledges being 'moved with a sense of grief at his lot, and a wish that he had been left with [them at the Grange]', such sentiments are characteristically hollow, and the more so as she has by then said that '[her] interest in him, consequently, decayed' (*WH*, p. 187). Also noteworthy during this time is Edgar's encouraging Nelly to 'gain information about Linton', and even telling her to 'ask the housekeeper whether he ever came into the village' (*WH*, p. 187). What Nelly learns from the housekeeper is that Linton 'had only been twice, on horseback, accompanying his father: and both times he *pretended to be quite knocked up for three or four days afterwards*' (*WH*, p. 187; italics mine). As we have seen before, the housekeeper seems to identify Linton's demonstration of physical weakness as simply the behaviour of a malingerer.[4] It is, incidentally, in this context that Nelly informs Lockwood that the unnamed housekeeper was, for reasons not given, replaced by Zillah 'two years after [Linton] came' (*WH*, p. 187), that is, in 1799, having served at the Heights for some fifteen years altogether.[5]

It is interesting to note that, having been housekeeper at the Heights for over a year or so already, Zillah at first comes across, not unlike her predecessor, as a sympathetic figure. But, unlike the unnamed housekeeper, whose physical appearance and age are nowhere specified, Zillah is described by Lockwood, on her entry into the house in order to put an end to his hapless struggle against the dogs, as 'a lusty dame, with tucked-up gown, bare arms, and fire-flushed cheeks' (*WH*, p. 5), and, next day, as 'the stout housewife' (*WH*, p. 14). Such details seem not inapposite as to someone who shows a certain violence not only when she subdues the dogs with 'a frying-pan' (*WH*, p. 5) but when, once aware of Lockwood's nose-bleed the following evening, she pours 'a pint of icy water down [his] neck, and pulled [him] into the kitchen' (*WH*, p. 14). The fact that Heathcliff soon afterwards 'told Zillah to give [Lockwood] a glass of brandy, and then passed on to the inner room' (*WH*, p. 14) may help to explain why Zillah should have assumed that he has left it to her to find Lockwood accommodation for the night. Not surprisingly, therefore, Zillah is nothing daunted in taking Lockwood up to a room where, as she admits, 'her master [...] never let anybody lodge [...] willingly' (*WH*, p. 15). When asked the reason for this prohibition, Zillah tells Lockwood that she 'did not know', for she had 'only lived there a year or two', adding, 'and they had so many queer goings on, she could not begin to be curious' (*WH*, p. 15). By thus detaching herself from a household where she has after all been employed for only a comparatively short time, Zillah is self-assured enough to act authoritatively once again on Lockwood's behalf. Certainly, in her bid to take the initiative for Lockwood's sake a third time, there is something admirable about the way in which she brushes aside the thought that she is taking a big risk in showing Lockwood to a room that she knows to have been declared out of bounds by her master. Indeed, it is for so acting that Zillah will have to pay dearly the next morning when, thanks to Lockwood's having sneaked on her, she is subjected to a severe scolding by Heathcliff in the house, as described thus by Lockwood: '[Heathcliff] stood by the fire, his back towards me, just finishing a stormy scene to poor Zillah, who ever and anon interrupted her labour to pluck up the corner of her apron, and heave an indignant groan' (*WH*, p. 25).

If Zillah so far gives the impression of being a 'good sort', and, indeed, enough so to have hardly deserved the upbraiding she has received from Heathcliff for putting Lockwood in the oak-panelled closet, it is nevertheless necessary to point out that she has for some time already been on bad terms with Cathy. This is amply hinted at towards the end of Chapter 3, when in her attempts to read a book by the light of the house fire, Cathy chides the housekeeper for 'covering her with sparks' while 'urging flakes of flame up the chimney with a colossal bellows' (*WH*, p. 25). Not that there has always been enmity between the two women, if we recall that Zillah was usually a most obliging hostess to Cathy at the time the latter was paying her illicit visits to Linton at the Heights, encouraged as the housekeeper probably was by Heathcliff to foster relations between the two cousins whom he intended to marry.[6] It is not until Cathy has returned to the Heights after her father's funeral that things turn sour between herself and Zillah, and that principally because Heathcliff has instructed the latter to 'follow her own business, and let his daughter-in-law look after herself' (*WH*, p. 259). And it is, as Nelly recalls, because Zillah 'willingly acquiesced' that Cathy 'evinced a child's annoyance at this neglect' and 'repaid it with contempt', thereby enlisting the housekeeper 'among her enemies, as securely as if she had done her some great wrong' (*WH*, p. 259). Cathy's animosity towards Zillah is then intensified by the latter's reluctance to help her to cope with Linton's critical illness, and is still manifest when she has come down to the house for the first time some two weeks after Linton's death; so that, by the end of Zillah's account, Nelly has learnt that Cathy is now at loggerheads with everybody at the Heights.[7]

Yet it is obvious that by the time she has so complacently finished her report to Nelly in Chapter 30, Zillah has ceased coming across to the reader as the more or less amiable person suggested in earlier narratives by Lockwood and Cathy. In any case, we have already been aware of Zillah's abject fear of Heathcliff since Chapter 2, when, mistakenly presuming that he and Hareton have been 'laying violent hands' on Lockwood, evidently because she has noticed them laughing at the latter after he has been borne down by the dogs, she 'turned her vocal artillery against the younger scoundrel' because, as Lockwood surmises, she dared not 'attack her master' (*WH*, p. 14). But if such desistence seems at the time to be a matter of good sense, it is quite another matter when fear of Heathcliff induces Zillah to decline to help Cathy to tend her severely ill husband Linton. Conspicuous in this context, for example, is the fact that, on Cathy's having come down to the house one morning, as Zillah observes, to ask 'all in a quiver if the doctor might be sent for? her cousin was very ill' (*WH*, p. 259), and then been flatly refused any such help by Heathcliff, Zillah remains utterly silent, evidently out of pure expedience. Significant, too, is Zillah's reaction to Cathy's subsequent requests for help: 'Then she began to bother me, and I said I'd had enough plague with the tiresome thing; we each had our tasks, and hers was to wait on Linton, Mr Heathcliff bid me leave that labour to her' (*WH*, p. 259). Even when Cathy now and again comes into the kitchen 'all wildered like' as if about to 'beg assistance', Zillah still declines, as she says, to 'disobey the master', adding: '— I never dare disobey him, Mrs Dean, and though I thought it wrong that Kenneth should not be sent for, it was no concern of mine, either to advise or complain; and I always refused to meddle' (*WH*, p. 260). Few utterances could better exemplify Zillah's lack of moral fibre, especially at a time when it is so badly needed. That such fecklessness on Zillah's part is testimony enough to her weak character can be seen when, despite at first ignoring Cathy's having ordered her one night to tell Heathcliff that his son is dying, she in the end feels compelled to deliver Cathy's message, overcome as she is by the moral force behind that message. Nor does Zillah's well-meaning gesture of giving 'a little wine' (*WH*, p. 260) to Cathy seated beside her dead husband do anything to make up for the housekeeper's failure to help her while Linton was still alive.

It is, however, in the wake of such incidents that Cathy becomes more than ever an object of Zillah's dislike for various reasons — a dislike that seems to date from the time when, on her return to the Heights after her father's funeral, Cathy ran upstairs, as Zillah complains, 'without even wishing good-evening to me and Joseph' (*WH*, p. 259). This dislike may be further sensed not only when, according to Nelly, Zillah said that, while visiting Cathy in her room 'twice a-day', she 'would have been rather more friendly, but her attempts at increasing kindness were proudly and promptly repelled' (*WH*, p. 261). It is again sensed when, having come down to the house a fortnight after Linton's death, Cathy 'turned up her nose at my civility', as Zillah puts it, namely that of offering 'my seat in the arm-chair' (*WH*, p. 262). Through all such complaints Zillah clearly betrays her inveterate respectability, a characteristic that perhaps encourages her to look upon herself as being much more than a mere servant. This is in part indicated by the way in which Zillah shows her resentment at the fact that, irrespective of her dire material circumstances, Cathy remains none the less her social superior through her genteel birth. This in turn explains why, though agreeing with Nelly that Cathy is 'too fine for Mr Hareton', Zillah asserts that she would 'love well to bring her pride a peg lower,' and why, in a bid to reduce Cathy's status further still, she goes on to say: 'And what will all her learning and her daintiness do for her, now? She's as poor as you or I — poorer, I'll be bound, you're saving — and I'm doing my little all, that road' (*WH*, p. 262). And when, towards the end of her account, Zillah tells Nelly that 'in spite of her pride', Cathy was forced to 'condescend to our company, more and more' (*WH*, p. 264), such words plainly indicate that the housekeeper is implying that she and Cathy are by now as good as social equals.

It is, then, easy to see that Zillah's criticisms of Cathy, understandable as they may be in some measure in view of the latter's continual off-handedness, are expressions of her fundamental class-consciousness. Yet we also realize the extent to which such criticisms show Zillah to be not only the 'narrow-minded, selfish woman' (*WH*, p. 259) that Nelly has by now declared her to be, but an utterly vain and stupid person. This is evident enough when Zillah tells Nelly that she 'took care there should be no further scorning at *my good nature* —', adding: 'ever since, I've been as stiff as herself' (*WH*, p. 264; italics mine). Amid her blatant vindictiveness, it is obvious that Zillah confuses 'good nature' with the 'civility' that she has now and then exhibited to Cathy, but which forms an integral part of the unconscionable respectability by which she is usually shown in a fairly satirical light. This we note when, for example, explaining why she has forgone attendance at her local (Dissenters') chapel on the Sunday morning Cathy is expected to come down to the house, she says: 'Young folks are always the better for an elder's over-looking' (*WH*, p. 261-62). Noteworthy in this connection is Zillah's further justifying her presence at the Heights that Sunday by adding: 'and Hareton, with all his bashfulness, isn't a model of nice behaviour' (*WH*, p. 262).[8] For it is through these words and others she will later utter about Hareton that Zillah will betray her snobbery and respectability at their cruellest levels. First of all, having warned

Hareton to 'leave his guns and bits of in-door work alone' because, as she explains, his cousin, who is about to make her appearance in the house, 'had been always used to see the Sabbath respected' (*WH*, p. 262), Zillah seems bent on referring to him as a somewhat contemptible figure. For example, by noting that Hareton 'coloured up at the news' of Cathy's imminent arrival, and then by 'laughing' at him when offering to help him make himself 'presentable', at the same time as she tells Nelly that she 'durst not laugh when the master is by' (*WH*, p. 262), Zillah seems all the more despicable for thus taking advantage of Hareton. Again, when she has later observed Cathy turning on Hareton for daring to touch her hair, she notices that he 'recoiled, *looking as foolish as he could do*' (*WH*, p. 263; italics mine).[9] Zillah's blatant disrespect for Hareton is finally confirmed when, instead of directly asking Cathy to read to them, as Hareton has requested her to do, the housekeeper blithely ignores his wish by saying this: 'Mr Hareton wishes you would read to us, ma'am [...]. He'd take it very kind — he'd be much obliged' (*WH*, p. 263).

At this juncture, Zillah might be said to have long ceased being the 'good sort' we have found her to be in earlier chapters of the novel. Indeed, our impression of her by now is that of a vain and stupid woman. Such an impression has already been gained at the beginning of Chapter 28, when, having arrived in her bedroom, and — as if to underline her inherent vanity — 'donned in her scarlet shawl, with a black silk bonnet on her head, and a willow basket swung to her arm' (*WH*, p. 246) in order to release Nelly from her incarceration there, she evinces a quite astonishing gullibility by continuing to assert her belief in the rumour going round the village about Heathcliff's rescue of Cathy and Nelly from Blackhorse marsh, and that even in the face of Nelly's outright denial of that rumour. At this stage, the reader might well be surprised enough at the oddness of Zillah's talk to wonder how far all this has to do with her role and function as a housekeeper. We note, for example, that

Zillah is a generally dutiful servant while Heathcliff is present in the Heights, and that, even when he is off the premises, she is dutiful enough to foster Cathy's relationship with Linton Heathcliff, aware as she supposedly is that Heathcliff is intent on marrying the cousins. There are also references to her usefulness as a housekeeper when we are told of her getting the house fire going in the early morning, helping Linton to dress or undress, milking cows, and even trying to deal with Cathy's highly emotional behaviour on the evening she and Linton have been turned out of the house by Hareton.[10] Nevertheless, it is noteworthy that, during the time Heathcliff is absent from the Heights for a week, Zillah is complained about by his son for, among other things, 'constantly gadding off to Gimmerton since papa went' (*WH*, p. 209) — a detail that seems to tie up with the fact that, unlike, say, the long-serving, loyal Joseph, Zillah has been employed at the Heights for 'only a year or two', and will leave her post not long afterwards. Moreover, Zillah's 'gadding off' should remind us that, like her unnamed predecessor, and despite those occasions when each of them is helpful, even kindhearted, towards such visitors to the household as Lockwood, Nelly and Cathy, both women are ultimately shown to take a fundamentally mercenary attitude to their jobs as domestics.

The question then arises: why has Emily Brontë given these two housekeepers rather more than the perfunctory roles generally assigned to servants in nineteenth-century English fiction? Certainly, Zillah is presented as something of a personality, as may be gathered easily enough from the fascinating mixture of dialect and educated speech with which she, like the unnamed housekeeper, makes her various utterances and pronouncements. There are, to be sure, contexts in which Zillah's presence at, or absence from, the Heights is crucial for the plot, especially as concerns Heathcliff's bringing about Linton's marriage to Cathy. Again, both housekeepers prove useful as narrators in providing Nelly with information about Cathy's and Linton's respective actions and situations at the Heights. Nor should we forget Zillah's function as a means whereby the seemingly rational Lockwood betrays a markedly irrational streak in his mental make-up when, in an attempt to propitiate Heathcliff, he complains to him about her putting him in the oak-panelled closet because, as he claims, she wanted 'another proof that the place was haunted, at [his] expense' (*WH*, p. 22). More important than the foregoing considerations, however, is the idea that Zillah and the unnamed housekeeper are ultimately of interest for the ways in which they indirectly shed light on the presentation of Cathy and Hareton. Thus we note, for example, that whereas Hareton's 'fearless nature' discourages Heathcliff from treating him 'physically ill' (*WH*, p. 174) and Cathy is shown time and again boldly standing up to the latter, usually at the risk of suffering his violence, both housekeepers are by contrast in constant fear of Heathcliff as their master. In Zillah's case, moreover, such fear reaches a point where she attaches more importance to keeping her job than to acting on the promptings of her conscience. It is also interesting to note that both housekeepers have a generally patronizing, even contemptuous, attitude towards Hareton, as if they saw him as little more than a benign idiot. Such attitudes may have done much to influence some Brontë scholars to overlook in him the intrinsic goodness and strength of character that Cathy in the end comes to recognize and to love him for. Again, it is almost certain that both the unnamed housekeeper's and Zillah's negative remarks about Linton Heathcliff have contributed to making him an unpopular character as much as Zillah's harsh criticisms of Cathy have helped to sustain the latter's poor image in the minds of many a reader over the years. In this connection, it is worthy of mention that, unlike both housekeepers as well as Nelly herself, Cathy is practically unique in not only showing compassion for Linton in his state of chronic ill-health but in continuing to show him love in spite of his persistently cantankerous talk and behaviour.

In view of the implicit contrast between Cathy, on the one hand, and the unnamed housekeeper, Zillah and Nelly, on the other, as to their respective attitudes to Linton Heathcliff, it is perhaps significant that, despite Lockwood's seeing her preparing tea on his second visit to the Heights and noticing her performing culinary tasks on his third visit there, Cathy at no time during her early widowhood at the Heights seems disposed to look upon herself as a servant. This is patent enough when, for example, she flatly refuses to do any work for Heathcliff in the house at the end of Chapter 3. The same may be said to be in some measure true of Hareton, especially when he objects to being treated like a servant by Cathy in Chapter 30, confirming as he does this attitude shortly afterwards by showing, in a spirit of contrition, his willingness to serve her particular needs, but only as an equal. Hareton's capacity for disinterested service is, moreover, the very opposite of that tendency in Zillah and the unnamed housekeeper to remain largely within the remit of their roles as hired servants, even if it is true that both women are by no means entirely devoid of humanity, being capable, as we have now and again seen, of friendliness and even of showing sympathy. Nevertheless, it is clear that, in their unsympathetic attitudes to Linton Heathcliff and Cathy, both housekeepers display an almost obtuse lack of understanding for the difficulties being undergone and endured by the targets of their relentless criticism. Such mental and moral limitations may be due partly to the mundaneness of the menial positions occupied by both the housekeepers under discussion and, of course, by Nelly Dean herself. This in turn might explain why, conscious as she surely was of the perennial need for more or less well-to-do families to employ servants to run their households in the eighteenth and nineteenth centuries, Emily Brontë seems intent, through the presentation of her two housekeepers, on disclosing an uncomfortable truth, namely, that domestic service has a tendency to harden the hearts of some of those carrying out such work and, in some degree, even to make them quite violent in both word and deed. This idea seems to be indirectly suggested when, on his return to Gimmerton in September 1802, Lockwood finds the Grange not in the hands of Nelly Dean, as he had expected it to be, but in those of a comparatively uneducated and simple-hearted woman, who, because barely familiar with the finer points of housekeeping, not only symbolically adumbrates the cosy atmosphere that has been prevailing at the Heights since the death of Heathcliff, but may also be thought somehow to point forward to an era when servants will once again have become as much 'part of the family' as they used to be in Mr Earnshaw's day.[11]

Brontë Studies, 45/3 (2020)

Notes

1   For quotations from the novel, see Emily Brontë, *Wuthering Heights*, ed. by Ian Jack and Patsy Stoneman (Oxford: Oxford University Press, 1998); hereafter *WH*. For the sake of convenience, the elder Catherine will be referred to as 'Catherine', the younger as 'Cathy'.

2   For Isabella's comments on the unkempt state of the kitchen and the house shortly after her arrival at the Heights as Heathcliff's bride, see *Wuthering Heights*, pp. 120-22.

3   By 'the house' is meant, throughout this essay, the family sitting-room of Wuthering Heights.

4   It is not unreasonable to suppose that Emily Brontë, who at the time she was writing *Wuthering Heights* was herself suffering from the same kind of disease that Linton Heathcliff is eventually to die of, readily identified with the boy, especially as regards the incomprehension, not to say lack of sympathy, of some of those attending him in his illness.

5   Although Zillah has been mentioned here and there in several essays on *Wuthering Heights*, no Brontë scholar has, to my knowledge, hitherto written extensively about her role in the novel. However, for some interesting explanations of Emily Brontë's choice of the name Zillah, see the following articles: Elliott B. Gose, Jr., '*Wuthering Heights*: The Heath and the Hearth', *Nineteenth-Century Fiction*, 21 (1966): 1-19; Ronald E. Fine, 'Lockwood's Dreams and the Key to *Wuthering Heights*', *Nineteenth-Century Fiction*, 24 (1969): 16-30; F. B. Pinion, 'Byron and *Wuthering Heights*', *Brontë Society Transactions*, 21, part 5(1995):

195-201; Marianne Thormählen, 'The Lunatic and the Devil's Disciple: The "Lovers" in *Wuthering Heights'*, *The Review of English Studies*, 48. 190 (1997): 183-97.

6   See *Wuthering Heights*, pp. 218-19.

7   See *Wuthering Heights*, p. 264. At the same time, by assuring Nelly at this stage that Cathy 'has no lover or liker among us' (*WH*. p. 264) at the Heights, Zillah seems utterly oblivious of Hareton's attachment to the latter, thereby showing an arrant presumptuousness that is of a piece with her portrayal as an essentially stupid woman.

8   The unnamed housekeeper herself has already referred to Hareton as 'not bad-natured, *though he's rough*—' (*WH*, p. 186; italics mine).

9   Something of the malicious pleasure underlying these references to Hareton's physicality can also be sensed in Zillah's earlier description of Cathy just after she has come to the house from upstairs: 'she made her appearance, donned in black, and her yellow curls combed back behind her ears, as plain as a quaker: she couldn't comb them out' (*WH*, p. 261).

10 See *Wuthering Heights*, pp. 25, 222, 241.

11 That Emily might well have imagined she was already living in such an era may be gathered from accounts of the very warm friendship that she and her family enjoyed at Haworth with their housekeeper Tabitha Aykroyd. For details, see especially Winifred Gérin, *Emily Brontë. A Biography* (Oxford, New York & Melbourne: Oxford University Press, 1978), pp. 29, 60, 225.

The Presentation of Mr Kenneth in *Wuthering Heights*

One character that deserves much more than the passing mention he generally receives in scholarly writings on *Wuthering Heights* is the village doctor, Mr Kenneth.[1] Indeed, in a novel where illness is by no means an uncommon occurrence, Kenneth's presence is substantial enough to warrant our giving it due critical attention. It is, moreover, through Kenneth that the reader gains some idea of the principal therapeutic methods resorted to by the medical profession in Britain during the late eighteenth century and beyond. Thus reference is made to such traditional practices as blood-letting and blistering as cures for practically every malady, including, most notably, Catherine's delirium.[2] At the same time, as well as playing a useful role in some dramatic moments of the narrative, Kenneth is especially interesting as a character in his own right, partly because in some sense he is quite representative of the essentially patriarchal ethos that permeates the society so ingeniously portrayed by Emily Brontë.[3] Let us now examine his presentation in some detail.

First of all, the reader might well wonder to what extent Kenneth is modelled on any of the medical doctors who attended members of the Brontë family for their respective ailments in Haworth. That Kenneth is more likely based on a composite of real-life physicians, if not mainly the product of the author's imagination, is suggested by the absence hitherto of any reference being made to an actual original by Emily's biographers.[4] In the novel itself, we are given very few personal details about Kenneth. All we learn in that respect is that, according to Nelly, he is 'a plain, rough man' (*WH*, p. 114) and that he has a house in Gimmerton; but we are told neither his age nor his marital status, nor anything about his personal appearance. What seems evident is that he is the only local doctor, and one who, as Nelly informs Lockwood, 'had enough to do in the parish where two or three miles was the ordinary distance between cottage and cottage' (*WH*, p. 78), travelling such distances as he does on his mare. Thus it would appear that, unlike general practitioners in Britain today, Kenneth does his work entirely in the dwellings of the patients he visits, though, interestingly enough, little is said about the fees he charges.[5] At the same time, Kenneth is shown to be a dutiful and hard-working doctor, as is well exemplified when, in complete contrast with the local parson, he is nothing daunted by bad weather to come to the Heights on the evening of Mr Earnshaw's death.[6] Similarly, on the night Nelly walked all the way to Gimmerton to get Kenneth to attend a delirious Catherine, we are told that, though he was 'just issuing from his house to see a patient in the village', and that as late as two o'clock in the morning, Nelly's 'account of Catherine Linton's malady induced him to accompany [Nelly] back immediately' (*WH*, p. 114). There are also other occasions when Kenneth duly arrives at the Heights very soon after he has been sent for.[7]

It is perhaps because Mr Kenneth is a conscientious doctor, as well as being the only doctor to turn to by those living in Gimmerton, that his authority is generally taken seriously. One example of this is suggested when the maidservant who has just announced Hareton's birth to Nelly adds this: 'But the doctor *says* missis must go; he *says* she's been in a consumption these many months' (*WH*, p. 56; italics mine). Presently, we note that to Hindley's enthusing about his newborn son, Nelly gives this answer: 'And the mistress? [...] the doctor *says* she's —' (*WH*, p. 57; italics mine). But although Hindley instantly repudiates what Nelly is about to utter, it is ironic to find him telling her this about his wife only a few moments later: 'I left her because she would not hold her tongue; and she must — tell her *Mr Kenneth says she must be quiet*' (*WH*, p. 57; italics mine).[8] Nelly, too, is quite deferential to Kenneth in certain ways. Thus we note that, when referring to Heathcliff as the easiest of Mr Earnshaw's children for her to nurse while they had measles, Nelly makes a point of saying this about the boy's recovery: 'He got through, and the doctor affirmed it was in a great measure owing to me, and praised me for my care. I was vain of his commendations, and softened towards the being by whose means I earned them' (*WH*, p. 33). Since measles was often a fatal illness in the eighteenth century, it is easy to understand Nelly's pride in this achievement. Nelly's fear of disobeying Kenneth is certainly apparent when, amid her attempts to cope with the effects of Catherine's delirium in Chapter 12, she tells of her nervous reactions to her mistress's appearance and behaviour: '[T]he expressions flitting over her face, and the changes of her moods, began to alarm me terribly; and brought to my recollection her former illness, and *the doctor's injunction that she should not be crossed*' (*WH*, p. 108; italics mine). For Nelly, illness almost invariably means sending for the doctor, as we see most plainly when, just after reporting Edgar's assumption that it is only through marriage to his nephew Linton that Cathy will be able to 'retain [...] the house of her ancestors', Nelly recalls that her master had no idea that Linton 'was failing almost as fast as himself', before adding: 'nor had any one, I believe; no doctor visited the Heights, and no one saw Master Heathcliff to make report of his condition, among us' (*WH*, p. 229). Later, having witnessed 'the greatest distress' in Linton during his second 'official' meeting with Cathy on the heath, Nelly, unaware as she is that the boy is cleverly feigning illness, gives Heathcliff the following piece of advice: 'To see him, I should say, that instead of rambling with his sweetheart on the hills, he ought to be in bed, under the hands of a doctor' (*WH*, p. 237).[9] And though even Zillah herself, mindful of Linton's acute ill health at the Heights after his marriage to Cathy, thinks it 'wrong that Kenneth should not be sent for' (*WH*, p. 260), her reason for not saying anything to Heathcliff is clearly due to her fear of losing her job as his housekeeper.

Kenneth's medical authority seems, then, to have been quite respectfully taken for granted both before and after the start of Nelly's narrative in Chapter 4. Certainly, in his diagnoses of particular illnesses he comes across as knowledgeable enough about his profession, at least as exercised in the eighteenth century. For example, having 'pronounced [Catherine] dangerously ill' as a consequence of her having spent the previous night in soaked clothing, Kenneth proceeds both to treat her and also to advise Nelly how to nurse her. As Nelly recalls: 'He bled her, and he told me to let her live on whey and water gruel; and take care she did not throw herself down stairs, or out of the window' (*WH*, p. 78). Noteworthy in this connection is that, after Kenneth has later heard Nelly's account of Catherine Linton's malady as described in Chapter 12, he 'made no scruple to speak his doubts of her surviving this second attack; unless she were more submissive to his directions than she had shown herself before' (*WH*, p. 114). How Kenneth knows about such disobedience on Catherine's part is, however, yet to be revealed. At the same time, it is clear that on account of 'odd reports' he has been given about life at Thrushcross Grange, Kenneth is astute enough to suspect that Catherine's illness has had an 'extra cause', convinced that '[a] stout, hearty lass like Catherine does not fall ill for a trifle' (*WH*, p. 114); in other words, that the cause has been psychological. Then, as soon as Nelly has given him a sort of summary of the showdown between Heathcliff and Edgar in the Grange kitchen and its aftermath, Kenneth reasserts his authority by saying this about the latter: 'Well, I told him to beware [...] and he must bide the consequences of neglecting my warning!' (*WH*, p. 115). That Kenneth is, however, less pessimistic in his prognosis regarding Catherine's second illness is evident from Nelly's following words: 'The doctor, on examining the case for himself, spoke hopefully to [Edgar] of its having a favourable termination, if we could only preserve around her perfect and constant tranquility' (*WH*, p. 116). This prognosis would have very probably proved correct had Nelly prevented the fateful tryst between Catherine and Heathcliff in Chapter 11, just as Edgar's neglect of Kenneth's earlier warning has predictably led to the 'consequences' in question. And though it is only to Nelly, not to Edgar himself, that Kenneth 'signified the threatening danger was not so much death, as permanent alienation of intellect' (*WH*, p. 116), he will nevertheless warn Edgar, during the time the latter is tending Catherine in her 'brain fever', that 'what he saved from the grave would only recompense his care by forming the source of constant future anxiety — in fact, that his health and strength were being sacrificed to preserve a mere ruin of humanity —' (*WH*, p. 118). That this prognosis, too, turns out to have been valid is evident enough if we recall that Catherine's mind henceforth continues to be more or less unbalanced until her death in Chapter 15.

Although Kenneth seems to have his authority honoured in several ways, it is nevertheless interesting to note the degree in which that authority is now and again resisted. Such resistance is usually encountered when Kenneth's diagnoses or prognoses, correct as they invariably prove to be, are thought too pessimistic to be acceptable. For example, the maidservant who announces Hareton's birth to

Nelly, having overheard Kenneth telling Hindley that Frances would die of consumption 'before winter', somewhat naively rejects this prognosis by saying this to Nelly: 'If I were [Frances] I'm certain I should not die. I should get better at the bare sight of [the baby], in spite of Kenneth. I was fairly mad at him' (*WH*, p. 56). A similar incredulity underlies Hindley's even stronger rejection of the same prognosis. Thus no sooner has Nelly begun to allude to Kenneth's fateful dictum than Hindley interrupts her as follows: 'Damn the doctor! [...] Frances is quite right — she'll be perfectly well by this time next week' (*WH*, p. 57). Later, when Kenneth warns Hindley that 'his medicines were useless at that stage of [Frances's] malady, and he needn't put him to further expense by attending her', Hindley retorts: 'I know you need not — she's well — she does not want any more attendance from you! She never was in a consumption. It was a fever; and it is gone — her pulse is as slow as mine now, and her cheek as cool' (*WH*, p. 57). Yet the more Hindley goes against Kenneth's prognosis with such talk, the more he seems to recognise what he knows to be an ineluctable truth, namely, that the doctor's prognosis will be sooner or later validated. And so we see how, through the account of Frances's fatal disease, Kenneth shows himself to be as medically efficient as he later does in respect of Catherine's two illnesses. Resistance to Kenneth is, to be sure, understandable in those for whom his prognoses mean the eventual loss of loved ones. On the other hand, Kenneth is sometimes resisted possibly because his therapeutic methods cause, as indeed they are known to have done in the eighteenth century, not inconsiderable discomfort to those subjected to them. Thus we are told that when, shortly after Heathcliff's return to Gimmerton, Isabella has been complaining about being victimized by everybody at the Grange, Catherine 'peremptorily insisted that she should get to bed; and, having scolded her heartily, threatened to send for the doctor'. The fact that '[m]ention of Kenneth caused [Isabella] to exclaim, instantly, that her health was perfect, and it was only Catherine's harshness which made her unhappy' (*WH*, p. 89) might suggest that Isabella dreads the probably painful treatment she would be obliged to undergo at Kenneth's hands.[10]

Isabella's rejection of Kenneth is somewhat foreshadowed by Lockwood's curiously chary attitude towards the doctor, which suggests certain contradictions not unlike those betrayed by Hindley. For example, at the beginning of Chapter 10, Lockwood complains of 'dilatory country surgeons', as if he were desirous of instant medical attention; yet, when actually visited by Kenneth, he laments his tendency to talk shop. That is why, while admitting with some resentment that Heathcliff is 'not altogether guiltless in this illness of mine', Lockwood writes of his own reluctance to 'offend a man who was charitable enough to sit at my bedside a good hour, and talk on some other subject than pills and draughts, blisters and leeches' (*WH*, p. 80). In a word, it is Kenneth's professionalism that irritates Lockwood, as we see presently confirmed when he shows impatience with Nelly not only for scrupulously obeying the doctor's instructions as to the exact time a particular medicine is to be taken, but also for exclaiming: 'The doctor says you must drop the powders' (*WH*, p. 80). In any case, Lockwood is now clearly far too concerned to know what Heathcliff did after his flight from the Heights to be bothered with medicines of any kind; hence his following instruction to Nelly: 'Keep your fingers from that bitter phalanx of vials' (*WH*, p. 80). Such annoyance at Kenneth's therapeutic measures somehow points forward to the fact that it is evidently thanks not so much to medical treatment as to Nelly's narrative that Lockwood will be restored to health sooner than Kenneth has expected him to be. Indeed, the idea that Lockwood's early recovery is due chiefly to his absorption in that narrative is suggested in that moment towards the end of Chapter 14, when, while referring to her dilemma as to whether or not to give Heathcliff's note to Catherine asking her to let him meet her at the

Grange, Nelly interrupts her narrative by saying: 'But here is Kenneth — I'll go down, and tell him how much better you are' (*WH*, p. 136). Moreover, it is no small irony that Lockwood is able to visit Heathcliff at the Heights already in January 1802, thereby not only proving how mistaken has been what he earlier said in his diary, namely, 'the terrible intimation of Kenneth that I need not expect to be out of doors till spring!' (*WH*, p. 80), but also in some sense suggesting what has been noted above, that is to say, that Kenneth is not only a conscientious doctor but, in some respects, also an unduly cautious one.

Since Kenneth seems to be exclusively depended on for his services by the entire population of the rather spacious village of Gimmerton, it is hardly surprising that he should come across to the reader as a very self-assured physician. Certainly, he cuts a much more engaging figure than many of those colleagues of his appearing in other nineteenth-century works of fiction, most of whom are only briefly described or mentioned in contexts of essentially medical interest. At the same time, it would appear that, competent though he may be as a general practitioner, he nevertheless has certain limitations. This is indicated not only by his perhaps undue reliance on the curative methods prevalent in his day, but, more particularly, by his inability to determine the cause of Heathcliff's death. Moreover, the fact that Kenneth seems by then to have been quite unaware of Heathcliff's psychological disorder, which is referred to by Nelly as 'a monomania' (*WH*, p. 288), is hardly to be wondered at, considering that this form of mental illness tended to remain hidden from all but the most expert eyes, principally because its victims otherwise generally enjoyed normal physical health. Thus, notwithstanding the anachronistic use of the term 'monomania', which was, in fact, not coined until about 1810, Kenneth's evident ignorance of this illness and his inability to recognize its symptoms admirably confirm the realism of Emily's portrayal of him as a comparatively ordinary eighteenth-century doctor.[11]

It is, however, useful at this juncture to be reminded that Kenneth is presented not merely as a physician, but also as something of a 'character' who, familiar as he appears to be with practically every household in Gimmerton, is much given to gossip and even to pontificating on the lives of some of the local inhabitants. That all this may be meant to raise certain doubts in the minds of readers as to Kenneth's medical competence is by no means to be altogether ruled out, and the more so on those occasions when his talk smacks of what the present-day reader might identify as machismo. Machismo is no doubt hardly an unusual thing in the very patriarchal society depicted in Emily's novel, instances of it being patently exemplified in Heathcliff's language and behaviour. Kenneth's machismo is doubtless due in some measure to his sense of having much the same respectable social status as that enjoyed by, say, a local parson in many a small community in eighteenth-century England. Such machismo is especially noticeable in certain things he says about people. Consider, for instance, the callous way in which Kenneth is overheard by the maidservant (who has informed Nelly of Hareton's birth) saying this to Hindley:

> Earnshaw, it's a blessing your wife has been spared to leave you this son. When she came, I felt convinced we shouldn't keep her long; and now, I must tell you, the winter will probably finish her. Don't take on, and fret about it too much, it can't be helped. And besides, you should have known better than to choose such a rush of a lass! (*WH*, p. 56)

The fact that the maidservant has by then referred to Kenneth as 'the old croaker' and told Nelly of being 'fairly mad at him' (*WH*, p. 56), presumably for his fatal prognosis, is probably also due to her awareness of Kenneth's blunt disregard of Hindley's feelings.

A similar insensitivity can also be felt in the bluff manner in which Kenneth informs Nelly of Hindley's death. Thus we note how he keeps her guessing, first, by putting this flippant question to her: 'Who's given us a slip now, do you think?', and then by advising her just as flippantly to 'nip up the corner of your apron; I'm certain you'll need it' (*WH*, p. 163). To Nelly's presuming that Heathcliff has died, Kenneth waggishly replies: 'What! would you have tears for him?' before continuing thus: 'No, Heathcliff's a tough young fellow; he looks blooming to-day — I've just seen him. He's rapidly regaining flesh since he lost his better half' (*WH*, p. 163). Here Kenneth seems to suggest in quite misogynistic vein that Heathcliff's health has actually benefited by his spouseless existence. And even when Kenneth discloses that it is Hindley who has died, he does so in much the same bluff manner in which he has earlier told the latter some painful truths about his moribund wife:

There! I said we should draw water — But cheer up! He died true to his character, drunk as a lord — Poor lad; I'm sorry, too. One can't help missing an old companion; though he had the worst tricks with him that ever man imagined, and has done me many a rascally turn — (*WH*, p. 163-64)

In view of what Kenneth has just said somewhat ironically about Hindley, the reader might well wonder why the doctor has bothered to cultivate the companionship of someone who has hitherto come across as a largely unsympathetic loner. That such a friendship seems to have been strangely intimate has already been suggested in Chapter 9, when, having just arrived home in a drunken state, Hindley threatens to make Nelly 'swallow the carving knife' before going on to say: 'You needn't laugh; for I've just crammed Kenneth, head-downmost, in the Blackhorse marsh' (*WH*, p. 65). Although such a vicious act might have been but a figment of Hindley's imagination, it nevertheless somehow foreshadows what Kenneth has said about Hindley's having 'done [him] many a rascally turn'. Yet despite such untoward behaviour on Hindley's part, it seems likely that Kenneth has made use of his company principally in order to obtain from him the scandalous gossip he evidently enjoys hearing and retailing. Perhaps the signal example of Kenneth's ear for gossip is shown on the night Nelly has come to Gimmerton in order to take him back to a delirious Catherine. And though, as we saw above, Kenneth believes that Catherine's illness has been psychologically induced, it is curious to note Kenneth seeking to draw Nelly out into informing him about what he has clearly already learnt by way of gossip, namely, that the illness has been brought on by Edgar's showdown with Heathcliff. Again, gathering that Heathcliff has now been forbidden to visit the Grange on account of his 'presumptuous aspirations after Miss Linton', Kenneth then asks: 'And does Miss Linton turn a cold shoulder on him?', even though, notwithstanding Nelly's saying that she is 'not in [Isabella's] confidence', he has already heard from someone he refers to as '[his] informant' that, during their encounter in the Grange grounds the previous night, Isabella has promised Heathcliff to elope with him 'on their first meeting after that' (*WH*, p. 115). What is puzzling about Kenneth's talk in this context is his preferring to wallow in gossip instead of, say, straightway advising Nelly to take immediate action to prevent Isabella's elopement. Indeed, knowing what he seems to have known for some twenty-four hours already, Kenneth could easily have informed Edgar of Isabella's intention in good time. In this connection, it is noteworthy that, in spite of having asked Nelly what she knows about Isabella's relations with Heathcliff, Kenneth proceeds to preface what he himself already knows about her romantic intentions with the following assertion: 'No, she's a sly one. [...] She keeps her own counsel! But she's a real little fool' (*WH*, p. 115) — words which, apart from putting us in mind of Kenneth's inveterate misogyny, might give the impression that he has all along been secretly hoping for Isabella's elopement rather than being concerned to do what he could already have done to prevent it.

It is, then, easy to surmise from the foregoing that Kenneth regards his respectable social status as the local village doctor such as to entitle him to make moral pronouncements on matters that have little to do with his profession. Accordingly, it might be asked whether Kenneth's self-importance in this respect, to say nothing of his apparent taste for gossip, is indirectly intended to make us cast some doubt on his medical reliability. Amid the attempt to answer that question, however, it is perhaps worth quoting the estimate he makes of Hindley's lifespan, which, because fundamentally unscientific, sits oddly with his role as a generally competent physician. Thus, when, just after saving Hareton from certain death, who has been dropped by his drunken father over the Heights bannister, Heathcliff expresses regret that Hindley 'cannot kill himself with drink', in spite of 'doing his very utmost', he goes on to say this to Nelly: 'Mr Kenneth says he would wager his mare, that [Hindley will] outlive any man on this side Gimmerton, and go to the grave a hoary sinner; unless some happy chance out of the common course befall him' (*WH*, p. 67). Kenneth's optimistic prediction is scarcely less mistaken than that whereby Heathcliff, amid the 'strange change' (*WH*, p. 287) he is experiencing through his mental illness, assures Nelly in Chapter 33 that he has 'neither a fear, nor a presentiment, nor a hope of death', before going on to make this false prediction about his own lifespan: 'Why should I? With my hard constitution, and temperate mode of living, and unperilous occupations, I ought to and probably *shall* remain above ground, till there is scarcely a black hair on my head —' (*WH*, p. 288-89). By that stage of the narrative, the reader will also have noted a similar optimism about longevity that colours Nelly's bid to distract a melancholy Cathy from her dread both of her father's death and the death of Nelly herself. Thus, though sensibly admitting to the girl that '[n]one can tell, whether you won't die before us,' Nelly nevertheless continues: 'we'll hope there are years and years to come before any of us go — master is young, and I am strong, and hardly forty-five' (*WH*, p. 203). Ironically enough, it turns out that being 'young' will not prevent Edgar from dying very soon afterwards at the age of thirty-nine. Mistaken, too, will prove to be the optimism with which, in defiance of Nelly's malicious prediction that Linton Heathcliff will 'not win twenty', Cathy gives the following reply: 'He's younger than I [...] and he ought to live the longest: he will — he must live as long as I do' (*WH*, p. 214).

And so, through our consciousness of such parallels, we become aware that, for all his scientific authoritativeness, Kenneth is after all just as fallible as any layman when confronted by the perennially vexed and seemingly unanswerable question of the relationship between the health of one's physical constitution and the length of one's life. Still, taken as it must needs be in conjunction with other aspects of his presentation as a man who, while more or less professionally competent, is nevertheless somewhat morally flawed, and as a man who is conspicuous for the way in which he keeps emotional involvement at bay through his constant recourse to trite metaphorical language, Kenneth's erroneous prediction about Hindley may be said to form an integral part of one of the most memorable portraits of a medical doctor ever drawn in English fiction.[12]

Brontë Studies, 43/2 (2018)

Notes

1 For quotations from the novel, see Emily Brontë, *Wuthering Heights*, ed. by Ian Jack and Patsy Stoneman (Oxford: Oxford University Press, 1998); hereafter referred to as *WH*. For the sake of convenience, the first Catherine will be referred to as 'Catherine', the second as 'Cathy'.

2 For historical accounts of such methods, see, among several studies, Dorothy Porter & Roy Porter, *Patient's Progress: Doctors and Doctoring in Eighteenth-Century England* (Stanford, CA: Stanford University Press, 1989).

3 For references to Kenneth's meetings with various characters, see *WH*, pp. 246, 248.

4 In this connection, it is notorious that whenever Emily fell ill she flatly refused not only to be visited by any doctor but also to receive medicine or medical treatments of any kind, even when her fatal illness was at its most acute just before her death. For details see especially Charlotte Brontë's letters to Ellen Nussey and W. S. Williams in *The Letters of Charlotte Brontë. With a Selection of Letters by Family and Friends*, ed. by Margaret Smith (Oxford: Clarendon Press, 2004) II, 130-31, 142-47, 154. See also Winifred Gérin, *Emily Brontë: A Biography* (Oxford: Clarendon Press, 1972), p. 255, and Katherine Frank, *Emily Brontë: the Chainless Soul* (London: Hamish Hamilton, 1996), pp. 253-54. That Emily's hostility to the medical profession, whom she is said to have dismissed as 'poisonous doctors', may have determined certain unsympathetic aspects of Kenneth's presentation is, accordingly, a quite plausible hypothesis.

5   For the only reference to fees, see *WH*, p. 57.

6   See *WH*, p. 38.

7   See *WH*, pp. 75, 165, 297.

8   Hindley's deference to Kenneth is also to be noted when Catherine has returned home after convalescing at the Grange in the wake of her delirium. As Nelly recalls: 'tutored by Kenneth, and serious threats of a fit that often attended her rages, her brother allowed her whatever she pleased to demand, and generally avoided aggravating her fiery temper' (*WH*, p. 78).

9   Although in a bid to propitiate Nelly just before he traps her with Cathy in the Heights, Heathcliff assures her that he will 'follow [her] advice concerning the doctor, without delay' (*WH*, p. 237), he is hardly likely to have done so, especially when we recall that, later, Cathy's own request as his daughter-in-law that 'the doctor might be sent for' on behalf of Linton is flatly rejected by Heathcliff, who, as Zillah informs Nelly, says this about his son: '[…] his life is not worth a farthing, and I won't spend a farthing on him' (*WH*, p. 259).

10 Isabella's refusal to see Kenneth is an ironic reminder of Emily's own tendency to do likewise.

11 For Kenneth's apparent ignorance of the nature of Heathcliff's mental illness, see Graeme Tytler, 'Heathcliff's Monomania: An Anachronism in *Wuthering Heights*', *Brontë Society Transactions*, 20. 6 (1992), 337-38.

12 Although 'Kenneth' is not cognate with 'ken' (to know), it is

nevertheless possible that Emily intended, albeit tongue in cheek, a direct connection between that name and that verb in so far as the village doctor comes across as something of a know-all.

Comedy in *Wuthering Heights*

The idea that *Wuthering Heights* should be of no little interest to us for elements which seem to belong to the realm of comedy might surprise those readers who remember the book first and foremost for its tragic love story. Yet a careful reading of the novel suggests that, central as is the tale of Heathcliff and Catherine, Emily Brontë is also much concerned with portraying a number of individuals of various social backgrounds and avocations, showing us how some of them are conspicuous for attitudes, talk or behaviour that could be categorised as falling somewhere on a scale ranging from farce to high comedy.[1] Indeed, though Emily Brontë's text is scarcely one to make us laugh out loud, there are incidents and episodes therein which, despite occurring amid some quite grim situations, may be deemed essentially amusing or comical.[2] Thus, to take a few examples at random, we may refer to Lockwood's giving vent to his rage after he has been knocked down by the dogs; to Mr and Mrs Linton's pompous reactions to Heathcliff's and Catherine's trespassing at Thrushcross Grange; to Isabella's bungled cooking of porridge in the Heights kitchen;

to Nelly Dean's tussle with 'a certain little boy', who has been acting as a go-between for Cathy and Linton Heathcliff, ending in their spilling between them the milk with which the Grange dairy maid has just filled his can; to Lockwood's nightmare of the Reverend Jabes Branderham's tediously long sermon and of the vicious fighting that breaks out among the members of his congregation.[3]

Lockwood's dream of such farcical violence in a chapel may be regarded as a grotesque foreshadowing of the sundry conflicts that take place in the narrative, some of which have patently comic implications, especially conflicts that he himself has with Nelly Dean. The fact that Lockwood exercises little control over the running of the household of which he is temporarily master may explain why, possibly owing to his apparent need to compensate himself for this undermining of his status, he is inclined to assert his authority now and then over his housekeeper. Thus, for example, he gets Nelly to tell him about '[his] landlord's family' (*WH*, p. 28) in his study one evening and, later that same evening, when she has remarked on the clock's being 'on the stroke of eleven', as if to suggest that it is now time to break off her narrative, he informs her that he is 'not accustomed to go to bed in the long hours' (*WH*, p. 54) — a confession that prompts Nelly to reprove him for leading such an irregular life. This reproof may in turn have induced Lockwood to assert his authority further still, not only by compelling Nelly to continue her narrative, but by refusing to let her 'leap over some three years', saying: 'No, no. I'll allow nothing of the sort!' (*WH*, p. 54). But if Lockwood triumphs over Nelly on this occasion, towards the end of Chapter 9 we learn that, having noticed the clock showing 1.30 a.m., Nelly 'would not hear of staying a second longer' (*WH*, p. 79); an utterance that shows such determination that Lockwood has to accept it, albeit with evident reluctance. At the beginning of Chapter 10, however, Lockwood once again asserts himself over

Nelly when, despite her dutifully reminding him of the medicine he is due to take in 'twenty minutes' on doctor's orders, he rejects this instruction outright, insisting instead that she forthwith continue 'the history of Mr Heathcliff' (*WH*, p. 80). But if all such details may be said to serve as a kind of foreshadowing of the earnest confrontations that Nelly has already had with some of the main characters, notably Heathcliff, Catherine and Edgar, the humour underlying her conflicts with Lockwood is rather redolent of those occasions when she is at odds with Joseph. Thus in Chapter 7 Nelly relates that on Christmas Eve, 'Joseph and [she] joined at an unsociable meal, seasoned with reproofs on one side and sauciness on the other' (*WH*, p. 49). Later, on the night of Heathcliff's disappearance from the Heights, Nelly recalls that when she had cooked the supper, she and Joseph 'began to quarrel who should carry some to Mr Hindley; and [they] didn't settle it till all was nearly cold' (*WH*, p. 73).

Joseph's conflicts with Nelly are, to be sure, mildly amusing, and have little of the vitriolic quality of those which the old servant has with some of his social superiors, Isabella and Edgar Linton in particular.[4] Such conflicts have doubtless played no small part in showing Joseph up as the ridiculous figure he occasionally cuts, and nowhere more so than when he is exhibiting his religious fanaticism. One thinks especially of those moments when he swings on to his knees in order to implore God for help in certain crises, a memorable instance being the occasion when, instead of mopping up Hindley's blood, as he has just been ordered to do by Heathcliff, he first 'joined his hands', as Isabella recalls, and 'began a prayer which excited [her] laughter from its odd phraseology' (*WH*, p. 157).[5] Yet if this sort of detail has helped to sustain an absurdly comical image of Joseph among readers and critics alike, it needs to be said that he is far from being merely the fanatical clown he is commonly adjudged to be. For, as well as being utterly loyal to the Earnshaws as his masters, and especially attached to Hareton, Joseph is a most diligent servant, and one who, because conscious of his very dependability, is prone to being 'cussed', especially when expected to carry out certain requests made by those whom he regards as outsiders. We see amusing examples of this when Lockwood pays his first two visits to the Heights.[6] Furthermore, it is probably mainly due to his self-confidence as a long-standing retainer that Joseph is capable of considerable wit, usually resorting to it most virulently when voicing his disapproval of, say, Isabella, Cathy and Linton Heathcliff.[7] Joseph is, of course, by no means the only character given to witticisms. Thus we may mention the ways in which someone's spoken words are used against them, as, for example, to Mr Earnshaw's asking Catherine: 'Why canst thou not always be a good lass, Cathy?', she impudently retorts: 'Why cannot you always be a good man, father?' (*WH*, p. 37).[8] Catherine's wit is generally caustic, and in some respects not unlike Heathcliff's, as is painfully obvious when one or other of them is addressing or talking about Edgar and Isabella.[9] Cathy's wit, too, tends to be caustic, especially when it is directed against Joseph or Hareton.[10] Nor should we forget to mention here the gentle wit with which Nelly responds to, say, Hindley's drunken talk in Chapter 9 or Joseph's rude comments to her in Chapter 32.[11]

Joseph's wit, on the other hand, is that of a man who, endowed with an acute sense of responsibility for the household he is in charge of, has acquired a keen eye and ear for what he as a devout Dissident considers egregious behaviour, and thereby developed a quite idiosyncratic language. Thus Nelly recalls entertaining herself in the Heights kitchen on Christmas Eve 'by singing carols, all alone; regardless of Joseph's affirmations that he considered the merry tunes [she] chose as next door to songs' (*WH*, p. 48). Nelly also recalls Joseph going to a neighbour's on Christmas Day, so that he may be 'removed from the sound of our "devil's psalmody", as it pleased him to call it' (*WH*, p. 53), namely, the music played at the Heights by the Gimmerton band.[12] Especially funny, however, is the moment when, having sneaked to Hindley about Catherine and Edgar's courtship antics during the time he (Hindley) is absent from, or has just arrived at, the Heights, Joseph proceeds to sneak on Nelly as follows: '— and Miss Nelly, shoo's a fine lass! shoo sits watching for ye i' t'kitchen; and as yah're in at one door, he's aht at t'other —' (*WH*, p. 77). Later, in Chapter 33, when Heathcliff, still unaware that Joseph is on the point of complaining about his uprooted currant bushes, tells the latter that he will 'interfere in no quarrels between [him] and Nelly', Joseph replies: 'It's noan Nelly! [...] Aw sudn't shift fur Nelly — nasty, ill nowt as shoo is. Thank God! *shoo* cannot stale t'sowl uh nob'dy! Shoo wer niver soa handsome, bud whet a body mud look at her baht winking' (*WH*, pp. 283-284). Joseph's final taunting of Nelly occurs when Lockwood, who has just turned up at the Heights for the last time and been offered 'a drink of our old ale' by her, hears him sardonically asking whether 'it warn't a crying scandal that she should have fellies at her time of life?' (*WH*, p. 275). And so it is thanks to Joseph's snide comments on Nelly's unprepossessing physical appearance and her possible love affairs that we are given an interesting glimpse of her personal life such as may seem otherwise quite unimaginable.

If some readers might think it acceptable, even legitimate, to smile at Joseph's witticisms, sardonic though they usually are, that is probably because they consider them the expressions of a loyal and trustworthy servant of no little moral integrity. Indeed, it is on account of the morality underlying Joseph's wit that one finds oneself much inclined, as it were, to laugh with him rather than at him. It is also noteworthy that Joseph's utterances, fraught as they are with malice or indicative of his religious fanaticism, are seldom, if ever, as silly as those made by some of the other characters. Especially comical on that head are some of the things said by the main figures during their childhood or adolescence. Thus we may refer to the occasion when, in the wake of Heathcliff's dashing the tureen of hot apple sauce against him, Edgar is blamed by Catherine for having spoken to him in the first place. Edgar, however, truthfully denies having done so, inasmuch as his remark on the length of Heathcliff's hair was addressed only to Hindley — a denial he then absurdly justifies by going on to make this feeble excuse: 'I promised mamma that I wouldn't say one word to him, and I didn't!' (*WH*, p. 52).[13] Then there is the episode in Chapter 7 when, suspecting that Catherine has become amorously interested in Edgar, a somewhat contrite young Heathcliff asks Nelly on Christmas morning to 'make [him] decent' because he is 'going to be good' (*WH*, p. 49). Yet in spite of Nelly's attempt to boost his self-confidence by assuring him that, being physically better built than Edgar, he could 'knock him down in a twinkling' (*WH*, p. 50), Heathcliff is nevertheless so enviously obsessed with the latter's personal appearance that, even from Nelly's suggestions of the ways in which he could improve his own looks, he naively draws the following conclusion: 'In other words, I must wish for Edgar Linton's great blue eyes and even forehead. [...] I do — and that won't help me to them' (*WH*, p. 50).

Of similar interest is much of what a fifteen-year-old Catherine says to Nelly while consulting her about Edgar's marriage proposal. Certainly, not a few of her utterances would elicit ironic smiles from a would-be onlooker, especially when, for example, she predicts that, being married to a rich man, she will 'like to be the greatest woman of the neighbourhood, and [...] proud of having such a husband' (*WH*, p. 69), and even presumes that she will be able to benefit Heathcliff by being wedded to Edgar. Furthermore, the fact that, once she has become aware that Heathcliff might have overheard most of the consultation, Catherine rather surprisingly remarks: 'What did I say, Nelly? I've forgotten. Was he vexed at my bad humour this afternoon? Dear! tell me what I've said to grieve him?' (*WH*, p. 74) — words that would suggest that her earlier talk, including her metaphorical images of the nature of her love for one or other of her two men, had been little more than hot air. Much the same comic effects can be felt in some of the utterances of Catherine's daughter in her early adolescence. Certainly, Emily Brontë admirably suggests the comicality of the overweening confidence with which Cathy looks forward to managing her relationship with her cousin Linton. Thus, as well as voicing the following pretentious claim to Nelly: 'I'm older than he is, you know, and wiser, less childish, am I not?' (*WH*, p. 213), she presently goes on to make a prediction that will prove to have been quite mistaken: 'He's younger than I [...] and he ought to live the longest: he will — he must live as long as I do' (*WH*, p. 214).[14] No doubt, the reader's reactions to these and other nonsensical statements of youngsters, testimony as they are to Emily Brontë's admirable understanding of the minds of children, are likely to betoken much milder amusement than they would to the silly things said by some of the adults portrayed in the novel, Zillah being perhaps the most notable case in point. Indeed, no character better deserves to be laughed to scorn than this housekeeper for her stupidity and her vanity, especially as manifest through the arrant respectability and snobbery with which she gives Nelly a quite heartless account of the widowed Cathy's behaviour at the Heights in Chapter 30.[15]

Zillah's vanity might be said to have been foreshadowed by that with which Lockwood tells himself early in his diary about his attractiveness to women. Such vanity is perhaps at its most glaring in Chapter 2 when he compares himself favourably with Hareton Earnshaw, and that to a point where, having presumed the young man to be married to Cathy, he speaks of the need to beware how he causes the latter to 'regret her choice', justifying this statement by presently adding: 'I knew, through experience, that I was tolerably attractive' (*WH*, p. 10). It is by virtue of such statements that, despite our initial impression of him as an intelligent and cultured young gentleman, Lockwood comes across as something of a comic figure. And though Lockwood's vanity is again evident on his third visit to the Heights, particularly through his patronising support of Hareton's quest to make himself literate, it is not until his final visit there that his vanity is to be seen in its most ridiculous guise. Thus, having witnessed Cathy and Hareton's reading lesson in 'the house' he has noiselessly entered, Lockwood presumes that he would be 'condemned in Hareton Earnshaw's heart, if not by his mouth, to the lowest pit in the infernal regions if [he] showed [his] unfortunate person in his neighbourhood then' (*WH*, p. 273). That is why, instead of, say, bravely confronting the couple and maturely wishing them well, a 'very mean and malignant' feeling Lockwood 'skulked round to seek refuge in the kitchen' (*WH*, p. 273). Later, having been told the last part of Heathcliff's history by Nelly in 'the house', Lockwood betrays his vanity once again when, 'disregarding [Nelly's] expostulations at [his] rudeness, [he] vanished through the kitchen' as Cathy and Hareton, back from their nocturnal ramble, 'opened the house-door' (*WH*, p. 300). Interestingly enough, Lockwood makes even further attempts to salvage his pride, not only when on his way out he drops a sovereign at Joseph's feet, as if in a bid to assure the latter that his meeting with Nelly has been perfectly respectable, but also when, as a clearly much disappointed lover, he utters to himself this pseudo-religious sentiment about Cathy and Hareton: '*They* are afraid of nothing. [...] Together they would brave Satan and all his legions' (*WH*, p. 300).

Lockwood's vanity is but one character trait of someone who, though outwardly a cultured person of genteel background, is also conspicuous for the kind of egotism by which he may be adjudged an essentially comic figure.[16] Such egotism may already be sensed when, because impressed by Heathcliff's conversation at the end of Chapter 1, Lockwood shows his resolve to ignore the latter's clearly wishing 'no repetition of [his] intrusion' by avowing: 'I shall go, notwithstanding' (*WH*, p. 5). Lockwood's determination to re-visit the Heights the next day, though at first weakened by the 'misty and cold' (*WH*, p. 6) weather, to the extent that he decides to spend the afternoon at the Grange, is then instantly revived once he has seen a servant-girl putting out his study fire. Then, no sooner has he reached the Heights entrance but found no one willing to open the front door to him, than he makes such dogged, even violent, attempts to get into the building as to disclose his egotism in a quite ludicrous light. We also note later that instead of, say, accepting the gloom amid which Heathcliff and members of his household are sitting round the tea-table, Lockwood inadvertently makes himself the centre of attention, chiefly through his tactlessly mistaken assumptions about their interrelationships. Such misguided sociableness on Lockwood's part is quite absurd when we recall that he has originally come to Yorkshire in order to get away from society. Moreover, it is odd to find that, misanthropic though he appears to be, Lockwood is much given to attention-seeking. Thus we may mention how, feeling unduly neglected after the evening meal as he watches some of the characters busy with their particular occupations, Lockwood reaches a point where, because impatient for immediate help in order to return safely to the Grange amid the heavy snow, he suddenly exclaims rather childishly: 'How must I do?' (*WH*, p. 11). Also worth mentioning here is that moment soon afterwards when Lockwood is so certain that Joseph's acrimonious criticism of Cathy is directed at himself that he 'stepped towards the aged rascal with an intention of kicking him out of the door' (*WH*, p. 11). Another risible example of Lockwood's attention-seeking occurs when, despite his hapless fight with the Heights dogs the day before, he nevertheless 'called the villain Juno, who deigned, at this second interview, to move the extreme tip of her tail, in token of owning [his] acquaintance' (*WH*, p. 7). As we see, even the friendliness of an animal with which he has been in recent conflict is welcome as a means of restoring his strong sense of self.[17]

In view of Lockwood's inveterate self-centredness, it is hardly surprising that he is prone to blaming others for his various predicaments and quandaries. Consider, for example, the inane way in which he blames Zillah for his second nightmare in Chapter 3, even going so far as to suppose that she 'wanted to get another proof' that the oak-panelled room 'was haunted, at [his] expense' (*WH*, p. 22). Consider, too, how, having already in the very first sentence of his diary spoken of Heathcliff as 'the solitary neighbour that I shall be *troubled with*' (*WH*, p. 1; italics mine), Lockwood refers to the latter at the beginning of Chapter 10 as follows: 'Scoundrel! He is not altogether guiltless in this illness of mine' (*WH*, p. 80), overlooking as he does the fact that he would probably not have been taken ill had he observed Heathcliff's request to him not to pay a second visit to the Heights. Again, even when at the end of Chapter 1 he speaks of 'the misbehaviour of a pack of curs' (*WH*, p. 5), it is obvious that he is far from ready to admit that it was he who caused the 'misbehaviour' in the first place.[18] It is, moreover, probably owing to his egotism that Lockwood evinces a marked tendency to jump to conclusions, basing them almost always on first impressions alone. One striking example among several others may be noted when he is anxious to find out whether the 'pretty girl-widow', namely Cathy, is 'a native of the country, or, *as is more probable*, an exotic that the surly indigenae will not recognise for kin' (*WH*, p. 28; italics mine).[19] Finally, Lockwood's frequent use of metaphors and similes, some of them distinctly fallacious, seems to confirm the inherent mark of the egotist who is hesitant to call a spade a spade; in other words, who seems reluctant to accept the actuality of the people or animals he encounters at the Heights as well as at the Grange.[20] Certainly, for all that he is a well-read intellectual with an exceptional ability to handle the English language at the highest level, Lockwood nonetheless betrays a somewhat disorderly mind in ways which, because largely rooted in his excessive sense of self, can hardly help making him a quite laughable figure in the eyes of the reader.

At this juncture, it is perhaps worth reflecting that a number of Brontë scholars have tended to regard Lockwood either as a figure detached from the story he relates as frame-narrator or as the reader's representative, even the reader himself.[21] Such views, however, would hardly seem to tally with the one implicitly held by various other scholars, namely, that since his presentation is thematically linked with that of some of the main characters in the novel, he should therefore be judged as impartially as any other character therein. This is in any case amply confirmed when we realise the extent to which, as we have already seen, Lockwood is shown to be something of a comic figure. In this connection, it is interesting to note that Nelly Dean, too, has sometimes been said to be also detached from her narrative, and even been identified with the reader. Nevertheless, there has been a general proclivity to judge Nelly as a character in her own right, even though opinions about her have been widely differing. Thus, whereas some scholars have drawn attention to Nelly's moral defects, notably her duplicity and her hypocrisy, other scholars have been content to declare her a normal, sensible, kindly woman of sound intelligence.[22] Such affirmative attitudes may have been encouraged, if not determined, by various cinematic and televisual adaptations of the novel in which she has been portrayed as a benign person who seems to exist virtually outside the grim stories she relates to Lockwood. One thinks in particular of her impersonation by Flora Robson as an essentially 'good sort' in the Hollywood film of 1939. Still, irrespective of conflicting evaluations of Nelly, no scholar to my knowledge appears to have contended that, like Lockwood, she at times comes across as a somewhat comic character. Let us now examine her presentation from this perspective in some detail, starting with the time when she is housekeeper at Thrushcross Grange.

First of all, we may refer to that moment when Nelly complains to herself about Heathcliff's accosting of Isabella in the Grange courtyard, yet loudly enough for Catherine to overhear her and then to reprove her thus: 'To hear you, people might think *you* were the mistress!' (*WH*, p. 99). Again, there is a moment when, already aware that Isabella has eloped with Heathcliff, yet too afraid to say anything to Edgar, Nelly clearly betrays her very uneasy state of mind when, in reaction to the following sudden announcement made to Edgar by one of the maids, whom she, incidentally, describes as 'a thoughtless girl': 'Oh, dear, dear! What mun we have next? Master, master, our young lady—', she angrily interrupts the maid in mid-sentence to tell her to 'hold [her] noise', enraged as she is, probably with a bad conscience, at 'her clamorous manner' (*WH*, p. 116). Such a bossy reaction on Nelly's part may be closely linked with the occasion when, sitting in the Grange parlour with the newborn Cathy on her knee and watching the snowflakes 'build up the uncurtained window', she hears someone entering the room 'out of breath and laughing!' and responds thus: 'My anger was greater than my astonishment for a minute; I supposed it one of the maids, and I cried, "[…] What would Mr Linton say if he heard you?"' (*WH*, p. 150). The comedy of such anger is, of course, enhanced by the fact that the intruder ironically turns out to be Isabella at the end of her snowbound flight from the Heights. Rather more memorable, however, is a previous occasion when, having no doubt pretentiously 'persuaded [her] conscience' that it was 'a duty to warn [Hindley] how people talked regarding his ways', especially since Heathcliff has been lodging with him, she shortly afterwards finds herself, while 'on a journey to Gimmerton', feeling an irresistible yearning to be at the Heights, partly because, having just seen young Hareton playing at the nearby guide post, she has momentarily mistaken the boy for Hindley doing the same thing with her 'twenty years before' (*WH*, p. 96). The consequence of all this are two of the funniest incidents in the novel. Thus not only does Nelly get hit on the bonnet by a flint flung at her by Hareton, evidently for addressing him as if he still remembered who she was, but, having, as she says, seen Heathcliff appear 'on the door stones' of the Heights instead of Hindley, she: 'turned directly and ran down the road as hard as ever [she] could race, making no halt till [she] gained the guide post, and feeling as scared as if [she] had raised a goblin' (*WH*, p. 98).

The three episodes just mentioned above are sufficient indicators of the fact that, since becoming Edgar's housekeeper, Nelly seems to have acquired a rather too strong sense of self-importance and respectability. Such characteristics are humorously plain to see at the beginning of Chapter 14, when, having arrived at the Heights in answer to Isabella's letter to her, and despite her awareness, from the content of that letter, of the writer's plight as Heathcliff's bride, Nelly is at first oddly concerned about the neglected state of the household, even going so far as to say this: 'I must confess that, if I had been in the young lady's place, I would, at least, have swept the hearth, and wiped the tables with a duster' (*WH*, p. 129). Having then spoken of her dismay at Isabella's bedraggled appearance, Nelly goes on to say this about Heathcliff's person: 'He was the only thing there that seemed decent, and I thought he never looked better. So much had circumstances altered their positions, that he would certainly have struck a stranger as a born and bred gentleman, and his wife as a thorough little slattern!' (*WH*, p. 130). In addition to this striking example of Nelly's snobbish respectability, we note that, in reply to Heathcliff's presuming that she has brought something for Isabella, Nelly instantly assures him that she has 'nothing', at the same time as she tells Lockwood that she thought it 'best to speak the truth at once' (*WH*, p. 130). Yet truthful though Nelly is indeed in that respect, the reader nevertheless can hardly help smiling at her then showing no hesitation whatever in going on to garble the message that Edgar has asked her to pass on to Isabella. Such a glaring inconsistency, though understandable in the circumstances, is one of several others in Nelly's narrative which cannot but show her in a ridiculous light. Consider, for instance, the ironic contrast between, on the one hand, the priggishness with which Nelly disapproves of Cathy's truthful account of her illicit visits to Linton Heathcliff (in Chapter 24), and, on the other, the sentimentality with which, just after being released from her five-day incarceration at the Heights and then perturbed by Linton's domineering attitude towards his new wife (in Chapter 28), she takes a diametrically opposite view of those same illicit visits by pleading with him thus:

> Master Heathcliff, [...] have you forgotten all Catherine's kindness to you, last winter, when you affirmed you loved her, and when she brought you books, and sung you songs, and came many a time through wind and snow to see you? She wept to miss one evening, because you would be disappointed; [...] and now you believe the lies your father tells, though you know he detests you both! And you join him against her. That's fine gratitude, is it not? (*WH*, p. 247)

Just as comical as the foregoing inconsistency are those that Nelly now and then shows between the resolutions she utters and her failure to carry them out. One particularly memorable example of this is her arranging for Heathcliff to visit a sick Catherine at the Grange, in spite of having originally refused to countenance such a visit by asserting: 'I say, Mr Heathcliff, [...] you must not—you never shall through my means. Another encounter between you and the master would kill her altogether!' (*WH*, p. 131). It is, therefore, curious to reflect that, though Nelly is eventually forced to promise to make such a visit possible, mainly because Heathcliff has otherwise threatened to detain her at the Heights, she could have broken that promise with impunity simply by warning Edgar of Heathcliff's nefarious intention and thus averted the tragic outcome she had more or less correctly foreseen. Much more comical, however, are the implications of the resolves made in Chapter 21 by Nelly on the afternoon Cathy encounters Heathcliff for the first time. To begin with, we note that, having been given permission by Edgar to have 'a ramble on the edge of the moors' with Cathy as long as they are both back at the Grange 'within the hour' (*WH*, p. 187), Nelly finds herself unable to fulfil this request, not only because she allows the girl to engage in prolonged conversation with Heathcliff, but because she fails to counter the latter's invitation to Cathy to meet his son. Moreover, even by the time Cathy has reached the Heights gate, and, having herself in the meantime been informed by Heathcliff that he is 'resolved' to marry the cousins, Nelly makes it plain that she has already resigned herself to the inevitable, as she retorts: 'And I'm resolved [Cathy] shall never approach your house with me again' (*WH*, p. 190). Yet even that resolve will prove utterly vain, as we recall the occasion when, instead of preventing Cathy from renewing her relationship with Linton, as Heathcliff has managed to persuade her to do outside Thrushcross park door (in Chapter 22), Nelly could easily have done so well before their departure for the Heights the following morning merely by reporting Cathy to her father in good time beforehand. Thus it is through her inability to be a consistent disciplinarian towards Cathy, and nowhere more disastrously so than on the afternoon the latter is lured into the Heights by Linton's cunningly feigning the invalid in order that the cousins' marriage may take place the next day, that Nelly's inability to carry out her worthy resolves cannot but show her up in an essentially comical light. Furthermore, we are thereby made strangely aware of the ironic contrast between Nelly's incapacity to control Cathy's movements and her apparent tendency to assert her authority aggressively over her domestic subordinates. Finally, mention should also be made of the contradiction between Nelly's readiness to suspect others of deceit and dishonesty and her own practice of resorting to prevarication, not to say blatant lies, out of pure expediency, as well as the sundry fallacies she is liable to, especially in her dialogues with youngsters.[23]

What we have just seen above, then, are some of the ways in which Nelly Dean may be appropriately designated a comic figure; indeed, like Lockwood himself, one tailor-made for high comedy. We have also seen other instances of comedy at various levels, and all of them in a text whose episodes and incidents might perhaps be thought too grim for us to be readily alive to the comic effects that have been signalled above. No doubt, there are comic moments that have been overlooked in our discussion, just as those pointed up might not be necessarily recognised as such by some readers. In this connection, it is interesting to note that E. M. Forster once went so far as to suggest that *Wuthering Heights* is one of those novels that expect of their readers a suspending of their sense of humour.[24] Such a suggestion would have been perfectly understandable, even acceptable, had the book been the unrelievedly gloomy Gothic tale it appears to have given many a reader the impression of being. In fact, a diligent perusal of the novel shows how extraordinary is the breadth of Emily Brontë's rendering of the talk and behaviour of people living in a comparatively isolated Yorkshire community towards the end of the eighteenth century and how, through judicious use of the characters she has created, the author can be truly said to have combined the comic and the tragic with commendable dramatic skill. Indeed, it is through this astute blending of the two genres that we are made aware of the remarkably comprehensive picture of human nature and human society which Emily Brontë has painted for us, and that in ways whereby we may come to realise why any reader of *Wuthering Heights* would be mistaken to remember this masterpiece for its famous love story alone.

Brontë Studies, 46/1 (2021)

Notes

1   To my knowledge, no monograph has hitherto been published about comedy in *Wuthering Heights*, even though some Brontë scholars have here and there made comments relevant to my chosen topic.

2   For quotations from the novel, see Emily Brontë, *Wuthering Heights*, ed. by Ian Jack and Patsy Stoneman (Oxford: Oxford University Press, 1998), hereafter *WH*. For the sake of convenience, the first Catherine will be referred to as 'Catherine', the second as 'Cathy'.

3   For these five episodes, see *Wuthering Heights*, pp. 13, 14, 43, 44, 125, 195, 18, 19, 20 respectively.

4   See *Wuthering Heights*, pp. 125, 126, 127, 179.

5   For other examples of Joseph's religious fanaticism, see *Wuthering Heights*, pp. 17, 35, 36, 75, 76, 157, 298.

6   See *Wuthering Heights*, pp. 4, 6.

7   See *Wuthering Heights*, pp. 121, 125, 126, 127, 182, 184.

8   For other examples, see *Wuthering Heights*, pp. 5, 13, 17, 39, 51, 62, 65, 70, 72, 74, 94, 107, 112, 113, 131, 184, 190, 194, 200, 211, 213, 214, 235, 247, 292, 296.

9   See *Wuthering Heights*, pp. 84, 92, 93, 101, 102, 107, 108, 112, 132, 133, 134.

10 See *Wuthering Heights*, pp. 11, 12, 266, 267, 268, 276.

11 See *Wuthering Heights*, pp. 65, 274.

12 For more examples of Joseph's idiosyncratic utterances being specially recalled by Nelly and other characters, see *Wuthering Heights*, pp. 74, 125, 154, 156, 222, 299.

13 For other references to young Edgar as a ridiculous figure, see *Wuthering Heights*, pp. 42, 49, 50.

14 For other examples of Cathy's inane utterances, see *Wuthering Heights*, pp. 173, 188, 191, 195.

15 For examples of Zillah's stupidity, see *Wuthering Heights*, pp. 247, 259-264.

16 In this connection, it is interesting to note a rare description of Lockwood in Brontë scholarship, namely, as 'the only genuinely comic figure in *Wuthering Heights*' in George Worth, 'Emily Brontë's Mr. Lockwood', *Nineteenth-Century Fiction*, 12 (1958), 320.

17 Significant in this connection are Lockwood's references to Joseph as 'my friend Joseph' and his addressing Nelly as 'my good friend'. It is interesting to note that the longest sentence in the novel, namely, the one with which Lockwood opens Chapter 4, contains five uses of the pronoun 'I'. For all these details, see *Wuthering Heights*, pp. 16, 28, 55.

18 Lockwood's habit of blaming others for his troubles may be said to foreshadow Catherine's blaming of Isabella and Edgar not only

for her early marital problems, but also for the latter's showdown with Heathcliff in Chapter 11. See *Wuthering Heights*, pp. 86, 87, 103.

19 For similar examples of Lockwood's presumptuousness, see *Wuthering Heights*, pp. 1, 2, 3, 7, 8, 9, 10, 11, 28, 54, 55, 58, 267, 269, 270, 273, 300.

20 For Lockwood's military metaphors, see *Wuthering Heights*, pp. 2, 3, 4, 18, 24, 25, 28, 80, 271.

21 For such views, see especially: Isobel Mayne, 'Emily Brontë's Mr. Lockwood', *Brontë Society Transactions*, 15. 3 (1968), 207-213; Terence McCarthy, 'The Incompetent Narrator of *Wuthering Heights*', *Modern Language Quarterly*, 42 (1981), 56; Jenny Oldfield, *Jane Eyre and Wuthering Heights. A Study Guide* (London: Heinemann, 1976), p. 52; Robert K. Wallace, *Emily Brontë and Beethoven's Equilibrium in Fiction and Music* (Athens: University of Georgia Press, 1986), p. 169; Barbara Hardy, *Wuthering Heights* (Oxford: Oxford University Press, 1987), p. 19; Cates Baldridge, 'Voyeuristic Rebellion: Lockwood's Dream and the Reader of *Wuthering Heights*', *Studies in the Novel*, 20 (1988), 275; U. C. Knoepflmacher, *Emily Brontë* (Cambridge & New York: Cambridge University Press, 1987), p. 10.

22 Although Nelly Dean has now and then been noted for her hypocrisy and her duplicity, most memorably in James Hafley, 'The Villain in *Wuthering Heights*', *Nineteenth-Century Fiction*, 13 (1958), 199-218, a good many Brontë scholars have regarded her as a normal, wholesome, mature, intelligent, kindly and good-natured character, or even identified her with the reader; in connection with which, see especially Jacques Blondel, 'Emily

Brontë: Récentes Explorations', *Études Anglaises*, 11 (1958), 329; Florence Swinton Dry, *The Sources of Wuthering Heights* (Cambridge: Cambridge University Press, 1937), p. 14; Laura L. Hinkley, *The Brontës: Charlotte and Emily* (London: Hammond, Hammond & Co., 1947), p. 259; Wendy A. Craik, *The Brontë Novels* (London: Methuen, 1968), p. 41; Q. D. Leavis, 'A Fresh Approach to *Wuthering Heights*' in F. R. and Q. D. Leavis, *Lectures in America* (London: Chatto & Windus, 1969), p. 93; Graham Holderness, *Wuthering Heights* (Milton Keynes & Philadelphia: The Open University Press, 1985), p. 8; Robert Liddell, *Twin Spirits: The Novels of Emily and Anne Brontë* (London: Peter Owen, 1990), p. 18.

23 For Nelly's lies, prevarications and fallacies, see *Wuthering Heights*, pp. 34, 35, 39, 56, 107, 112, 129, 130, 137, 147, 165, 168, 171, 180, 181, 182, 200, 205, 214, 215, 293.

24 See Thomas Moser, 'What is the Matter with Emily Jane?: Conflicting Impulses in *Wuthering Heights*', *Nineteenth-Century Fiction*, 17 (1962), 2.

Aesthetic Attitudes in
Wuthering Heights

One of the most intriguing aspects of *Wuthering Heights* is the presence of sundry aesthetic attitudes throughout the narrative.[1] By 'aesthetic attitude' is meant essentially the sensitive and perceptive appreciation or evaluation not only of works of art, but also of the beauty or physicality of human beings, natural phenomena, inanimate objects, etc.[2] It is within the bounds of this definition that the term 'aesthetic' and its cognates shall be used here. In this connection, it should be acknowledged at the outset that various aesthetic attitudes informing the poetry and prose of the European Romantics from the late eighteenth century onwards constitute an essential background against which Emily Brontë's novel may be in part historically understood. Certainly, they can be said to provide a sort of basis for Lockwood's presentation as a gentlemanly aesthete or dilettante, whose diary entries now and again betoken a marked literary, not to say poetic, disposition, as is well illustrated by the much admired paragraph with which he brings the novel to close. Aesthetic attitudes may also be discerned in some of the utterances or reactions of the other characters, and assume a wide variety of guises ranging from, say, Cathy's elaborate description of her ideal summer's day to Heathcliff's monomaniacal obsession with his images of Catherine's ghost, and including, aptly enough, passages relating to music, literature and the fine arts. Yet if aesthetic attitudes may be thought praiseworthy in themselves, especially as manifest in some of the written or spoken sentiments of Lockwood and Nelly Dean, there can be little doubt that they are sometimes problematic enough to raise certain awkward questions. Thus, it might be asked: what place should aesthetic attitudes have in our lives and in our relations with our fellow human beings? What are their moral implications? What are their limitations and drawbacks? These are some of the questions which Emily seems to be inviting us to ponder, and to which in the course of our discussion some answers will be hazarded.

As a primary object of aesthetic interest and inquiry, human beauty has, of course, been a central motif in fiction from time immemorial, what with its innumerable handsome heroes and heroines, and is indeed a prominent one in *Wuthering Heights*, a work notable for the sensitivity with which the characters observe and analyse one another's physical appearances, and hence in some measure indicative of the influence that Lavater's physiognomic theories were exerting on nineteenth-century European fiction in general.[3] This influence is nowhere more perceptible than in Nelly Dean's and Isabella's keen awareness of family resemblances, each description of which usually bespeaks the aesthetic response at its most delightful.[4] The same is true of Lockwood's and Nelly's analyses of Cathy's face, not least because they subtly illustrate Lavater's theory of the correlation between beauty and virtue.[5] Moreover, such analyses are structurally important because they foreshadow Cathy's presentation as someone who, notwithstanding her failings and foibles in childhood and adolescence, proves to be endowed with the finest moral qualities. Noticeable, too, is the tendency of the characters to show an acute sense of all kinds of beauty, not only the beauty of a human being, but that of an animal, a landscape, a room, or a book, described as they are with such epithets as 'handsome', 'beautiful', 'pretty', 'admirable', 'graceful', 'winsome', 'bonny' and the like. But though responses to, or affirmations of, human beauty, however subjective or perfunctory, seem reasonable enough, and are even implicitly acknowledged by Emily to be legitimate in love relationships, as is amply suggested in the mutual physical attraction existing between Cathy and Hareton, the author seems none the less intent on turning the traditional function of beauty and handsomeness in fiction somewhat on its head.[6] This is already ironically first hinted at in Hindley's seemingly innocuous response to the sight of Catherine's transformed personal appearance on her return to the Heights after her five-week sojourn at Thrushcross Grange: 'Why, Cathy, you are quite a beauty! I should scarcely have known you — you look like a lady now — Isabella Linton is not to be compared with her, is she, Frances?' (*WH*, p. 46).

What is significant about Hindley's complimentary words just quoted is their supposed effect on Catherine. Indeed, like Frances's endeavours to 'raise [Catherine's] self-respect with fine clothes and flattery' (*WH*, p. 46) while the latter is still at the Grange, Hindley's encomium may have encouraged his sister to become unduly conscious of her appearance as an asset to be exploited in relations between the sexes. We sense this partly in the condescending manner in which, during her reunion with Heathcliff shortly afterwards, and not without having already spoken of being 'used to Edgar and Isabella Linton' (*WH*, p. 47), she advises him to clean and tidy himself up. This, in turn, may explain why, in spite of Nelly's efforts in Chapter 7 to help him to improve his personal appearance, Heathcliff naively conjectures at one point that all he needs are those characteristics of

Edgar's particular handsomeness that he has now come to covet.[7] Thus we see how an unwonted concern with beauty on the part of the young hero and heroine marks an ominous turning-point in their relationship. Further, as well as apparently eroding her love for Heathcliff, Catherine's new awareness of beauty accounts for her making it one of the criteria for her decision to marry Edgar. Thus, when asked by Nelly why she loves Edgar, Catherine replies: 'Well, because he is handsome, and pleasant to be with', presently confirming this answer both by saying that she 'love[s] all his looks' and by averring that she would 'only pity him — hate him, perhaps, if he were ugly, and a clown' (*WH*, p. 69). Yet if Nelly counters Catherine's childish assertions by sensibly pointing out, among other things, that Edgar's handsomeness will not last, and that there may be other handsome men, even handsomer ones, for Catherine to choose from, her words can scarcely be said to mitigate the fact that she, too, has already acknowledged and affirmed Edgar's handsomeness with the rather tendentious comparison she has already drawn between him and Heathcliff at the time of the former's visit to the Heights in Chapter 8. As Nelly recalls: 'Doubtless Catherine marked the difference between her friends as one came in, and the other went out. The contrast resembled what you see in exchanging a bleak, hilly, coal country for a *beautiful* fertile valley; and his voice and greeting were as opposite as his aspect' (*WH*, p. 61f.; italics mine).

It will be seen from the foregoing, then, that Nelly's preoccupation with beauty is a mark of her respectability and social snobbery, characteristics that may account for some of her untimely aesthetic judgements. For example, despite learning from Isabella's letter that she is deeply unhappy as Heathcliff's bride, Nelly surprises the reader, on her arrival at the Heights soon afterwards, by being perturbed not only by the disorderly interior of the house but, more importantly, by the change in the personal appearances of Isabella and Heathcliff, her description of whom she concludes as follows: 'He was the only thing there that seemed decent, and I thought he never looked better. So much had circumstances altered their positions, that he would certainly have struck a stranger as a born and bred gentleman, and his wife as a thorough little slattern!' (*WH*, p. 130). Such a snobbish comparison, tasteless as it seems in view of Isabella's particular plight, is perhaps easy to comprehend if we remember the importance that Nelly implicitly attaches to health and strength, notably in contexts where she is describing or alluding to the physicality of Heathcliff, Catherine, Cathy, Hareton and Linton Heathcliff.[8] It is undoubtedly because of her admiration for the strong and the fit that, not unlike the village doctor Kenneth or Zillah, the Heights housekeeper, Nelly shows a lack of compassion for those suffering from chronic ill-health, such as Frances Earnshaw and Linton Heathcliff, and even a certain impatience with the acute forms of mental illness suffered by Catherine. Thus as if mindful of Kenneth's comment to her that, by looking after a sick Catherine, Edgar is sacrificing his health and strength 'to preserve a mere ruin of humanity' (*WH*, p. 118), Nelly evinces much the same hardness when, noticing Catherine's apparent unconsciousness at the end of her tryst with Heathcliff, she says this to herself: 'She's fainted or dead [...] so much the better. Far better that she should be dead, than lingering a burden and a misery-maker to all about her' (*WH*, p. 143).

Nelly's intolerance of physical and mental illness may, then, explain why her aesthetic disposition reveals a new dimension once Catherine has died. This may be already noted just before Heathcliff's tryst with a moribund Catherine in Nelly's description of the latter's face: 'Her appearance was altered [...] but when she was calm, there seemed unearthly beauty in the change' (*WH*, p. 137). It is, however, shortly after her death that Catherine's beauty is at its most sublime, as if to suggest that she has been rehabilitated in Nelly's eyes, and that Nelly herself has in some sense atoned for her own guilt in having indirectly caused her mistress's death. As Nelly recalls: '[…] no angel in heaven could be more beautiful than she appeared' (*WH*, p. 145).[9] Yet if this and analogous descriptions serve, as it were, to apotheosize the principal heroine, they are of interest chiefly for throwing light on Nelly's mentality. For example, the idea that Nelly seems to have a curious, albeit unconsciously aesthetic, fascination with death is plain enough from her following comment on Edgar as seen lying beside his dead wife: 'I noticed on that occasion how much selfishness there is even in a love like Mr Linton's, when he so regretted Catherine's blessed release!' (*WH*, p. 145f.).[10] Clearly, Catherine's death is too important to Nelly for her not to belittle Edgar's perfectly natural way of mourning the loss of his wife. No less interesting here is Nelly's inferring from Catherine's beauteous face that she has already gone to heaven, and even her corroborating that inference by recalling the latter's words to her: 'Incomparably beyond and above us all!' (*WH*, p. 145). Certainly, Nelly's assumption that Catherine is already with 'her Maker', and that despite having just doubted, 'after the wayward and impatient existence she had led', whether she 'merited a haven of peace at last' (*WH*, p. 146), seems hardly different from the kind of talk which, in their grief at Mr Earnshaw's death, young Catherine and Heathcliff are apparently given to with their childish image of heaven as a place of permanent happiness to which departed loved ones are perforce destined. Such thinking with respect to the after-life is also conspicuous in Edgar's own assumption about Catherine's heavenly destination as well as in his abnormally prolonged mourning of her death; which latter process seems to have a certain futility about it mainly because it turns him into a recluse.[11]

But over and above their pseudo-theological implications, parts of Nelly's descriptions of Catherine's appearance in death show her to possess a distinct propensity for aesthetic contemplation. This can be seen when, referring to her vigil over Catherine's corpse, she says this to Lockwood: 'My mind was never in a holier frame than while I gazed on that untroubled image of Divine rest' (*WH*, p. 145). Such words suggest that, however well she may know her Bible, Christianity is for Nelly at times much less a religion to be practised devoutly in everyday life than a kind of aesthetic sentimentalism. This is especially apparent when, having described Edgar lying beside Catherine on the morning after her death, she digresses from her narrative as follows:

> I don't know if it be a peculiarity in me, but I am seldom otherwise than happy while watching in the chamber of death, should no frenzied or despairing mourner share the duty with me. I see a repose that neither earth nor hell can break; and I feel an assurance of the endless and shadowless hereafter — the Eternity they have entered — where life is boundless in its duration, and love in its sympathy, and joy in its fulness. (*WH*, p. 145)

What is remarkable about this impressive piece of poetic prose is that, in its inherent idealization of the real world, it epitomizes Nelly's tendency to enjoy certain experiences in her somewhat hectic existence as aesthetically perfect moments. Among several such instances one thinks of the occasion when, having come upstairs to the Grange parlour to announce Heathcliff's unexpected arrival, Nelly describes Catherine and Edgar thus:

> They sat together in a window whose lattice lay back against the wall, and displayed, beyond the garden trees and the wild green park, the valley of Gimmerton, with a long line of mist winding nearly to its top [...]. Both the room, and its occupants, and the scene they gazed on, looked wondrously peaceful. I shrank reluctantly from performing my errand. (*WH*, p. 83).

As may be seen from the excerpt just quoted, Nelly's aesthetic disposition is sometimes manifested through descriptions of nature — its sights, its sounds, its fragrances.[12] One example is the following passage concerning the day after Catherine's funeral: 'On the morrow one could hardly imagine that there had been three weeks of summer: the primroses and crocuses were hidden under wintry drifts: the larks were silent, the young leaves of the early trees smitten and blackened — And dreary, and chill, and dismal that morrow did creep over!' (*WH*, p. 150). And though this passage, not unlike passages containing references to, say, moonlight, sunsets, rain, storms and so on, may have some symbolic meaning, it is primarily interesting as a commendable example of Nelly's aesthetic view of nature. The same is also true of Lockwood's references to nature, especially in Chapter 32. Thus his account of the fine, warm weather in Gimmerton on his return there in September 1802 and of his noticing 'by the aid of [his] nostrils' that 'a fragrance of stocks and wall flowers, wafted on the air, from amongst the homely fruit trees' (*WH*, p. 273) is at once symbolic of a new and happier era at the Heights and testimony to an equally commendable aesthetic response to nature. Like Lockwood, Nelly is acutely aware of the weather and the seasons, her comments on them, sometimes in detail quite extraordinary because remembered after so many years, being among the most moving parts of her narrative. Especially noticeable in this connection are Nelly's references to sunshine, her pleasure in which she expresses both through her comments about its beneficial effects on mind and body, and through metaphors with which she conveys certain examples of human happiness.[13]

It is, nevertheless, noteworthy that Nelly's affirmative references to sunny weather and to other natural phenomena are sometimes essentially ironic. For example, it is on a day remembered by Nelly for the heat of 'the July sun' (*WH*, p. 169) that Cathy will break bounds and hence discover the existence of the Heights for the first time. Again, it is on her sixteenth birthday, which falls on 'a beautiful spring day' (*WH*, p. 187), when Cathy will first encounter Heathcliff. And there are other idyllic descriptions of weather that serve a like ironic function. This is true, for example, of Nelly's account of the September evening when she has been gathering apples at the Grange as a prelude to her suddenly happening upon Heathcliff there: 'I set my burden on the house steps by the kitchen door, and lingered to rest and draw in a few more breaths of the *soft, sweet air*' (*WH*, p. 82; italics mine). We may also refer to the remarkable detail given by Nelly both just after she has described Catherine on the Sunday afternoon when the latter is about to be visited by Heathcliff, and just before she gives her his note:

> Gimmerton chapel bells were still ringing; and the *full, mellow flow* of the beck in the valley came *soothingly* on the ear. It was a *sweet* substitute for the yet absent murmur of the summer foliage, which drowned that music about the Grange when the trees were in leaf. At Wuthering Heights it always sounded on quiet days, following a great thaw, or a season of steady rain — and of Wuthering Heights Catherine was thinking as she listened; that is, if she thought, or listened, at all. (*WH*, p. 138; italics mine)

Yet for all its poetic charm, this seemingly disinterested passage might well be adjudged a self-deluding attempt on Nelly's part to mask her sense of disloyalty to Edgar. Similarly ironic is the way in which Nelly ascribes to Edgar, on his return from church that same Sunday afternoon, and only a few moments before he will catch Heathcliff in the final stages of his tryst with Catherine, something of her own aesthetic bent when relating that, on opening a Grange gate, he 'sauntered slowly up, probably enjoying the *lovely* afternoon that *breathed as soft as summer*' (*WH*, p. 143; italics mine). Yet touching as Nelly's words may be, the reader cannot but think how ironic this as well as her other digressive references to nature can appear, occurring as they often do in contexts where she is, as it were, about to be caught unawares by events or where her sense of moral responsibility is in conspicuous abeyance.

Nelly's aesthetic responses to nature are also interesting for sometimes suggesting an apparent indifference on her part to grim human situations. Consider, for instance, the following reference to Catherine's corpse: 'Next morning — *bright* and *cheerful* out of doors — stole *softened* in through the blinds of the silent room, and suffused the couch and its occupant with a *mellow, tender glow*' (*WH*, p. 145; italics mine). As with references to Catherine's beauty in death, this painterly detail, with its alliterations and assonances, would appear to be more deserving of interest to Nelly than, say, the irretrievable loss of the human being it concerns. Nelly's nature descriptions are also problematic with respect to her relations with Cathy. Thus, although uneasy about the latter's quest to ramble on the moors in search of birds' nests, Nelly recalls the early part of their excursion together in Chapter 21 as follows:

> I found plenty of entertainment in listening to the larks singing far and near; and enjoying the *sweet*, warm sunshine; and watching her, my pet, and my delight, with her *golden* ringlets flying loose behind, and her *bright* cheek, as *soft* and *pure* in its bloom as a wild rose, and her eyes *radiant* with cloudless pleasure. She was a happy creature, and an angel, in those days. It's a pity she could not be content. (*WH*, p. 188; italics mine)

For Nelly all this doubtless represents another aesthetically perfect moment, which, while forming an ironic prelude to Cathy's first meeting with Heathcliff, is significant mainly as an expression of her desire to keep the girl well within the confines of childhood, and permanently so, were that possible. This has already been symbolically manifested when Nelly is made uneasy by Cathy's interest in Penistone Craggs as stimulated most particularly when they are exposed by 'the setting sun' (*WH*, p. 168). Indeed, not for Nelly any landscape existing beyond the limits of the familiar! As she says to Cathy: 'The moors, where you ramble with [Edgar], are much nicer; and Thrushcross park is the finest place in the world' (*WH*, p. 168). One wonders what Cathy's fate might have been as an adult, had she heeded Nelly's cautious (and fallacious) advice.

More questionable, however, is Nelly's aesthetic talk in her dialogue with Linton Heathcliff on their ride to the Heights in Chapter 20. For though Nelly's remarks to the boy about the pleasures of nature might be thought harmless enough as far as they go, their patent insincerity in this particular context must come home to her at the time she is giving Lockwood the account of that journey. That Nelly's love of nature has a certain heartiness about it is already apparent when, in her efforts to get Linton out of bed at five o'clock in the morning, she makes this specious comparison: 'An early ride on such a *beautiful* morning is much preferable to an hour's more sleep' (*WH*, p. 180; italics mine). Nelly's aphoristic utterance is doubtless justified when soon afterwards she attributes something of her own aesthetic sensibility to Linton: 'The *pure heather-scented* air, and the *bright* sunshine, and the *gentle* canter of Minny relieved his despondency, after a while' (*WH*, p. 181; italics mine). Yet what Nelly describes so poetically is, of course, a cunning means of distracting the boy from his apprehensiveness. Thus when asked by him whether Wuthering Heights is 'as pleasant a place as Thrushcross Grange', Nelly avoids the negative answer she might otherwise have given in less delicate circumstances by referring to the physical and spiritual advantages of the Heights' setting as being such that one can 'see the country *beautifully*, all round; and the air is healthier [...] — fresher, and dryer' (*WH*, p. 181; italics mine). Nelly also deceives Linton with the notion that living at the Heights will enable him to enjoy other aspects of nature. As she says: 'And you will have such *nice* rambles on the moors! Hareton Earnshaw [...] will show you all the *sweetest* spots; and you can bring a book *in fine weather*, and make a *green hollow* your study' (*WH*, p. 181; italics mine). Thus Nelly encourages Linton to be hopeful about his new life with a string of prevarications, conscious as she comfortably is that she will not have to be at the Heights to see to it that her aesthetic prognostications are fulfilled.

Just as nature elicits aesthetic responses from Nelly, so, too, do objects, whether natural or man-made. Perhaps the most memorable example of this may be noted in the pleasurable sensations she experiences while sitting alone in the Heights kitchen on Christmas Eve: 'I smelt the *rich* scent of the heating spices; and admired the *shining* kitchen utensils, the *polished* clock, decked in holly, the *silver* mugs ranged on a tray ready to be filled with mulled ale for supper; and, above all, the *speckless purity* of my particular care — the *scoured* and *well-swept* floor' (*WH*, p. 48; italics mine). As well as stirring up a sentimental memory of Mr Earnshaw's generosity to her every Christmas, such aesthetic awareness prompts a sudden, and hardly less sentimental, concern on her part for Heathcliff's welfare, and yet a concern that will, ironically enough, lead in the end to his being punished and excluded from the festivities the following day.

Nelly's description of the kitchen may also be seen as a kind of compensation for her solitude in much the same way as Lockwood's very detailed inventory of 'the house' in Chapter 1 may be undersood, albeit retrospectively, as a facet of his tendency to take psychological refuge in things, no less than in nature, to offset his loneliness. This is especially noticeable as regards the visual comfort he draws from the fires mentioned both in Chapter 2 and on his last visit to the Heights in Chapter 32. Further, Lockwood's description of 'the house' foreshadows Isabella's own sensitive responses to the place shortly after her arrival at the Heights as Heathcliff's bride. The fact that Isabella is by then in considerable despair doubtless explains her attempts as something of a loner herself to seek comfort in the house interior as she nostalgically includes this detail in her letter to Nelly: 'There was a *great* fire, and that was all the *light* in the *huge* apartment, whose floor had grown a uniform grey; and the once *brilliant* pewter dishes which used to *attract my gaze* when I was a girl partook of a similar obscurity, created by tarnish and dust' (*WH*, p. 122; italics mine). Isabella's and Lockwood's aesthetic responses to 'the house' are significantly linked with the enthusiasm that Frances, an outsider like themselves, evinces at the sight of the interior of the Heights on her arrival there as Hindley's wife. Thus Nelly recalls: 'Every object she saw, the moment she crossed the threshold, appeared to delight her' (*WH*, p. 39). Indeed, as Nelly adds, Hindley would have 'carpeted and papered a small room for a parlour', had not Frances 'expressed such *pleasure* at the *white* floor, and *huge glowing* fire-place, at the pewter dishes, and delf-case, and dog-kennel, and the wide space there was to move about in, where they usually sat' (*WH*, p. 39f.; italics mine). And yet, worthy as Frances's responses to the exoticism of the Heights might be thought, they should also be understood, like Lockwood's and Isabella's responses, as the expression of an undue dependency on things for psychological well-being and hence, by implication, of a certain misanthropy, which, in Frances's case, will be betrayed not only through her exclusive relationship with Hindley and her somewhat mercenary attitude to Catherine as Edgar's prospective wife, but, more especially, through her aiding and abetting Hindley's ill-treatment of Heathcliff.

Is it, then, any wonder that Frances's aesthetic sensitivity should be conspicuous at the time Heathcliff is locked up in a garret on Christmas Day? This is clearly borne out while the Gimmerton band and singers are entertaining the Earnshaws and their guests downstairs, whereby Nelly recollects this detail: 'After the usual carols had been sung, we set [the musicians] to songs and glees. Mrs Earnshaw *loved* the music, and so they gave us plenty' (*WH*, p. 53; italics mine). And since music can be powerfully distracting, it enables Frances to be utterly oblivious of Heathcliff's sufferings while it is being played or sung, indeed as oblivious as Nelly herself must have been when, amid words such as 'pleasure', 'respectable' and 'first-rate treat', she took careful note of the very instruments making up the 'fifteen strong' band. By way of contrast with professionally performed music, which seems to have negative associations here, is the humble musicality of the characters in the form of singing or humming, those most primordial of artistic endeavours undertaken, say, to entertain a loved one, to lull a child or an adult to sleep, to amuse, console or compensate oneself, to express joy or contentment. Certainly one of the most affecting of Nelly's aesthetic responses, testimony though it is to her inveterate (unconscious) desire to keep Cathy in a permanent state of childhood, is a passage in which she recalls that '[i]n summer' the girl would climb up to a high branch of a tree and, as well as either watching birds or meditating, would '[f]rom dinner to tea [...] lie in her breeze-rocked cradle, doing nothing except singing old songs— my nursery lore — to herself' (*WH*, p. 203).

If music-making in its more or less skilled forms, as against its more modest ones noted in the foregoing, is implicitly given a negative connotation, so, too, in certain respects, are the fine arts, references or allusions to which are usually unfavourable. Take, for example, the negative allusion to an effigy when, in response to Joseph's scolding of her in Chapter 2, Cathy is overheard by Lockwood threatening the old servant with having him 'all modelled in wax and clay' (*WH*, p. 12). This foreshadows the moment when, while reading one of Catherine's books in the oak-panelled bed, Lockwood comes upon 'an excellent caricature of [his] friend Joseph, rudely yet powerfully sketched' (*WH*, p. 16). In both latter instances the artistic achievements are clearly grim means of self-compensation, rather like that which, after her quarrel with Hareton in Chapter 31, Cathy doubtless seeks when she is noticed by Lockwood 'retiring to a stool by the window, where she began to carve figures of birds and beasts, out of the turnip parings in her lap' (*WH*, p. 265). Similarly, it is surely in order to divert her frustration that Cathy, after yet another failed attempt to be reconciled with Hareton, is observed by

Nelly 'beguiling an idle hour' with, among other activities, 'drawing pictures on the window panes' (*WH*, p. 277).

Even the professional portrait painting seems to be implicitly questioned here for its peculiar limitations, notably when Lockwood uses Edgar's portrait, which for him 'formed a sweet picture', as sufficient reason for him to understand why Catherine 'could forget her first friend [Heathcliff] for such an individual' (*WH*, p. 58). The irony of Lockwood's judgement of Edgar's physical beauty here, however, is that he is yet to learn from Nelly's subsequent account that this good-looking man did not necessarily deserve the admiration his portrait has thus elicited. Even Nelly seems momentarily indifferent to defects of character when, speaking of the portraits of Edgar and Catherine as seen by moonlight in Chapter 29, she once again betrays her habitual concern with beauty by referring to 'the *splendid* head of Mrs Linton, and the *graceful* one of her husband' (*WH*, p. 253; italics mine). That the portrait painting can give only a limited idea of the person it represents has been ironically underlined several years earlier when, just before leaving the Grange for good, Isabella 'kissed Edgar's and Catherine's portraits' (*WH*, p. 161), as if to suggest that, with such a token farewell, she had clean forgotten her unpleasant experiences of those two people. All this may, in turn, explain why the word 'picture', whether as a noun or a verb, tends to be used as a negative metaphor. One memorable example may be noted when, having adversely described Heathcliff's character with a good deal of insensate figurative language in order to discourage Isabella's amatory interest in him, Catherine concludes her diatribe with the words: 'There's my picture' (*WH*, p. 91).[14] The irony of 'picture' in that phrase is that it not only contradicts the commendatory remarks that Catherine has shortly beforehand uttered to Edgar about the newly returned Heathcliff, but confirms that, here as elsewhere, she sees the latter chiefly in terms of essentially aesthetic images.

Of like interest are the metaphors now and again drawn from

the literary genres. Consider, for example, those contexts in which the drama is alluded to with such words and phrases as 'act', 'scene', 'perform', 'play a part', etc., most of them used with respect to highly emotional language and behaviour, and with sinister connotations.[15] For example, we note that, after her quarrel with Heathcliff towards the end of Chapter 3, Cathy is presently observed by Lockwood on a seat 'playing the part of a statue during the remainder of [his] stay' (*WH*, p. 26). Indeed, Emily seems to suggest thereby that some of her characters turn moments of their everyday lives, especially tense moments, into a kind of drama. Noteworthy in this connection, too, is the way in which Lockwood himself seems to turn Nelly's account of real people into a kind of fiction. This is especially evident at the beginning of Chapter 10, when, having sent for Nelly to 'finish her tale', he remembers that 'her *hero* had run off, and never been heard of for three years: and the *heroine* was married' (*WH*, p. 80; italics mine), and that in spite of having just noted in his diary that he was visited by the real-life Heathcliff only a few days earlier! Similarly, we see that, whereas Lockwood has already met Cathy at the Heights in Chapter 2, her reality for him has been determined first and foremost by what Nelly has told him about her in subsequent chapters, to say nothing of the 'picture' of Cathy he has asked his housekeeper to 'hang [...] over [his] fireplace' (*WH*, p. 226). As he informs a somewhat withdrawn Cathy on his third visit to the Heights: '[Y]ou are not aware that I am an acquaintance of yours? so *intimate*, that I think it strange you won't come and speak to me' (*WH*, p. 266; italics mine). Paradoxically enough, this intrinsically aesthetic view of Cathy amply suggests that Lockwood is, in fact, anxious, albeit unconsciously, to remain detached from the characters in Nelly's 'tale' and their lives as flesh-and-blood creatures. In any case, the literary allusions he has occasional recourse to as analogies to his own experiences probably prevent him from looking upon such experiences as both real and unique, one comical example of this being given when, having been released from beneath the Heights dogs that have knocked him down, he orders their 'malignant masters' to let him out of the house at once 'with several incoherent threats of retaliation that, in their indefinite depth of virulency, smacked of King Lear' (*WH*, p. 14).[16]

Lockwood's literary allusions, like the elegance of his written and spoken language, presuppose no mean familiarity on his part with books, reminding us that books play a prominent part in the novel, and one much more important than music or the fine arts. But although, for example, Nelly Dean, Joseph, Catherine, Edgar, Linton Heathcliff and the groom Michael have to do with books in one way or another, whether for religious purposes, for cultural snobbery, for self-improvement, for distraction, for consolation, even for writing commentaries or diaries in, it is obvious that none of these characters matches Cathy in her constant and consistent love of books both for their content and for what they are as artefacts. It is true that her bibliophily and her pride in her literacy sometimes argue aesthetic snobbery at its most arrogant, as, for example, when, having blamed Hareton in Lockwood's presence for his part in depriving her of her books at the Heights, she smugly adds: 'But I've most of them written on my brain and printed in my heart, and you cannot deprive me of those!' (*WH*, p. 267). Such language, no less than her humiliation of Hareton presently for his bumbling attempts to read aloud, is, to be sure, the very antithesis of the spirit with which Cathy will soon afterwards offer to teach the latter to read. At the same time, it is curious to note that a number of critics have condemned Cathy's education of Hareton as a kind of emasculation of the young man, encouraged as they may have been thereto in part by the knowledge that, as Cathy informs Lockwood in Chapter 31, Heathcliff 'never reads' and that, accordingly, he 'took it into his head to destroy [her] books' (*WH*, p. 266), doubtless in the frame of mind of the leisure-hating workaholic he seems to have gradually become as master of the Heights.[17] And yet for all their objections to Cathy's cultural influence on Hareton — objections which after all smack of little more than mere apologies for the tenets of machismo — those critics would appear to have overlooked Emily's tacit recognition here of the idea that, thanks in no small measure to the aid of the imagination, books have the power to liberate us from the physical and mental restrictions of the human condition.

It is in the same dialogue that Lockwood, wondering how Cathy can live without books, says this to her: 'Though provided with a large library, I'm frequently very dull at the Grange — take my books away, and I should be desperate!' (*WH*, p. 266). Thus the most literate of all Emily's characters suggests that, even for him, books are at best a sort of convenience and, rather like the women in his life, at their most appealing when they are least available. Further, however admirable Lockwood's aesthetic responses and reactions may be by virtue of his perceptive descriptions and analyses of human beauty, nature, landscapes and inanimate objects, one cannot help thinking that they also enable him to take partial refuge from life and, more importantly, to avoid the rough-and-tumble of personal relationships such as, by striking contrast, Cathy and Hareton prove eminently capable of entering into and sustaining.[18] For both cousins, moreover, books bid fair to become no bloodless substitute for the business of living, but an integral and wholesome part of their life together as much as any other aesthetic pursuits of theirs mentioned in the final chapters.[19] And perhaps it is through a careful reading of *Wuthering Heights* that we may come to understand why this should be so.

Brontë Studies, 37/1 (2012)

Notes

1   For references to the novel, see Emily Brontë, *Wuthering Heights*, ed. Ian Jack and Patsy Stoneman (Oxford: Oxford University Press, 1998), the edition used here being the second 1998 impression consisting of 330 pages; hereafter *WH*. For the sake of convenience, the first Catherine will be referred to as 'Catherine', the second as 'Cathy'.

2   For an instructive essay on the 'aesthetic attitude' as something held with respect to everyday life as much as to works of art, see Edward Bullough's influential paper 'Psychical Distance as a Factor in Art and as an Aesthetic Principle', *British Journal of Psychology*, 5 (1912), 87-117. Although there has, to my knowledge, been no publication on *Wuthering Heights* specifically concerned with my chosen topic, the following studies may be said to have some bearing on the content of my essay: Butler Wood, 'The Influence of the Moorlands in Charlotte and Emily Brontë', *Brontë Society Transactions*, 6 (1922), 79-87; T. W. Hanson, 'The Local Colour of *Wuthering Heights*', *Brontë Society Transactions*, 6 (1925), 201-19; W. Thompson Elliott, 'Atmosphere in the Brontë Works', *Brontë Society Transactions*, 7 (1928), 119-36; Wilson Midgley, 'Sunshine in Haworth Moor', *Brontë Society Transactions*, 11 (1950), 309-26; Dorothy J. Cooper, 'The Romantics and Emily Brontë', *Brontë Society Transactions*, part 62 (1952), 106-12; Hilda Marsden, 'The Scenic Background of *Wuthering Heights*', *Brontë Society Transactions*, 13 (1957), 111-30; Jeremy Cott, 'Structures of Sound: The Last Sentence of *Wuthering Heights*', *Texas Studies in Literature and Language*, 6 (1964), 280-89; Margaret Homans, 'Repression and Sublimation of Nature in *Wuthering Heights*', *Publications of the Modern Language Association of America*, 93 (1978), 9-19; N. S. Kiernan, 'The Seasons in the Brontë Novels', *Brontë Society*

Transactions, 18 (1981), 36-38; Paul Simpson-Housley, Andrea O'Reilly and Deborah Carter Park, 'Geographic Reality: Symbolic Landscapes of *Wuthering Heights*', *Brontë Society Transactions*, 19 (1989), 369-75; Christopher Heywood, 'Yorkshire Landscapes in *Wuthering Heights*', *Essays in Criticism*, 48 (1998), 13-34.

3   See Graeme Tytler, 'Physiognomy in *Wuthering Heights*', *Brontë Society Transactions*, 21 (1994), 137-48.

4   See *Wuthering Heights*, pp. 121, 160, 167, 177, 182, 286f.

5   See *Wuthering Heights*, pp. 7f., 167. See also Graeme Tytler, *Physiognomy in the European Novel: Faces and Fortunes* (Princeton, NJ: Princeton University Press, 1982), pp. 68-70.

6   For Cathy and Hareton's mutual awareness of the other's good looks, see *Wuthering Heights*, pp. 192, 261, 263.

7   See *Wuthering Heights*, p. 50.

8   See *Wuthering Heights*, pp. 49f., 84, 171, 173, 189, 190, 240. For Nelly's references to Linton Heathcliff as 'weakling', 'invalid', etc., see *Wuthering Heights*, pp. 178, 182, 190, 208f., 214, 240.

9   Nelly's references to the beautification of Catherine's face both before and after her death bear out what Lavater says about the physiognomy of the dying and the dead. See Tytler, *Physiognomy in the European Novel*, pp. 254-59.

10 Nelly's fascination with death may also be sensed in one or two sentimental comments of hers relating to the deaths of Hindley and Isabella. See *Wuthering Heights*, pp. 119, 164f.

11 For Edgar's aesthetic comments with respect both to his memory of Catherine and to his anxiety about Cathy's future after his own death, see *Wuthering Heights*, pp. 162, 187, 226f.

12 In this connection, it is interesting to compare the two heroines as to their strong love of nature, and nowhere more poignantly than in moments when they are helplessly longing to be in its midst. See *Wuthering Heights*, pp. 110, 111, 118f., 266.

13 See *Wuthering Heights*, pp. 81, 88, 119, 190, 204, 271.

14 For other metaphorical uses of 'picture' with negative implications, see *Wuthering Heights*, pp. 91, 133, 160, 220, 229, 254.

15 See *Wuthering Heights*, pp. 14, 20, 25, 26, 59, 68, 77f., 100, 104, 107, 148, 239.

16 For Lockwood's allusions to *Twelfth Night* and *Macbeth*, see *Wuthering Heights*, pp. 3, 24.

17 For negative attitudes to Cathy's education of Hareton, see, for example, Dorothy Van Ghent, 'On *Wuthering Heights*' in *Wuthering Heights. An Anthology of Criticism*, ed. by Alastair Everitt (London: Frank Cass, 1967), p. 169; Terence Dawson, '"An Oppression Past Explaining": The Structure of *Wuthering Heights*', *Orbis Litterarum*, 44 (1989), 64; Beth Newman, '"The Situation of the Looker-On": Gender, Narrative and Gaze in *Wuthering Heights*', *Publications of the Modern Language Association of America*, 105 (1990), 1036; Claire Jones, *Wuthering Heights. Emily Brontë* (London: York Press, 1998), p. 59.

18 Lockwood's fear of love relationships is amply suggested when, by way of answer to Nelly's fancying that 'no one could see Catherine Linton and not love her', he says: 'It may be very possible that *I* should love her; but would she love me? I doubt it too much to venture my tranquillity by running into temptation' (*WH*, p. 224). It is, moreover, Lockwood's inordinate reliance on his attractiveness to women that surely accounts for his passivity as well as his diffidence in his relations with Cathy.

19 As a noble example of such pursuits, one may refer to Cathy's (and Hareton's) planting of flowers at the Heights. See *Wuthering Heights*, pp. 282-84, 290.

The Workings of Memory in *Wuthering Heights*

*W*uthering Heights is a text purportedly made up for the most part of some quite extraordinary feats of memory.[1] Such feats comprise not only Lockwood's recording of Nelly's 'history of Heathcliff', but Nelly's version of that history, with its highly detailed accounts of events, many of them experienced or observed by her several years earlier, and incorporating a number of other narratives provided by major and minor characters alike. There are, to be sure, moments in the novel when both principal narrators make it plain that each possesses a memory much like that of any normal human being. Thus Nelly prefaces some episodes with 'I remember' or 'I recollect' as if to invest them with a touch of verisimilitude.[2] Sometimes, too, Nelly confesses to lapses of memory on her part, and on occasion suggests that she has forgotten about certain resolutions she has made. More curious, however, are contexts in which Lockwood's memory seems somewhat shaky, and surprisingly so in someone who, we are led to suppose, has so faithfully reproduced Nelly's narrative. Such shakiness is already apparent when, concerning the time she has lived at Thrushcross Grange, he asks Nelly: '[…] did you not say sixteen years?', only to be corrected by her with the reply, 'Eighteen, sir' (*WH*, p. 28). Again, when, at the beginning of Chapter 10, Lockwood decides to have Nelly up to his study to 'finish her tale', he (supposedly) writes this in his diary: 'I can *recollect* its chief incidents, as far as she had gone. Yes, I *remember* her hero had run off, and never been heard of for three years: and the heroine was married' (*WH*, p. 80; italics mine). It is not difficult to deduce from such words that, while Lockwood can remember the 'chief incidents', he may well have remembered little else besides. Moreover, he seems to imply that he has not yet even started to write up Nelly's account as given him from Chapter 4 to Chapter 9. The reader's credulity is further strained when, on his return to the North in Chapter 32, Lockwood describes his reaction to the ostler's mention of Gimmerton thus: '— my residence in that locality had already grown dim and dreamy. "Ah! I know! How far is it from this?"' (*WH*, p. 271). Why, we might wonder at this point, should Lockwood have more or less forgotten a place he has been mentally and emotionally so involved with barely eight months earlier?

What has just been said about Lockwood should, nevertheless, not obscure the fact that the diary entries making up the first three chapters, though remarkable enough for their detail, are not altogether improbable as testimonies to his apparently retentive memory. In any case, the accounts of his first two visits to the Heights could well have been written up by him each time after he has returned to the Grange. Somewhat unusual for their detail, however, are Lockwood's descriptions of his two nightmares in Chapter 3, in view of the difficulty one ordinarily has in remembering the content of one's dreams for more than a few moments after waking up. No doubt Lockwood is able to recall both dreams vividly partly because of his sense of the unwontedness of his night in the oak-panelled bed: 'I *don't remember* another that I can at all compare with it since I was capable of suffering' (*WH*, p. 18; italics mine). That Lockwood's dreams seem to be symbolic transmutations of his memories of unpleasant experiences undergone at the Heights in Chapters 1 and 2, of books and names read in the oak-panelled bed, and of the episode of his disappointed love at the sea-coast, admirably exemplifies the author's understanding of the way in which recent memories lodged in the unconscious may determine the quality of one's dreams. Certainly, literary scholars of a Freudian turn of mind have managed to distinguish between the manifest and the latent content of Lockwood's dreams.[3] Yet the chief interest of these dreams lies for us here in their reminding us that, during the time he is asleep, Lockwood is under the control of his unconscious memory, and, no less importantly, that the power of his unconscious memory to keep him thus in thrall foreshadows the mental problems of the two main protagonists of the novel.

Noteworthy in this connection, first of all, are the links that may be drawn between Lockwood's two nightmares and Catherine's own troubled dreams, some of which are possibly based on unpleasant memories.[4] For example, her dream of being cast out of heaven by the angels seems symbolic (as she herself is apparently conscious) of the carking doubts she has been having about her amatory relationship with Edgar. Much more significant, however, is the fact that, even after her marriage to Edgar, Catherine is beset by memories of her childhood with Heathcliff. This is especially apparent in Chapter 12 with respect to her blackout in her bedroom when, after waking up from it, she finds her mind trapped in a twilight zone between the conscious and the unconscious that induces her intermittently to confuse the past with the present. At the same time, it is interesting to note that Catherine's conscious memory is by no means impaired at this stage. This is confirmed by such utterances of hers as '*memory burst in*' (*WH*, p. 110; italics mine); '*I did not recall* that [the last seven years of my life] had been at all' (*WH*, p. 110; italics mine); 'my heart ached with some great grief which, just waking, *I could not recollect*' (*WH*, p. 110; italics mine); 'Oh dear! I thought I was at home [...]. I thought I was lying in my chamber at Wuthering Heights' (*WH*, p. 109). Yet though normal enough to suggest that she is at worst only partially insane, Catherine's conscious memory nevertheless continues to weaken from the time her 'brain fever' is diagnosed in Chapter 13 until her death two chapters later. This is suggested in some measure when Nelly, in her attempt to discourage Heathcliff from visiting Catherine at Thrushcross Grange, and notwithstanding his presumptuous claim that she is constantly thinking of him, warns him that she has 'nearly forgotten' (*WH*, p. 131) him. It is further suggested when, having just received Heathcliff's note from Nelly, Catherine is momentarily unable to register who it is from. But what finally underlines the deterioration of Catherine's conscious memory is Nelly's following statement about her dying: 'Her senses never returned — she recognised nobody from the time you left her' (*WH*, p. 147). Indeed, such is the weakness of Catherine's conscious memory at this time that, as Nelly somewhat perversely informs Heathcliff, she did not once mention his name on her deathbed.

It is, therefore, ironic that Heathcliff should spend the rest of his life remembering someone whose memory of himself was defective, not to say eroded, shortly before her demise. Among several possible reasons for this, the most important are not only Catherine's omitting to mention his name but the resentment with which he reacts to her asking him at their final meeting whether his children will not be 'dearer to [him] than she was' (*WH*, p. 140) at the approach of his own death: 'Do you reflect that all those words will be *branded in my memory*, and eating deeper eternally, after you have left me?' (*WH*, p. 140; italics mine). That Heathcliff's memory of Catherine's words will have been instrumental in bringing about his subsequent obsession with her is prefigured in what he says to her just after her death: 'You said I killed you — haunt me, then!' (*WH*, p. 148). No doubt, it is Heathcliff's constantly remembering or thinking about Catherine that will partly account for the visual and auditory hallucinations symptomatic of that peculiar mental illness which afflicts him and which will be tentatively designated by Nelly, appropriately enough, as 'a monomania' (*WH*, p. 288). Yet if, through the ineluctable influence of his unconscious memory, Heathcliff, too, eventually succumbs to partial insanity, his conscious memory, unlike Catherine's, remains perfectly intact to the end of his life in ways characteristic of those suffering from monomania.[5] This is poignantly suggested when, acutely aware of the malfunction of that part of his memory governing habit, he says this to Nelly: 'I have to *remind myself* to breathe — almost to *remind* my heart to beat!' (*WH*, p. 289; italics mine). Nevertheless, even his conscious memory now and again proves inadequate to his intentions, as, for example, when he has sat down to meals prepared for him. Thus Nelly recalls this detail two days before Heathcliff's death: '[…] if he stretched his hand out to get a piece of bread, his fingers clenched, before they reached it, and remained on the table, *forgetful of their aim*' (*WH*, p. 295; italics mine). But although such behaviour may elicit no little compassion for the hero from some readers, other readers may be wondering to what extent Heathcliff and indeed Catherine herself are to blame for their respective mental illnesses. Certainly it is difficult to deny that both illnesses are in large measure due to the abuses to which they have each subjected their memory systems, Catherine by remaining, consciously and unconsciously, fixated on her childhood memories, Heathcliff by allowing his memories of her to turn into an incurable mental illness. Further, the fact that Catherine and Heathcliff both end up outright victims of their much-abused faculties of memory might induce us to call in question their hallowed status as heroic figures, especially in the light of the importance that Emily Brontë seems to attach elsewhere in her novel to the possession of a sound memory.

If, as we have seen, then, memory plays a crucial part in causing mental illness, it does so undoubtedly when it operates in the form of extreme nostalgia.[6] This idea is suggested when, in the throes of his monomania, Heathcliff says this to Nelly about Catherine: 'The entire world is a dreadful collection of *memoranda* that she did exist, and that I have lost her!' (*WH*, p. 288; italics mine). That Catherine's mental illness, too, may have been determined by her own proclivity to nostalgia is indicated not only by her memories of her childhood, but by the way in which she betrays this proclivity in a conversation with Edgar during her convalescence in Chapter 13. Thus to Edgar's saying, 'Catherine, last spring at this time, I was longing to have you under this roof —', she replies, '[...] Next spring you'll long again to have me under this roof, and you'll look back and think you were happy to-day' (*WH*, p. 118). What is especially striking here is Catherine's awareness of Edgar's own strong tendency to nostalgia; a tendency that will manifest itself in him most powerfully after her death. Nelly herself puts this idea in a nutshell when she says: 'He *recalled her memory* with ardent, tender love (*WH*, p. 162; italics mine).[7] But if Edgar's nostalgia for his late wife is just as sympathetically conveyed by Nelly in other contexts, it is none the less an inherently harmful nostalgia mainly because it prevents him from leading a constructive life in the present. The same is to some extent true of Isabella, for whom happiness is something that belongs principally to the past, if not to the future, as is only too evident both from her letter to Nelly and from her dialogue with her in Chapter 17.[8] Characteristic of Isabella's nostalgic disposition is one of several memories she evokes thus: 'When I *recollect* how happy we were — how happy Catherine was before [Heathcliff] came — I'm fit to curse the day' (*WH*, p. 160; italics mine). Yet, as is so often the case with someone recalling past happiness, Isabella appears to have overlooked what Nelly will later tell Lockwood, namely, that life at the Grange during the early days of Catherine and Edgar's marriage was often anything but happy for her.[9] This may, in turn, explain why Isabella's nostalgia in regard to disappointed love takes the form of a conflation of good and bad memories, as is apparent when she says this to Nelly about Heathcliff: '— Monster! would that he could be blotted out of creation, and *out of my memory!*' (*WH*, p. 152; italics mine).

Just as nostalgia, especially in the extreme forms noted above, may be said to be a sort of abuse of the memory, so some kinds of forgetfulness may be designated as a misuse thereof. We think, for example, of the promises which Mr Earnshaw has made to Nelly and his children before his journey to Liverpool, but which he appears to have forgotten about or inadequately fulfilled on account of his concern for the foundling he has brought home with him. In this connection, it is noteworthy how often in the narrative resolutions are hastily made and then not adhered to. This holds especially for those voiced by Hindley concerning Heathcliff.[10] No doubt, this is one aspect of the state of chronic forgetfulness in which Hindley lives his life as master of his household. Thus, for example, it is Joseph's reporting Catherine and Heathcliff to him for failing to go to church that '*reminded* [Hindley] to order Heathcliff a flogging, and Catherine a fast from dinner or supper' (*WH*, p. 40; italics mine). Again, whenever Frances expresses her dislike of Heathcliff, that is enough to '*rouse* in [Hindley] all his old hatred of the boy' (*WH*, p. 40; italics mine). A similar unawareness sometimes informs Hindley's actual behaviour, and that most patently when, just before he drops Hareton over the bannister, Nelly notices him '*almost forgetting* what he had in his hands' (*WH*, p. 66; italics mine). This unawareness is cast in much the same mould when Isabella, having arrived at the Heights as Heathcliff's bride shortly beforehand, suffers Hindley's indifference to her as she watches him walk 'up and down, with his hands in his pockets, apparently quite *forgetting [her] presence*' (*WH*, p. 122; italics mine).

The forgetfulness that seems characteristic of the Earnshaws is to be seen in some of its most pathetic forms in Catherine. And though Catherine's forgetfulness seems somehow bound up with her precarious mental health, especially as manifest in Chapters 12 and 13, it may also be understood as the mark of a certain thoughtlessness. Consider, for example, how in full consciousness she answers Heathcliff's accusation of her for having treated him 'infernally' with the following question: 'How have I treated you infernally?' (*WH*, p. 100), as if she were utterly oblivious of what had caused him to leave the Heights three years earlier. More serious, however, are the contradictions Catherine is liable to through her failure to remember things she has said. For example, when, in her attempt in Nelly's presence to neutralize Isabella's infatuation with Heathcliff by portraying him as a kind of monster, she appears to have clean forgotten telling Nelly only a short time beforehand about Edgar's 'melting into tears because [she] said that Heathcliff was now worthy of any one's regard, and it would honour the first gentleman in the country to be his friend' (*WH*, p. 87). Yet nowhere in the narrative is Catherine's forgetfulness more glaring than when, informed by Nelly that, just before slipping out of the kitchen, Heathcliff 'had heard a good part of what [Catherine] said' there during their dialogue about Edgar's offer of marriage, Catherine is, oddly enough, quite unable to recall anything she has uttered in that context, including even the highly poetic comparisons she has made between her two men: 'What did I say, Nelly? *I've forgotten.* Was he vexed at my bad humour this afternoon? Dear! tell me what I've said to grieve him?' (*WH*, p. 74; italics mine). Ironically, it is precisely what Catherine has said to 'grieve' Heathcliff which, together with all the other sufferings he has endured in childhood, he will persist in carrying wilfully in his memory, and, as we have already noted, with tragic consequences. Moreover, it is by harbouring grudges of all kinds for years on end that Heathcliff seems to be the very antithesis of Hareton, another Earnshaw conspicuous for forgetfulness, but a forgetfulness that seems constructive enough through his disinclination to allow any resentment or anger aroused in him by, say, Lockwood, Cathy or Linton Heathcliff to have an adverse influence on his subsequent relations with any of them.[11]

The readiness to 'forgive and forget' is a trait that may often be predicated of a dog, to which creature Hareton is sometimes compared, with the implication, too, that he shares something of its good nature.[12] Such readiness is in some sense prefigured when, on the day after his fight with the Heights dogs, Lockwood notices that the bitch pointer Juno 'deigned, at this second interview, to move the extreme tip of her tail, in token of owning [his] acquaintance' (*WH*, p. 7). This is a touching illustration of that remarkable propensity in dogs to bear no ill will against those human beings with whom they have been in conflict. Noteworthy, too, is the ability of dogs to remember people long after they have last seen them.[13] Such a mnemonic gift is no doubt rare in human beings and practically non-existent in children. As Nelly herself rightly surmises concerning Hareton, from whom she was separated when he was only five: 'I've no doubt he has *completely forgotten* all about Ellen Dean and that he was ever more than all the world to her, and she to him!' (*WH*, p. 79; italics mine) — a surmise sadly realized for her some three years later when, at first mistaking him for his father at the guidepost, she presently addresses an uncomprehending Hareton as follows: 'Hareton, it's Nelly — Nelly, thy nurse' (*WH*, p. 97), only to have a stone thrown at her by the boy for her pains. The tendency in young children to forget those they have known earlier is again suggested in the first reunion between Cathy and her cousin Linton. As Nelly recalls: '[Linton's] features had waxed so dim in [Cathy's] memory that she did not recognise him' (*WH*, p. 186). It is, therefore, perhaps only to be expected of Heathcliff that, with his almost pathologically retentive memory, he should mildly rebuke the two cousins for being unable to remember each other, first by saying this to Cathy: 'Ah! you have *a short memory*' (*WH*, p. 190; italics mine); and then by addressing his son thus: 'Linton, *don't you recall* your cousin, that you used to tease us so with wishing to see?' (*WH*, p. 190; italics mine).

Since people are for some reason or other prone to forgetfulness, they sometimes need, indeed may depend on, reminders from their fellow creatures. At the same time, reminders may throw some light on the character of those giving them. We note, for example, how Heathcliff takes advantage of Nelly's presence by saying this to her about the invective with which Isabella has just broken out against him: 'If you are called upon in a court of law, you'll *remember* her language, Nelly!' (*WH*, p. 134; italics mine). Much the same self-interest seems to lie behind the fact that, in answer to Nelly's insistence on Hindley's funeral being respectable, Heathcliff 'desired [her] to *remember* that the money for the whole affair came out of his pocket' (*WH*, p. 165; italics mine). Nelly Dean, too, not unlike Joseph in his tendency to remind Mr Earnshaw or Hindley of their respective duties as masters of the Heights, reveals something of her domineering disposition through some of the reminders she readily gives to her superiors. For example, just before going to the Heights to see to Hindley's funeral, Nelly '*reminded* [Edgar] that the child, Hareton, was his wife's nephew' (*WH*, p. 164; italics mine), thereby disclosing her proneness to go beyond her official province as Edgar's housekeeper. It is, however, with respect to the children under her care that Nelly's reminders seem almost blatant. For example, we note that, in reply to Cathy's earnest vow to maintain unswerving devotion to her sick father, Nelly says: 'Good words [...]. But deeds must prove it also; and after he is well, *remember you don't forget* resolutions formed in the hour of fear' (*WH*, p. 204;

italics mine). The irony of this somewhat pleonastic exhortation is that, while Nelly is thus counselling someone who scarcely needs any such martinet-like advice, she may well have forgotten having signally failed to stick to the odd well-intended resolution that she has made to herself several years earlier as Edgar's trusted servant.[14]

What has just been said in the foregoing would suggest how much easier it is to remind others of their obligations than it is to remind oneself of one's own obligations. The importance of the latter idea, betokening as it does the functioning of the human memory at one of its noblest levels, is perhaps in no respect better illustrated than through the presentation of Cathy. Indeed, rather more than most of the characters discussed hitherto, Cathy shows time and again how much her awareness of those she is in close relationship with has to do with her sound memory. Such awareness is, to be sure, apparent to some extent in the aesthetic sensitivity with which, say, Lockwood, Nelly Dean, Isabella and even Heathcliff, remember sundry details of the physicality of the characters they observe and describe.[15] And yet there is perhaps something worthier about the anxious tenderness with which, for example, Cathy remarks on the change in Linton's appearance at their first official reunion on the heath: '[you are] worse than when I saw you last — you are thinner, and —' (*WH*, p. 230), as if she lovingly remembered what he had looked like at their previous meeting. More significant in the same context, however, is the way in which Cathy can still vividly recall a conversation she has had with Linton several months earlier: 'You *recollect* the two days we agreed to spend in the place and way each thought pleasantest? This is nearly yours, only there are clouds; but then, they are so soft and mellow, it is nicer than sunshine' (*WH*, p. 231; italics mine). The fact that Linton '*did not appear to remember what she talked of*' (*WH*, p. 231; italics mine) makes it abundantly clear which of the two cousins has been truly aware of the other. It is through such seemingly minor details that we come to realize the significant part played by the memory for the kind of thoughtfulness that Cathy so often shows to Linton, and that not least through a capacity seldom matched by the other characters, namely, that of remembering to carry out where possible the promises she has made to him in much the same spirit as those that she will later make to her father, to Nelly and to Hareton.[16]

It might be asked at this juncture whether Cathy's ability to remember her obligations to others is not in some way connected with the fact that she possesses a well-trained memory. This is no idle question if we recall those parts of the novel concerned with rote-learning and memorization. We note, first of all, that, being a more or less arduous process, rote-learning is sometimes imposed on the young by way of punishment, as is evident from references to Catherine and Heathcliff paying for their respective transgressions by being ordered to 'get by heart' (*WH*, p. 40) several chapters of the Bible or to 'learn a column of Scripture names' (*WH*, p. 41). Diametrically opposite in motivation, on the other hand, is the love with which Cathy commits favourite literary passages to memory, as she somewhat arrogantly suggests when, having complained to Hareton about depriving her of the books he has illicitly 'borrowed' from her, she says: 'But I've most of them written on my brain and printed in my heart, and you cannot deprive me of those!' (*WH*, p. 267). It is doubtless her capacity to memorize literary texts that makes Cathy eminently fitted to become Hareton's tutor shortly afterwards. This is suggested when, while teaching him the correct pronunciation of 'contrary', with the stress on the second syllable, she humorously admonishes him for his forgetfulness thus: '*Recollect*, or I pull your hair!' (*WH*, p. 273; italics mine). This lesson is secretly witnessed by Lockwood, and appropriately so if we remember his defence of Hareton in Chapter 31 against Cathy's mockery of the latter's bumbling attempts to teach himself to read. The fact that on that occasion Lockwood has stood up for Hareton in the light of certain basic pedagogic principles indirectly evokes the idea of the education that he himself has undergone, as indicated partly through his allusions or references to Shakespeare and the Bible in the first three chapters.[17]

It is, nevertheless, noteworthy that, for all such knowledge as he possesses, Lockwood appears to be interested above all in history, a word which, incidentally, he mentions some half-dozen times.[18] That Lockwood is, moreover, something of a historian himself is confirmed by the diary he (supposedly) keeps during his tenancy of the Grange. Yet notwithstanding that a diary may serve, among other things, as a means of conversing with oneself, passing the time, or distracting oneself from painful reality, as is true, for example, of Catherine's diary quoted by Lockwood in Chapter 3, it is otherwise not dissimilar from any historical text in being a kind of repository of memories, whereby the past, which a diary is by its very nature designed to represent, even at the moment an entry is being indited, is, as it were, wrapped up and settled once and for all.[19] Accordingly, the question inevitably arises: does not a diary, like any other historical document, excuse someone keeping it from having to retain in their memory whatever has been written down therein? This notion seems to be ironically suggested when, as we saw above, Lockwood remarks, in the context of his return to the North in September 1802, that his residence in Gimmerton has by then 'already grown dim and dreamy' (*WH*, p. 271). Such a comment, made only a few months after his departure from the Grange, may indicate either that Lockwood has not yet recorded any of Nelly's narrative, or that, if he has done so, he has scarcely bothered to think about it since it is now on paper for him to resort to at will. In any event, Lockwood's supposed memorization of Nelly's narrative, to say nothing of Nelly's own memories of 'Heathcliff's history', seems to go well beyond the bounds of normal mnemonic capacity to the point of being utterly freakish. Hence it is that, for all the reader's willingness to suspend disbelief and to make allowance for this peculiar use of poetic licence, *Wuthering Heights* continues none the less to raise certain awkward, not to say unanswerable, questions. At the same time, it is through such mnemonic anomalies and contradictions that Emily Brontë may well be using her frame narrator to foreshadow or evoke symbolically the extremes of the range within which the strengths and weaknesses of the human memory play their part in the presentation of her characters.

Brontë Studies, 37/1 (2012)

Notes

1 For quotations from the novel, see Emily Brontë, *Wuthering Heights*, ed. by Ian Jack and Helen Small (Oxford: Oxford University Press, 2009). For the sake of convenience, the first Catherine will be referred to as 'Catherine', the second as 'Cathy'.

2 See *Wuthering Heights*, pp. 30, 33, 37, 187.

3 For interpretations of Lockwood's dreams, see especially Edgar F. Shannon, Jr., 'Lockwood's Dreams and the Exegesis of *Wuthering Heights*', *Nineteenth-Century Fiction*, 14 (1959), 95-109; Ronald E. Fine, 'Lockwood's Dreams and the Key to *Wuthering Heights*', *Nineteenth-Century Fiction*, 24 (1970), 16-30; Cates Baldridge, 'Voyeuristic Rebellion: Lockwood's Dreams and the Reader of *Wuthering Heights*', *Studies in the Novel*, 20 (1988), 274-87.

4 Significant in this connection are Catherine's following words to Nelly in Chapter 12: 'I dread sleeping, my dreams appal me' (*WH*, p. 109).

5 See Graeme Tytler, 'Heathcliff's Monomania: An Anachronism in *Wuthering Heights*', *Brontë Society Transactions*, 20 (1992), 331-43.

6 That nostalgia is, of course, a universal and usually harmless emotion is suggested now and again by Nelly's occasional bouts of it. See *Wuthering Heights*, pp. 48, 164, 167.

7 For conspicuous signs of Edgar's nostalgia, see *Wuthering Heights*, 226f.

8 See *Wuthering Heights*, pp. 121, 122, 124f., 154.

9   See *Wuthering Heights*, p. 81.

10 See *Wuthering Heights*, pp. 33, 45, 47, 77.

11 See *Wuthering Heights*, pp. 13, 173, 222.

12 For a discussion on Hareton's characterization in this respect, see Graeme Tytler, 'Animals in *Wuthering Heights*', *Brontë Studies*, 27 (2002), 122-24.

13 See *Wuthering Heights*, pp. 46, 127, 139.

14 See *Wuthering Heights*, p. 136.

15 See *Wuthering Heights*, pp. 3, 7f., 82, 84, 121, 137f., 145, 173, 269, 288.

16 See *Wuthering Heights*, pp. 197, 200, 220f., 226, 286.

17 See *Wuthering Heights*, pp. 3, 14, 18-20, 24.

18 See *Wuthering Heights*, pp. 2, 28, 29, 89, 275.

19 In this connection, see Rebecca Steinitz, 'Diaries and Displacement in *Wuthering Heights*', *Studies in the Novel*, 32 (2000), 407-19.

Facets of Time
Consciousness in
Wuthering Heights

Critical discussions on time in *Wuthering Heights* in the past several decades have centered chiefly on its structural or symbolic function in the art of narrative.[1] Comparatively little, on the other hand, appears to have been written by scholars concerned with this novel on the relationship between time and human psychology, or what might be designated simply as time consciousness. But if time consciousness is a universal human phenomenon, being part and parcel of our experience of the world through our awareness of time present, past and future, it may also be a signpost to one's character, one's mode of life, one's personal circumstances, and so on. This notion is illustrated in *Wuthering Heights* in ways striking enough to warrant special critical attention. Emily Brontë also shows how complex, even complicated, is our relationship with time, principally owing to the limits and limitations of the human mind as manifest most palpably through our emotional, not to say careless, use of language. Noteworthy, too, is how, occurring as they do now and again in various negative contexts, a good many time references in the narrative seem to suggest that time itself is for the author something of a metaphysical problem.

Emily's interest in time consciousness is discernible in sundry comments in her text indicating how the interplay between the conscious and the unconscious can determine one's experience of time. Thus we may mention that moment when, doubtless as a consequence of his two seemingly endless nightmares, Lockwood is astonished to gather from his watch how slowly real time has passed. As he says to himself in Heathcliff's presence: 'Not three o'clock yet! I could have taken oath it had been six — time stagnates here — we must surely have retired to rest at eight!'.[2] This detail foreshadows a similar reaction when, to Nelly's informing her that she locked herself in her bedroom on 'Monday evening' and that it is now 'Thursday night, or rather Friday morning', Catherine exclaims: 'What! of the same week? [...] Only that brief time?', presently adding, 'Well, it seems a weary number of hours. [...] it must be more' (*WH*, p. 110). Through Catherine's account of her blackout in Chapter 10, then, we are given an instructive illustration of the power of the unconscious to upset our sense of so-called normal or objective time. Pertinent here, too, is Emily's recourse to a familiar experience to show how time can seem much longer than usual because we are trying to hurry it on. We note this when, for instance, Nelly Dean remarks that 'the three days of [Mr Earnshaw's] absence' from the Heights 'seemed a long while to [them] all' (*WH*, p. 31). By the same token, Catherine suggests how a painful spell may yet be accelerated when she relates (in the form of a diary) that, after being 'hurled' with Heathcliff into the Heights back-kitchen by Hindley one Sunday evening, she has used the blank spaces of a book in which to record the day's events and thus 'got the time on with writing for twenty minutes' (*WH*, p. 17). By contrast, the passing of time may be quite unnoticed by dint of a mental distraction of some kind. For example, while observing the recently reconciled Cathy and Hareton poring over a book together by 'the house' fire, Nelly 'felt so soothed and comforted to watch them, that [she] did not notice how time got on' (*WH*, p. 286). Also of interest here is Nelly's reminding us of the well-known difference between children and adults as to a sense of the duration of time when, by way of a specious answer to Linton Heathcliff's wondering whether or not his father visited him during his early childhood, for, as he adds, he remembers 'not a single thing about him', she replies, '[...] ten years seem very different in length to a grown up person, compared with what they do to you' (*WH*, p. 182).

The anomalies of man's relationship with time, as suggested to some extent in the foregoing, help to explain our heavy dependence on the clock. We have already seen how by looking at his watch in the room where he has spent the night, Lockwood notes a glaring difference between real time and subjective time. And though Lockwood is sometimes imprecise as to the number of hours or minutes a particular action has lasted, he nevertheless seems to be quite obsessed with clock-time.[3] Thus he makes a point of saying that, on his return to Thrushcross Grange at the end of Chapter 3, 'the clock chimed twelve as I entered the house' (*WH*, p. 26). Again, regarding his third visit to the Heights one morning, Lockwood notes this in his diary: 'It was eleven o'clock, and I announced [to Hareton] my intention of going in, and waiting for [Heathcliff]' (*WH*, p. 265). Just as clock-conscious as Lockwood is Nelly Dean herself, as the former scrupulously notes by observing that, on reaching the end of the first part of her narrative, she 'chanced to glance towards the time-piece over the chimney; and was in amazement on seeing the minute-hand measure half-past one', whereat she 'would not hear of staying a second longer' (*WH*, p. 79). Clearly, Nelly's narrative has by then so come to occupy her mind as to unsettle her usually keen awareness of real time, manifested as that awareness is now and again by some rather punctilious references to clock-time in other contexts. Certainly, Nelly's punctiliousness in respect of time is, not unlike Lockwood's, underlined by the apparent gratuitousness of some such references. This is suggested when, for example, she tells of arriving at the Heights with Linton Heathcliff at 'half-past six' (*WH*, p. 182); when she speaks of going downstairs in the Grange at 'three o'clock' in the morning to 'fetch a jug of water' (*WH*, p. 250); or when she recalls how, though not yet aware that Isabella has already eloped with Heathcliff, she 'repeatedly caught the beat of horses' feet galloping at some distance' and that she found it 'a strange sound, in that place, at two o'clock in the morning' (*WH*, p. 114).[4]

If clock time is, strictly speaking, time at its most accurate and therefore at its most objective, we may nevertheless wonder how reliable are the references to it mentioned above. It is noteworthy in this connection that references to clock time in the novel happen to entail every one of the twelve hours, whether ante or post meridiem, there being only a handful of references indicating half-past a particular hour. Indeed, apart from the occasion when Hindley assures Isabella that he is going to kill Heathcliff by saying, 'Promise to hold your tongue, and before that clock strikes — it wants three minutes of one — you're a free woman!' (*WH*, p. 155), nowhere in the novel are we told of a minute-hand pointing to any part of the clock other than the hour or the half-hour. This is, of course, by no means an unusual thing in fiction, where references to time are almost invariably given in round figures. We see this plainly enough even in the case of the time span 'years'. Thus Nelly recalls that, on returning to the Heights on the death of her father, Hindley was 'altered considerably in the three years of his absence' (*WH*, p. 39);

that Edgar married Catherine 'three years subsequent to his father's death' (*WH*, p. 79); that Isabella died 'some thirteen years after the decease of Catherine' (*WH*, p. 162). But although such figures seem as acceptable as, say, 'for years', 'so many years', 'all these years', 'in a few years', etc., they may still prompt such doubts as are aroused by references to 'month' or 'months', when such references are preceded by specific cardinal numbers. For whereas, say, Lockwood's phrases 'the next six months' (*WH*, p. 264) and 'beyond the twelvemonths' (*WH*, p. 269) with respect to his sojourns in London and at the Grange respectively are presumably bona fide through being written in a diary, we may ask ourselves whether Nelly Dean's phrases such as 'three months' service' (*WH*, p. 47), 'ten months since' (*WH*, p. 97), 'in those two months' (*WH*, p. 118), 'a four months' indisposition' (*WH*, p. 169), confidently uttered as they are a long time after the periods they pertain to, can be altogether taken on trust. Indeed, our doubts as to their authenticity may be in some measure justified when we recall Nelly's telling Lockwood on his fourth visit to the Heights in September 1802 that Heathcliff has been dead '[t]hree months since' (*WH*, p. 275), even though it is obvious that he died in April that year, namely, five months earlier. That is why the various references made to weeks, days, hours, months or seconds should perhaps be viewed with caution, especially where they are in each case preceded by a specific number.

But whereas 'year', 'month', 'week', 'day' and 'hour' are generally straightforward temporal concepts, the same is by no means always true of very brief time spans such as 'minute', 'second', 'moment' and 'instant'. Take, for example, the use of 'minute' in the following phrases: 'we had not a minute's security that she wouldn't be in mischief' (*WH*, p. 36); 'she couldn't be still a minute' (*WH*, p. 176); 'no amusement usurped a minute' (*WH*, p. 214). In each phrase it is obvious that 'minute' serves a rhetorical or an emotional function, and not a measurable temporal one. We also find that the temporal meaning of 'minute', 'moment' or 'instant' is elusive when, because preceded by the definite article, those words mean 'as soon as'.[5] Noteworthy, too, is the way in which 'minute', 'moment' or 'instant' when preceded by 'this' has the sense of 'here and now', sometimes as part of a very emotional utterance. Thus when Heathcliff in his rage wonders who put Lockwood in the room with the oak-panelled closet, he goes on to add: 'I've a good mind to turn them out of the house this moment!' (*WH*, p. 22). Similarly, when Cathy is trying to get Hareton to talk amid her attempts to be reconciled with him, he at one point angrily says, 'Side out of t'gait, now; this minute!' (*WH*, p. 278).[6] These idiomatic uses of 'minute' and 'moment' are a reminder of the extent to which human beings have, as it were, come to dominate, not to say abuse, time through the medium of language. Such dominance may in some sense also be apparent through the use of such terms as 'presently', 'often', 'directly', 'at length', 'frequently', 'generally', 'sometime', 'seldom', 'soon', 'constantly', 'now and then', 'ever and anon', 'twice or thrice', 'by and bye', as well as numerous other temporal adverbs and adverbial phrases which, employed here and there by Emily's characters, can give us only a vague or approximate idea of the actual time, or the actual number of times, a particular action or process occurs or has occurred.[7]

Among the most interesting — and the most problematic — of temporal adverbs is 'always'. For example, in view of Catherine's amatory involvement with Edgar Linton since her five-week sojourn at the Grange, we may be not a little inclined to question the use of that adverb when, during her consultation with Nelly about Edgar's proposal of marriage, she says this about Heathcliff: '— he's always, always in my mind — not as a pleasure, any more than I am always a pleasure to myself' (*WH*, p. 73). Clearly, 'always', in this context, far from bearing a genuinely factual meaning, has an intrinsically emotional connotation, and not without such ironic implications as are to be descried, for example, in the following utterances of three women servants. Consider, first of all, the unnamed Heights housekeeper's following complaint to Nelly about Linton Heathcliff: '[…] he must always have sweets and dainties, and always milk, milk for ever' (*WH*, p. 186). Here we see how easily a perfectly valid temporal concept can be somewhat invalidated within the confines of an angry sentiment. Again, we may question Zillah's use of 'always' when, in partial explanation of the reason why she kept Cathy and Hareton company at the Heights one Sunday morning instead of going to chapel, she says this to Nelly: 'Young folks are always the better for an elder's over-looking' (*WH*, p. 261f.). The power of 'always' to reinforce a dubious aphorism has been suggested earlier in the novel when, in answer to Edgar's anxious sentiments about Cathy's future, Nelly not only reassures him that she will continue to support her after his death and that, being 'a good girl', Cathy will not go 'wilfully wrong', but goes on to comfort him further with these words: '[…] and people who do their duty are always finally rewarded' (*WH*, p. 227).[8]

Of like interest here are the temporal adverbs 'ever' and 'never'. Consider, for instance, the liberties taken with 'ever' in sentences containing superlatives. Thus, recollecting her care of Heathcliff while he was down with measles, Nelly refers to him as 'the quietest child that ever nurse watched over' (*WH*, p. 33); or, again, when on learning that Catherine has accepted Edgar's marriage proposal, she warns her that, if she happens to be Heathcliff's choice, he will be 'the most unfortunate creature that ever was born!' (*WH*, p. 72). Such uses of 'ever' are, of course, fallacious for being ultimately unverifiable, as is its use in Mr Kenneth's following comment about Hindley, shortly after he has announced the latter's death: 'he had the worst tricks with him that ever man imagined' (*WH*, p. 163). Again, consider Hindley's mention of 'never' when, in answer to Mr Kenneth's telling him that he (Kenneth) need no longer attend the fatally ill Frances, he retorts, 'I know you need not — she's well — she does not want any more attendance from you! She never was in a consumption. It was a fever; and it is gone —' (*WH*, p. 57). The 'never' with which Hindley stubbornly denies the nature of his wife's illness is not dissimilar in spirit from the 'never' that Nelly falls back on in order to buttress her noble intentions with respect to both Catherines: first, when in response to Heathcliff's determination to visit Catherine at the Grange, she assures him that 'you never shall through my means' (*WH*, p. 131); and, secondly, when, to Heathcliff's saying that he is resolved to marry his son to Cathy, she gives this reply: 'And I'm resolved she shall never approach your house with me again' (*WH*, p. 190). To both of Nelly's sentences could indeed be applied the well-known dictum 'famous last words'![9] The discrepancies we have noted, then, between the literal meaning of some temporal adverbs and the hyperbolic uses to which they are put may be indirectly linked with the more or less imprecise meanings conveyed by other temporal adverbs or adverbial phrases, some of which have been mentioned above. Yet it is this very imprecision which indicates how much it is owing to the medium of language, or rather the elasticity of language, that we are able, as it were, to dominate, not to say tyrannize over, time. This idea we see nowhere more conspicuously rendered in *Wuthering Heights* than through Nelly Dean's presentation.

As principal narrator, Nelly Dean is in a good position to 'control' all the time references in her narrative, even though she sometimes admits to non-omniscience in some such references, and notwithstanding that allowance should be made for the fact that Lockwood's memory seems here and there faulty enough to make us wonder how faithfully he has recorded her accounts. Be that as it may, Nelly's strong sense of the annual calendar, as borne out by her mentioning or alluding to every month except May, and every day of the week except Wednesday, together with her awareness of the season, the weather, the time of day, even the hour or hours when a particular episode has taken place, makes her narrative sound for the most part historically plausible. It is, therefore, hardly surprising that, time-conscious as she is in several remarkable ways, Nelly should be now and again tempted, as it were, to domineer over time. This we see more especially in contexts where she is concerned with the ages of the main characters, especially in their childhood or adolescence and, occasionally, mentions a character's birthday.[10] That Nelly might nevertheless have been mistaken in some of these references is not altogether improbable when we consider what she has said to Heathcliff shortly before his death: 'You are aware, Mr Heathcliff, [...] that from the time you were thirteen years old, you have lived a selfish, unchristian life' (*WH*, p. 296). The presumptuousness of this reference to Heathcliff's age is presently confirmed when Nelly soon afterwards admits that no dates could be inscribed on his grave 'because [they] could not tell his age' (*WH*, p. 293).[11] Such a contradiction seems to be of a piece with Nelly's habit of estimating life-spans as optimistically, if also as mistakenly, as, say, Mr Kenneth, who predicts that Hindley will 'outlive any man on this side Gimmerton' (*WH*, p. 67); or as Heathcliff, who is confident that he will 'remain above ground, till there is scarcely a black hair on [his] head' (*WH*, p. 289); or even as Cathy, who thinks that, because Linton Heathcliff is 'younger than [her]', he 'ought to live the longest' (*WH*, p. 214). Nelly's own optimism in this respect is particularly noticeable when she is trying to comfort Cathy in her dread that her father may die soon:

> It's wrong to anticipate evil — we'll hope there are years and years to come before any of us go — master is young, and I am strong, and hardly forty-five. My mother lived till eighty, a canty dame to the last. And suppose Mr Linton were spared till he saw sixty, that

would be more years than you have counted, Miss. And would it
not be foolish to mourn a calamity above twenty years beforehand?
(*WH*, p. 203f.)

The fallaciousness of this well-meaning argumentation not only
suggests how far Nelly seems to be expecting time to act at her
behest but will be ironically corroborated by Edgar's death at the
early age of thirty-nine.

Just as Nelly evinces a propensity to dominate time, so she may be
said to be also a slave to time. This we have to some extent gathered
from the references she makes to clock-time. Such references are
quite appropriate to Nelly's presentation as a rather fastidious servant
bent on performing her sundry domestic duties according to a regular
daily timetable. That Nelly attaches perhaps too much importance to
time, notably from a quantitative viewpoint, is ironically manifest
when, in response to Cathy's having spoken of 'loving' her cousin
Linton through their exchange of letters, she retorts:

> *Loving!* Did anybody ever hear the like! I might just as well talk of
> loving the miller who comes once a year to buy our corn. Pretty
> loving, indeed, and both times together you have seen Linton
> hardly four hours in your life! (*WH*, p. 200)

Nelly's implicit hostility towards Linton Heathcliff here becomes
quite overt when, amid her growing impatience with Cathy's
attempts to comfort him in the wake of his tantrum (in Chapter 23),
she addresses the boy as follows: 'Miss has wasted too much time on
you, already; we cannot remain five minutes longer' (*WH*, p. 212). In
fact, in spite of Nelly's 'strenuous objections', Cathy will continue to
entertain her cousin with several ballads until, as Nelly recalls, 'the
clock struck twelve' (*WH*, p. 213). There are also occasions when
Nelly resorts to the clock in order to get Cathy to go back with her
to the Grange: first, when, annoyed at the girl's wilfully staying on at

the Heights after her first meeting with Hareton, she says, 'It will be dark in ten minutes' (*WH*, p. 171); and, secondly, when, increasingly uneasy both about Cathy's long conversation with Heathcliff after their chance meeting on the moors for the first time and about her own neglect of Edgar's earlier instructions, she says, 'Miss Cathy, [...] it will be three hours instead of one that we are out, presently' (*WH*, p. 189).

Noteworthy among similar references to Cathy is Nelly's remark that, on the day she discovered the existence of the Heights, '[t]he naughty thing never made her appearance at tea' (*WH*, p. 170), for it reminds us that meals mark important stages in the housekeeper's daily timetable.[12] Of particular interest, too, is Nelly's recourse to the clock when she thinks it is time for someone to go to bed or to take sustenance. In this connection, we may mention Nelly's solicitude for Lockwood while he is laid up with a bad cold when, to his annoyance, because he wishes her to continue her narrative forthwith, she says, 'It wants twenty minutes, sir, to taking the medicine' (*WH*, p. 80). Lockwood's momentary irritation with Nelly's concern here may have a little to do not only with her having at the outset dictated the hours when he shall have his dinner, but with her having more recently rebuked him for keeping late hours: 'You shouldn't lie till ten. There's the very prime of the morning gone long before that time. A person who has not done one half his day's work by ten o'clock, runs a chance of leaving the other half undone' (*WH*, p. 54).

No less fastidious about time than Nelly Dean is Heathcliff himself, especially while he is master of the Heights. This is evident when, to Lockwood's having remarked on the shortness of the night he has spent at the Heights and then concluded that '[they] must surely have retired to rest at eight', Heathcliff gives this laconic reply: 'Always at nine in winter, and always rise at four' (*WH*, p. 23). The punctiliousness of that elliptical statement may help to explain why Heathcliff hates wasting time. This is already apparent when Lockwood, on his first visit to the Heights, is discouraged from requesting 'a short history' of the place because his landlord's attitude at the door 'appeared to demand my speedy entrance, or complete departure' (*WH*, p. 2). There are, moreover, occasions when Heathcliff is in such a hurry as if to seem intent on being one step ahead of time itself. We see this plainly in Chapter 14 when he tells Nelly of his desire to visit Catherine at the Grange, and that, as he insists, 'without delay' (*WH*, p. 134); and, again, when, finding Nelly still obstinately reluctant to oblige him, he says, 'Decide! because there is no reason for my lingering another minute, if you persist in your stubborn ill-nature!' (*WH*, p. 135). Another striking example of this is Heathcliff's sending Joseph to the Grange to fetch his son Linton on the very night of the boy's arrival there from the south. Again, Heathcliff's ability to outdo others by taking full advantage of time is memorably illustrated in Nelly's account of how she and Cathy, when trapped at the Heights as his prisoners, were too slow to respond to the sound of voices they have all three heard coming from outside. As Nelly recalls, 'Our host hurried out, instantly; *he* had his wits about him; *we* had not. There was a talk of two or three minutes, and he returned alone' (*WH*, p. 243). Certainly, no character in *Wuthering Heights* is quite like Heathcliff in his shrewd recognition of the timeliness of actions, especially those undertaken to his own ends. And though Nelly is perhaps unduly nervous about Heathcliff's intentions since his return to Gimmerton, and especially so after overhearing his altercation with Catherine in Chapter 10, her image of him as 'an evil beast' that is 'waiting his time to spring and destroy' (*WH*, p. 95) has no little bearing on what has just been said about him above.[13]

Although Heathcliff often seems to be one step ahead of others in the matter of time, he is none the less remarkable for his stoical endurance of periods ranging from one hour to several years. For instance, when Nelly has chanced upon him outside the Grange on the evening of his unexpected return to the neighbourhood, Heathcliff addresses her thus: 'I have waited here an hour [...] and the whole of that time all round has been as still as death' (*WH*, p. 82). Heathcliff's capacity to wait is very characteristic of the final stages of his involvement with Catherine, as we gather when, in the midst of trying to persuade Nelly (in Chapter 14) to let him visit the latter, he says, 'Last night, I was in the Grange garden six hours, and I'll return there to-night; and every night I'll haunt the place, and every day, till I find an opportunity of entering' (*WH*, p. 134f.). Again, when on the morning after Catherine's death, Nelly finds Heathcliff 'leant against an old ash tree', she surmises that he has been 'standing a long time in that position' (*WH*, p. 146) partly because a pair of ousels have been unaffected by his presence while building their nest nearby. Yet it is partly through his ability to endure time that Heathcliff in the end becomes its helpless victim. The seeds of such victimisation can be said to have been sown principally during his final meeting with Catherine, whose taunting utterances to him have at one point prompted him to say this to her: 'Do you reflect that all those words will be branded in my memory, and eating deeper *eternally*, after you have left me?' (*WH*, p. 140; italics mine). This rhetorical question, taken in conjunction with the request 'Be with me *always*' (*WH*, p. 148; italics mine) with which he apostrophizes Catherine after her death, is almost certainly the root of that continuous obsession with her that will eventually lead to his mental illness in the form of monomania.[14]

That Heathcliff's obsession with Catherine will have been continuous for many years after her decease is evident enough when, to Nelly's objection to his having disturbed the latter's grave (in Chapter 29), he retorts, 'No! she has disturbed me, night and day, through eighteen years — incessantly — remorselessly — till yesternight — and yesternight, I was tranquil' (*WH*, p. 255).

Much of what Heathcliff goes on to tell Nelly in the same chapter is concerned with the nature of Catherine's haunting of him, whereby time itself seems to have become intolerably protracted not only through its duration but through its repetitiousness. Such sufferings are, moreover, made worse for Heathcliff through his having to endure the constant presence of Cathy, who bears a striking resemblance to her late mother. This is evidenced when, for example, he says this to a somewhat recalcitrant Cathy, in Lockwood's presence, towards the end of Chapter 3: 'You shall pay me for the plague of having you *eternally* in my sight' (*WH*, p. 25; italics mine); and again when, clearly annoyed by her frivolous behaviour at the breakfast table with Hareton in Chapter 33, he addresses her as follows: 'What fiend possesses you to stare back at me, *continually*, with those infernal eyes? Down with them! and don't remind me of your existence again' (*WH*, p. 283; italics mine).[15] In light of these particular utterances, it is, then, little wonder that time should figure quite often in contexts where Heathcliff is violent or is threatening violence of some kind. For example, when, riled both by Catherine's rebuking him for making advances to Isabella and by her then complacently offering him the latter as a wife, Heathcliff has reproached her for having 'treated [him] infernally', he goes on to warn her thus: '— and if you fancy I'll suffer unrevenged, I'll convince you of the contrary, *in a very little while!*' (*WH*, p. 99; italics mine). Later that day when, enraged with Edgar for punching him on the throat, and then warned by Catherine that Edgar will have him evicted with the help of armed servants, Heathcliff retorts, 'Do you suppose I'm going with that blow burning in my gullet? [...] By Hell, no! I'll crush his ribs in like a rotten hazelnut, *before I cross the threshold*! If I don't floor him now, I shall murder him *some time*' (*WH*, p. 103; italics mine). Oddly enough, the last two words quoted are the very ones he will use when, having seized Cathy viciously by the hair, because she has angered him with her taunting accusations, and then suddenly released her, he addresses her as follows: 'You must learn to avoid putting me in a passion, or I shall really murder you, *some time!*' (*WH*, p. 285; italics mine).[16]

There are, to be sure, other contexts where references to time occur within utterances that have much the same violent or portentous implications we have noted in Heathcliff's language above. Instances of this are conspicuous in Hindley's dialogues with some of the main characters. Consider, for example, the episode in which he says this to Isabella as to his intention to commit suicide after he has carried out his resolve to kill Heathcliff: 'Nobody alive would regret me, or be ashamed, though I cut my throat this minute — and it's time to make an end!' (*WH*, p. 155). Significant, too, is the use of 'minute' and 'minutes' in respect of Edgar's uneasy relationship with Heathcliff. Thus Nelly recalls that on seeing the latter's appearance at the Grange after a long absence, Edgar 'remained *for a minute* at a loss how to address the ploughboy, as he had called him' (*WH*, p. 85; italics mine). Several years later Nelly also observes that, when informed by Joseph that he has been sent by Heathcliff to take his newly-arrived son back with him to the Heights, 'Edgar Linton was silent *a minute*; an expression of exceeding sorrow overcast his features' (*WH*, p. 179; italics mine). Ironically, a multiple of the same time unit has been used by Edgar himself when, having ordered Heathcliff's 'instant departure' from the Grange, he adds, '*Three minutes' delay* will render it involuntary and ignominious' (*WH*, p. 101; italics mine).[17] It is also interesting to note fractionalized time being mentioned in connection with ominous or tragic events. For example, while Mr Earnshaw is assumed to have fallen asleep, even though it turns out that he has in fact died, Nelly recalls that the rest of the household 'all kept as mute as mice a full half-hour' (*WH*, p. 37). Of similar significance, it seems, is Nelly's saying that, reluctant as she was to be present at Cathy's final meeting with her dying father, she 'stood outside the chamber-door a quarter of an hour, and hardly ventured near the bed, then' (*WH*, p. 251). The negative symbolic function of fractionalized time is, however, perhaps nowhere more ironically overt than when, in her long confession to Nelly about her illicit evening visits to Linton Heathcliff, Cathy says: 'I was at the Heights by half-past six, and generally stayed till half-past eight' (*WH*, p. 217).[18]

References to time, whether precise or imprecise, we have found to be unusually pervasive in *Wuthering Heights*, and enough so to raise questions as to the author's ultimate intentions therewith. That some such references are meant to play their part in the presentation of Nelly Dean and Heathcliff, as they are to a lesser extent in that of the other characters portrayed, has been suggested in our discussions above. It is, moreover, through her characters that Emily has illustrated the anomalous relationship that exists between time and the human mind, and between time and language. The prominence of time references here may not be unconnected with the fact that the novel is written in the form of a diary, which in turn can be said to be a kind of history. Lockwood himself is presented as an amateur historian through his keen interest in the past lives of those people he has encountered in the first two chapters, as he is also through his curiousity about the Heights and other buildings he has visited in the local neighbourhood. Further, Lockwood confirms his historical bent by being the only character to be concerned with the century as a time span, using as he does '1801' and '1802' as headings of his two main diary entries rather than, say, a month or a day, as might normally be expected.[19] In any event, it is thanks to this bent that Lockwood (presumably) takes the trouble to write down what he himself designates as 'the history of Mr Heathcliff' (*WH*, p. 80).

Nevertheless, it is curious to note that Nelly suddenly ends the first part of her narrative by presuming that 'these tales cannot divert' Lockwood and by reproaching herself for 'chattering on at such a rate', especially since he is 'nodding for bed' (*WH*, p. 54). And although, despite having presently said, 'The clock is on the stroke of eleven, sir', Nelly is asked by Lockwood to 'sit still, another half hour' (*WH*, p. 54), she will in fact do so for two and a half hours, by which time she will have told of Heathcliff's disappearance from the Heights and of Catherine's marriage to Edgar Linton, both events constituting the mainsprings of the tragic content of the novel. Could these events, then, be the reason why, at the end of the first part of her narrative, Nelly says this to Lockwood, 'I could have told Heathcliff's history, all that you need hear, in half-a-dozen words' (*WH*, p. 54)? Such brevity would have scarcely satisfied the historian in Lockwood, for whom a history is after all a detailed succession of happenings inevitably narrated with all manner of references and allusions to time.[20] But since we have seen how often in 'the history of Mr Heathcliff' such references are to be found in contexts fraught with negative connotations, we may be induced to speculate whether, in the eyes of the author, the problems of the human condition are not inseparable from, indeed caused by, time itself.[21] If so, we might accordingly go so far as to assume that Nelly is speaking for Emily when, referring to her vigil over Catherine's corpse in Chapter 16, she declares how happy she is 'watching in the chamber of death' because she feels 'an assurance of the endless and shadowless hereafter — *the Eternity* they have entered — where life is boundless in its duration, and love in its sympathy, and joy in its fulness' (*WH*, p. 145; italics mine).

Brontë Studies, 40/1 (2015)

Notes

1   See, for example, Charles Percy Sanger, *The Structure of Wuthering Heights* (London: Hogarth Press, 1926); Charles Travis Clay, 'Notes on the Chronology of *Wuthering Heights*', *Brontë Society Transactions*, 12.2 (1952), 100-05; Robert F. Gleckner, 'Time in *Wuthering Heights*', *Criticism*, 1 (1959), 328-38; Stuart A. Daley, 'A Revised Chronology of *Wuthering Heights*', *Huntington Library Quarterly*, 37 (1974), 337-53; Patricia Dreschel Tobin, *Time and the Novel. The Genealogical Imperative* (Princeton, NJ: Princeton University Press, 1978); Conal Boyce, 'A Map: Plotting 300 Pages of "Longitude" Against 300 Years of "Latitude" to Elucidate the Nested Narratives of Emily Brontë's *Wuthering Heights*', *Brontë Studies*, 38.2 (2013), 93-110.

2   Emily Brontë, *Wuthering Heights*, ed. by Ian Jack and Helen Small (Oxford: Oxford University Press, 2009), p. 23; hereafter *WH*. For the sake of convenience, the first Catherine will be referred to as 'Catherine', the second as 'Cathy'.

3   For Lockwood's imprecise time references, see *WH*, pp. 26f., 79, 80, 271.

4   For Nelly Dean's other references to clock time, see *WH*, pp. 31, 49, 54, 75, 145, 169, 180, 204, 213, 215, 216, 222, 244, 292. Not without significance here is Nelly's mention of 'the polished clock, decked in holly', which she admires among other objects in the Heights kitchen on Christmas Eve. See *WH*, p. 48. Also worth mentioning here is Isabella's concern with clock time in accounts of her life at the Heights as Heathcliff's hapless bride. See *WH*, pp. 120, 123, 153, 154.

5   See *WH*, pp. 40, 66, 77, 89, 128, 129, 131, 139, 156, 178, 214, 217, 248, 282, 297.

6   For other examples of such uses of 'minute', 'moment' and 'instant', see *WH*, pp. 66, 113, 120, 163, 178, 194, 208, 237.

7   This is especially true of phrases containing the nominal form of 'while'; see *WH*, pp. 49, 53, 64, 73, 76, 106, 119, 163, 173, 181, 201, 207, 212, 216, 234, 244, 262, 270, 271, 276, 284, 296.

8   For other similarly problematic uses of 'always', see *WH*, pp. 36, 37, 50, 59, 61, 65, 90, 167, 210, 216, 248.

9   For other similarly problematic uses of 'ever', see *WH*, pp. 7, 33, 35, 38, 56, 72, 90, 143, 147, 163, 166, 167, 210, 214, 220; for other similarly problematic uses of 'never', see *WH*, 3, 11, 14, 35, 36, 50, 71, 72, 76, 77, 84, 85, 90f., 100, 103, 106, 107, 108, 112, 129, 131 133, 141, 191 192 193, 197, 199, 209, 213f, 216, 221, 224, 228, 236, 246, 247, 287.

10 See *WH*, pp. 79, 171, 187, 189, 190, 227.

11 For Nelly's other errors as to Heathcliff's age, see *WH*, pp. 49, 59, 181.

12 See *WH*, pp. 40, 49, 56, 105, 214, 251, 285, 292, 294.

13 Notwithstanding that Nelly's prediction here will not be altogether fulfilled when, some years later, she learns that Heathcliff has decided not to see his plans of vengeance against the two families through to the end, it is nevertheless interesting to note how time-conscious he continues to be as he says this to

Nelly in the context of that decision: 'My old enemies have not beaten me — *now would be the precise time* to revenge myself on their representatives — I could do it; and none could hinder me' (*WH*, p. 287; italics mine).

14 See Graeme Tytler, 'Heathcliff's Monomania: An Anachronism in *Wuthering Heights*', *Brontë Society Transactions* 20.6 (1992), 331-43.

15 See Graeme Tytler, 'Physiognomy in *Wuthering Heights*', *Brontë Society Transactions*, 21.4 (1994), 137-48 (p. 144).

16 For other similar combinations of violence and time in Heathcliff's utterances, see *WH*, pp. 53, 94, 95, 132, 133, 134, 135, 157, 186, 205, 239, 241, 242, 243, 246, 247, 254, 255, 275, 283, 284, 285. Interesting in connection with this episode is the way in which Heathcliff has only a short while earlier momentarily reacted to Hareton's resemblance to Catherine as follows: '[...] when I look for his father in his face, I find *her every day more*! How the devil is he so like? I can hardly bear to see him' (*WH*, p. 269; italics original and mine).

17 For other uses of 'minute' or 'minutes' with violent or portentous connotations, see *WH*, pp. 6, 8, 14, 15, 17, 23, 26 36, 49, 51, 70, 75, 85, 99, 102, 108, 115, 123, 139, 147, 150, 164, 176, 186, 194, 197, 205, 211, 232, 239, 243, 245, 246, 251, 262, 267, 275, 279, 288, 294. For similar uses of 'second' or 'seconds' with negative or portentous connotations, see *WH*, pp. 4, 47, 79, 105, 110, 120.

18 For references to the 'half-hour' with similarly negative implications, see *WH*, pp. 8, 49, 54, 57, 120, 142, 158, 182, 231, 232, 252, 263, 282; for similar references to 'a quarter of an hour', see *WH*, pp. 21, 39, 74, 211, 260.

19 Not without pertinence here is Lockwood's finding a book in the oak-panelled closet with Catherine's name in it and bearing 'a date *some quarter of a century* back' (*WH*, p. 16; italics mine).

20 This is confirmed by Lockwood's wanting Nelly to 'continue minutely'. See *WH*, p. 54.

21 It is noteworthy how often the word 'time' occurs in sentences or phrases with negative or portentous connotations both in Nelly's narrative and in the utterances of some of the other characters; in which connection, see *WH*,pp. 20, 24, 28, 35, 40, 49, 52, 57, 59, 61, 66, 71, 73, 74, 81, 85, 98, 100, 113, 123, 124, 130, 138, 139, 143, 147, 168, 177, 187, 188, 193, 194, 198, 206, 209, 210 217, 223, 224, 226, 237, 247, 287, 289, 298.

Weeping and Wailing in *Wuthering Heights*

It would be a rare author who had not made some reference or other to crying or the shedding of tears in a novel he or she had written. At the same time, even when this form of behaviour is mentioned in a work of fiction, it is for the most part consonant with the reader's own experience of life. Accordingly, the idea of viewing such references as a worthy topic of literary criticism might be thought largely unnecessary, not to say barely justified. In some novels, however, the presence of these physical expressions of emotion is frequent enough to warrant our paying them more than the perfunctory attention they might otherwise elicit. This is especially true of *Wuthering Heights*, in which tears help to throw light on the presentation of the characters therein as well as reinforcing our awareness of the essential realism of Emily Brontë's masterpiece.[1]

The terms used in Emily's novel to convey the different types of crying, ranging as they do in volume from the silence of weeping to the clamour of wailing, play a useful part in telling us something essential not only about some of the characters given to crying but even about those who hold particular attitudes to crying in general. Whether or not Nelly Dean has accurately recalled everything from a distant past, there can be little doubt that some of her references to crying are quite memorable for their emotional intensity. For example, the fact that Catherine's and Heathcliff's faces are described as 'washed by each other's tears'[2] at one point during their last tryst may be thought by some readers to be utterly appropriate to their view of them as supreme lovers.[3] Just as memorable, too, and perhaps even more so for its peculiar pathos, is the curiously frivolous manner in which a moribund Frances Earnshaw responds to Nelly's message from Hindley, namely, that only as long as she promises 'not to talk' will he visit her upstairs in her bedroom: 'I hardly spoke a word, Ellen, and there he has gone out twice, crying. Well, say I promise I won't speak, but that does not bind me not to laugh at him!'.[4] There can be few readers who are not moved by those words, and that in spite of the fact that these two characters have hitherto been shown to be utterly unsympathetic. Much the same pathos has probably already been felt by many a reader when Nelly relates that a fourteen-year-old Hindley, who appears hitherto to have done nothing untoward, 'blubbered aloud' on discovering that the 'fiddle' his father promised to bring him from Liverpool has been completely destroyed on the return journey.[5]

Hindley's tearful reaction is one example of the various ways in which the characters respond to their sufferings in childhood. To be sure, there is nothing unusual about children crying, whether it be because they have been scolded by an adult, mistreated by an older sibling, or made aware of the unexpected death of a parent.[6] Certainly, the tears shed by, say, Edgar and Isabella while quarrelling as youngsters over a dog are scarcely to be wondered at.[7] Much more touching, because quite unexpected from Nelly, are the references to the tears Catherine sheds out of sympathy for Heathcliff after he has been thrashed and excluded from the Christmas dinner, not least for showing us an unwontedly sensitive side to her otherwise quite boisterous nature. Of like interest is Catherine's 'crying outright' on the night Heathcliff has disappeared from the Heights, underscored as it is by Nelly's remarking that the girl 'beat Hareton, or any child, at a good, passionate fit of crying'.[8] All such details are palpable testimonies to Catherine's early affection for Heathcliff.

Significant, too, in respect of our introduction to Linton Heathcliff, are the tears he sheds both on his arrival at the Grange and, later, at his first encounter with the father he had previously thought never to have existed. Such behaviour in an eleven-year-old boy who has recently lost his mother is perfectly understandable. Nevertheless, it is after having led a rather loveless life at the Heights for a few years that Linton shows a tendency to cry as if for the sake of crying. This is at first made obvious when, having had his chair violently pushed by Cathy at the climax of their vicious quarrel over the love lives of their respective parents, Linton is seized with a 'suffocating cough' such as to cause the girl to weep profusely. And though Cathy denies striking him, as he claims her to have done, Linton is nonetheless determined to take advantage of her tearfulness on his behalf, especially when, having spoken of his sufferings with 'nobody near [him]', he begins to 'wail aloud for very pity of himself'.[9] And whereas some readers might continue to feel sorry for Linton even at this stage, others are likely to share Nelly's suspicion that there is an obvious duplicity behind the boy's tears.[10] In this respect, it is noteworthy that one of Cathy's illicit meetings with Linton later at the Heights is marked by their continually crying the whole time they are together, as if symbolically to confirm the problematic nature of their early love relationship, not to mention its inherent childishness.[11]

Similarly, there are one or two equally unfavourable references to Catherine's crying in her early adolescence; for noble as are the tears she sheds on account of Heathcliff's maltreatment on Christmas Day, there are occasions when she resorts to crying for selfish, not to say childish, reasons. One notable instance is the moment just after Edgar has shown his determination to leave the Heights because Catherine has, among other things, not only 'struck' him but also 'told a deliberate untruth' during their rendezvous in 'the house'.[12] Thus, instead of honestly acknowledging the truth of these accusations, Catherine tells Edgar that he may leave, though not without adding this threat: 'And now I'll cry — I'll cry myself sick', whereby, as Nelly recalls, she 'dropped down on her knees by a chair and set to weeping in serious earnest'.[13] That such a reaction may have partly encouraged Edgar to rescind his decision to depart exemplifies one of the ways in which Catherine sometimes takes advantage of tears to gain her ends. This we see again three years later when, now married to Edgar, she succeeds, with the help of both husband and Hindley, in forcing Nelly against her will to accompany her to the Grange, and that at a time when she (Nelly) has begun to teach a five-year-old Hareton 'his letters'.[14] As Nelly says of herself and the latter: 'We made a sad parting, but Catherine's tears were more powerful than ours'.[15] Most other references to Catherine's tears occur in the last six months of her life, and almost entirely in contexts where she is undergoing a second bout of delirium, or convalescing thereafter, or nostalgically yearning for the Heights of her childhood.[16] And it is partly through such references that we may discern the extent to which, notwithstanding the sincerity of the tears which in her distress she silently or loudly sheds on account of Heathcliff, Catherine remains a fundamentally immature and self-centred young woman to the end.

Just as prone to crying is Isabella Linton, especially as a young adult. Crying is already a prominent feature of her childhood, as we noted earlier, and will again note when she is described 'weeping to go home' after Edgar has had his 'face and neck' struck by Heathcliff with the apple-sauce tureen provided for the Christmas dinner at the Heights.[17] Isabella's tendency to weep is, however, made especially conspicuous in episodes during which, while dominated by Catherine at the Grange, she betrays her love for Heathcliff. We see examples of this when Isabella is complaining to Catherine of deliberately depriving her of Heathcliff's company on their walks together and, later, when she has been hurt by Catherine's advising her to renounce her infatuation. Moreover, coddled as she appears to have been by her upper-class parents and endowed with a high-strung temperament, not to mention an intensely romantic outlook on life, Isabella perhaps inevitably falls victim to her sister-in-law's domineering disposition, thereby doubtlessly exacerbating her own sense of being an irremediable weakling. It is not surprising, therefore, that Isabella relates this in the letter she has written to Nelly after arriving at the Heights as Heathcliff's unhappy bride: '[I] filled the interim with wild regrets and dismal anticipations, which, at last, spoke audibly in irrepressible sighing and weeping'.[18] Noteworthy too is Isabella's typifying that tendency in many a well-born lady to be daunted by an outspoken senior retainer serving in a household other than her own. We gather this notion from the detail about Joseph's early insubordination towards her at the Heights hitherto: 'I recovered spirits sufficient to hear Joseph's eternal lectures without weeping; [...] You wouldn't think that I should cry at anything Joseph could say, but he and Hareton are detestable companions'.[19] Nevertheless, this passage indicates that Isabella has begun to overcome her chronic habit of crying, thanks largely to her ability to create some degree of independence for herself in a very gloomy household. Indeed, by the time she has fled from the Heights, she seems to have toughened up considerably. This we see when, just after arriving at the Grange, and then begging Nelly to 'put poor Catherine's baby away',[20] she presently says: 'Listen to that child! It maintains a constant wail — send it out of my hearing, for an hour; I shan't stay any longer'.[21] And though Isabella has by then spoken of having, like her infant niece, 'cried too, bitterly — yes, more than any one else has reason to cry', partly since she and Catherine 'parted unreconciled',[22] it is because Heathcliff has, as she avers, 'destroyed [her heart]', that she goes on to say this: 'I have not power to feel for him, and I would not, though he groaned from this to his dying day, and wept tears of blood for Catherine! No, indeed, indeed, I wouldn't!'.[23] What is striking about those words is the measure in which they indicate that Isabella, not unlike some of the other characters, now become slightly hardened in her attitude to such expressions of emotion.[24]

That tears are at times frowned upon as a shameful weakness, and sometimes even thought quite unnecessary, is illustrated now and again in the narrative. One of the earliest examples of this is Catherine 'contemptuously' saying this to Edgar just after the apple-sauce tureen incident: 'Well, don't cry! [...] You're not killed' before going on to say this to his sister for the same reason: 'Give over, Isabella! Has any body hurt *you*?'[25] — words that ironically foreshadow Catherine's bossy treatment of both Lintons during the early months of her marriage. One is reminded that Catherine disapproves of Edgar crying because, as she tells Nelly, she 'gave a few sentences of commendation to Heathcliff' on the night of the latter's visit to the Grange.[26] Much more churlish, however, are Linton Heathcliff's objections to Cathy's persistent crying shortly after they have married. Even on the day before their marriage, he humiliates his imprisoned bride-to-be as she is about to hand him a cup of tea: 'Now, Catherine, you are letting your tears fall into my cup! I won't drink that. Give me another'.[27] Heartless, too, are Linton's later complaints about Cathy's crying, as we gather when he tells Nelly that she is 'a naughty thing for crying continually' in their room together.[28] And here it may be worth mentioning that two housekeepers at the Heights seem more or less helpless, not to say unhelpful, in the face of the tears shed by their social superiors. This we see when, for example, the unnamed housekeeper complains about Linton Heathcliff's occasional crying, and when Zillah proves too afraid to act on Cathy's behalf even while aware that she is weeping for want of the help she badly needs in tending her fatally ill young husband. Such details tell us not a little about the moral limitations of the two serving women, as do the reactions of somewhat case-hardened characters such as Hindley, Joseph and Mr Kenneth who, whether jocularly or impatiently, taunt those crying, or about to cry, over the death or disappearance of a loved one.[29]

Of all the characters in the novel, however, none could be said to harbour a greater or more frequent antipathy to crying than Heathcliff. This may seem odd when we recall that, though taken by Lockwood at first as a seemingly normal, if morose, country gentleman, Heathcliff will, to the astonishment of his guest, be observed 'bursting [...] into an uncontrollable passion of tears' while frantically entreating Catherine's ghost to come back in through the lattice he has just 'wrenched open'.[30] These tears are among those that will subsequently be shown to have been due to Heathcliff's ill-fated love for Catherine during their childhood and adolescence, and at their last tryst as adults.[31] Such strong displays of emotion on Heathcliff's part undoubtedly lend a certain nobility to his continuous attachment to Catherine, and may even be said to enhance his role as a sort of ideal lover. Yet it is easy to forget that as a boy Heathcliff is remarkable for not crying on occasions when most children are likely to have done so. Thus, as Nelly recalls, Heathcliff 'would stand Hindley's blows without winking or shedding a tear'.[32] Such apparent self-restraint is further manifested just after Heathcliff has suffered 'a violent blow' from Hindley for forcing him to hand over his colt.[33] This may well explain why as a youngster Heathcliff (with Catherine) is contemptuous of Edgar and Isabella for crying while squabbling in the Grange drawing-room over the possession of a young dog. As he says scornfully to Nelly about the 'screaming' and 'weeping' of both Linton children:

> The idiots! That was their pleasure! to quarrel who should hold a heap of warm hair, and each begin to cry because both, after struggling to get it, refused to take it. We laughed outright at the petted things, we did despise them! When would you catch me wishing to have what Catherine wanted? or find us by ourselves, seeking entertainment in yelling, and sobbing, and rolling on the ground, divided by the whole room?[34]

All such details may have contributed to turning Edgar and Isabella into somewhat unsympathetic figures they have tended to be adjudged, albeit mistakenly, while substantiating the idea of Heathcliff as a model of tough masculinity.

Heathcliff's contempt for Isabella's and Edgar's tears as adults is just as pronounced as it was when he saw them as youngsters. For example, amid his sardonically detailed account of Isabella's behaviour since their elopement, Heathcliff tells Nelly that 'the very morrow of [their] wedding, she was weeping to go home'.[35] Similarly, just before his showdown with Edgar in the Grange kitchen, he ironically puts this question to Catherine: 'Is he weeping, or is he going to faint for fear?'[36] just before giving Edgar's chair the push that will immediately induce the latter to punch him hard on the throat. Heathcliff's contempt for tears in this and other contexts is clearly evidence of his deep-seated machismo. We see glaring examples of this in his treatment of his son Linton, and that already when the boy has only just arrived at the Heights for the first time. Thus perhaps because painfully aware that Linton looks like his late mother but not himself, Heathcliff is, not surprisingly, unwilling to sympathise with the perfectly understandable unease and nervousness of an eleven-year-old child who clearly feels a sense of alienation in the place he has brought to against his will. Again, on noticing his son weeping on Nelly's shoulder, Heathcliff drags him roughly between his knees, saying: 'Tut, tut! [...] None of that nonsense!',[37] as if to make plain that crying is an utterly unmanly thing. That Linton remains a chronic weeper for quite a long time thereafter presumably has its roots in the loveless life he is compelled to lead at the Heights. We see striking examples of this at his two "official" meetings with Cathy on the moors.[38] But whether at the second of these meetings Linton is persistently crying out of a sense of guilt for the deceit he has been supposedly ordered by his father to practise, or he is feigning his tears of his own accord in order to lure Cathy into the Heights for their marriage, cannot be known for certain. Either way, Linton's behaviour enables Heathcliff to ensure the success of his scheme, as he indirectly alludes to his own hand in it by characteristically re-asserting his machismo thus: 'Has the whelp been playing that game long? I *did* give him some lessons about snivelling'.[39]

That Heathcliff is also quite ruthless to young Cathy once he has presently made her his prisoner in the Heights is obvious enough when at one point he says this to her: 'Weep away. As far as I can see, it will be your chief diversion hereafter: unless Linton make amends for other losses'.[40] Heathcliff's constant indifference to both Cathy's and Nelly's tears during this time is especially underlined just before he imprisons them in Zillah's room. Thus Nelly recalls that, because they had failed to call out to the Grange servants sent to fetch them, she and Cathy 'gave vent to our grief without control', whereby, as she adds, Heathcliff 'allowed us to wail on till nine o'clock'.[41] Heathcliff's somewhat malicious pleasure in Cathy's and Nelly's tears in that context may be thought to stand in ironic contrast to the resentment he has earlier shown Nelly for weeping over Catherine's death by addressing her thus: 'Put your handkerchief away — don't snivel before me. Damn you all! she wants none of *your* tears!'[42] Through these words Heathcliff has already revealed in blatantly egotistic fashion his apparent inability to identify with others in a state of grief, even with those crying for the same reason as he himself has been doing. Moreover, sincere as seem to be the tears that Heathcliff now and again sheds for Catherine, one may well wonder whether they are not after all but expressions of morbid self-pity. For what little crying he is given to, it is seldom, if ever, an expression of that sympathetic concern for others which is so characteristic of Cathy's own tears.

Cathy's tendency to weep, cry and sob is especially interesting for marking stages of her moral development. It is a tendency that does not, however, come to the fore until she has reached the age of thirteen and has met Hareton Earnshaw for the first time while on her illicit excursion to Penistone Craggs.[43] What is striking about that meeting is the way in which Cathy asserts her pride in her privileged background and upbringing by very tearfully refusing to accept the fact that Hareton is her cousin. Few scenes could be more comical in the novel than the one where with fitful crying she stubbornly rejects the idea of such a consanguinity. Cathy's childish behaviour has doubtless done much to lend her the rather unfavourable reputation she scarcely deserves. Indeed, perhaps that is why it is easy to forget that Cathy's tears are sometimes shed out of a genuinely compassionate concern for others. A good example of this may be noted when, despite her bitter quarrel with Linton over their respective parents, as referred to above, Cathy nevertheless displays exceptional compassion for the boy once he has soon afterwards been seized by 'a suffocating cough', a physiological reaction that frightens even Nelly Dean herself.[44] At the same time, however, Nelly suggests how diametrically opposite in spirit to her own fundamental lack of sympathy for Linton on that occasion is Cathy's own response to his involuntary reaction to her angrily pushing his chair: 'As to his cousin, she wept with all her might, aghast at the mischief she had done, though she said nothing'.[45] Realizing soon afterwards that Cathy looks as if she is about to abandon him, Linton 'slid from his seat on to the hearthstone' and, as Nelly maliciously adds, 'lay writhing in the mere perverseness of an indulged plague of a child, determined to be as grievous and harassing as it can'.[46] And whereas Nelly's hostility to the boy is such as to make her think that 'it would be folly to attempt humouring him', she nevertheless goes on to say this: 'Not so my companion: she ran back in terror, knelt down, and cried, and soothed, and entreated, till he grew quiet from lack of breath, by no means from compunction at distressing her'.[47]

It is evident from this episode how easily Nelly is inclined to show a lack of compassion for tears. It is not that she herself is incapable of crying, even though it would appear that she tends to cry for more or less sentimental reasons. For example, her nostalgic thoughts about the late Mr Earnshaw's generosity to her every Christmas arouses tears in her such as to prompt her to go out to help the old man's erstwhile favourite Heathcliff, though, ironically, not without adverse consequences for the boy soon afterwards. Although the tears she sheds over the deaths of Mr Earnshaw, Hindley, and Catherine seem quite heartfelt, as are those she sheds for Catherine and Heathcliff's recklessness under Hindley's dominance and, later, during her first reunion with young Hareton, there is, nevertheless, something fundamentally derogatory about her attitude to tears in other contexts.[48] An early example may be noted when, in answer to young Heathcliff's wishing that he was as handsome as Edgar Linton and 'had a chance of being as rich as he will be',[49] she says this: 'And cried for mamma, at every turn — [...] and trembled if a country lad heaved his fist against you, and sat at home all day for a shower of rain'.[50] Such a tough sentiment may well explain Nelly's inability to sympathise with, let alone understand, the tears that Cathy sheds on certain occasions. For example, when she finds Cathy crying in her bedroom on the evening of her second visit to the Heights, that is, after she has been forbidden to go there again, she learns that the girl is doing so because Linton will be disappointed at her not visiting him the next day as she has promised. Nelly not only dismisses the idea of such a disappointment, but goes on to make this fallacious utterance: 'Not one in a hundred would weep at losing a relation they had just seen twice, for two afternoons'.[51] Further, the fact that Nelly has only moments before assured Cathy that she 'never had one shadow of substantial sorrow'[52] suggests how little able she was to identify with the 'passionate tears and lamentations'[53] that Cathy had given vent to on learning that, on the very day after his arrival at the Grange, Linton had unexpectedly departed. There is something of a dismissive attitude to tears, too, when, noting Cathy crying on their walk through Thrushcross park, Nelly gives her this advice: 'You mustn't cry because papa has a cold; be thankful it is nothing worse'.[54] Cathy retorts that 'it *will* be something worse'.[55] These words will have been far more prescient than Nelly's will have been with the complacently optimistic, albeit utterly mistaken, prediction she has made about Edgar's lifespan (a prediction made to assuage Cathy's anxiety).

Through these episodes, then, we see that, weeping as she does quite naturally and understandably at the prospect of her beloved father's untimely passing, Cathy seems, at least for now, to be no longer the crybaby she showed herself to be earlier. This change is manifested especially in her tendency to weep silently, as Nelly herself notices while on their walk together in Thrushcross park: '[O]ften, from the side of my eye, I could detect her raising a hand, and brushing something off her cheek'.[56] Again, having soon afterwards been persuaded by Heathcliff's account of his son's near fatal condition since she ended her correspondence with him, Cathy shows how much more mature she has become when, while both are sitting in the library after their return to the Grange, Nelly notices that the girl 'recommenced her silent weeping', dismissing it somewhat as her 'favourite diversion'.[57] And though Nelly tries to talk her out of her distress over Linton, while conscious of the seriousness of the girl's tears, it is because she usually hates to see her unhappy. Perhaps that is why she finds herself obliged, albeit reluctantly, to accompany her to the Heights the following morning to visit Linton, thereby demonstrating once again her inability to keep the girl under control in accordance with Edgar's instructions. Nevertheless, Cathy's growing maturity is finally affirmed by Nelly's description of her mourning the death of her father all night at his bedside: 'Whether Catherine had spent her tears, or whether the grief were too weighty to let them flow, she sat there dry-eyed till the sun rose'.[58]

This is not, however, to suggest that the incidences of Cathy's tears mark out in strictly linear fashion her gradual development to the mature young woman she will have become by the end of the narrative. For notwithstanding the essential selflessness of her tears in respect of her father and Linton, Cathy now and again reverts not only to childishly self-pitying tears, as may be noted after she and Linton have been turned out of 'the house' by an angry Hareton, but also to the ridiculous pretentiousness characteristic of her utterances. Such pretentiousness we see when, having promised Heathcliff that she will marry his son while pleading with him to let her visit her sick father afterwards, she goes on to say somewhat presumptuously that she has 'given over crying'.[59] She does this at the same time as she flatteringly attributes to Heathcliff all sorts of splendid qualities of character in what proves a vain attempt to propitiate him in her favour. Later, when Heathcliff has come to the Grange to take her back to the Heights, telling her of Linton's resentment at '[her] desertion' and of the likely viciousness of his behaviour towards her, Cathy utters a reply which shows that she has still hardly abandoned her tendency to make naïve judgments about people associated with her. This is evident not only from her smug comments on her love relationship with her young husband, but also from the assessment she imparts to her father-in-law thus: 'Mr Heathcliff, *you* have *nobody* to love you', presently going on to make this vindictive prediction: '*Nobody* loves you — *nobody* will cry for you, when you die! I wouldn't be you!'[60] That Cathy's prediction will have been ultimately proved mistaken is ironically demonstrated in perhaps the most unforgettable act of weeping in the entire narrative, namely, Hareton's passionate grieving over the death of Heathcliff, an emotional tribute which may be said to have done a good deal to help sustain the latter's heroic status.

Hareton's floods of tears both while sitting all night at a dead Heathcliff's bedside and, later, while digging his grave, are clearly sincere expressions of his staunch loyalty to, and abiding love for, someone by whom he has, sadly enough, never been cherished for his own sake in return.[61] At the same time, Hareton's tears for Heathcliff are as "normal" as any that he has shed from time to time since early childhood. Indeed, though possibly remembered by some readers principally for his uncouthness and violence, Hareton shows through his very sincere tearfulness over Heathcliff's death a signal aspect of his essential normality as a human being. This we sense already even in his early childhood when he is described frantically crying while struggling in the arms of his inebriated father. Such normality is again manifest when, having had his patent attempt to apologise to Cathy for having violently turned her and Linton out of 'the house' rebuffed with a paranoid threat on her part to have him 'put in prison and hanged', Hareton 'commenced blubbering himself, and hurried out to hide his cowardly agitation', as if painfully aware of the ineluctable power exerted over him by this high-born young lady.[62] But if Cathy seems to have been wilfully blind to Hareton's well-meaning approach to her, it is likely that she will have later attached no little importance to his tears on that occasion, especially during her eventual realization of his intrinsic lovableness, a quality that is surely one of the main reasons she strives to be reconciled with him. And here it is important to note that, owing to her seemingly hopeless attempts at first to rekindle Hareton's friendship, Cathy is now and again described in a more or less tearful condition. For example, Nelly notes that because of a failed attempt on her part to get Hareton to speak to her, she, 'as a last resource, cried and said she was tired of living, her life was useless'.[63] A similar emotional reaction occurs when, in the wake of a second such failed attempt, she is referred to as 'retreating to the window-seat, chewing her lip, and endeavouring, by humming an eccentric tune, to conceal a growing tendency to sob'.[64] Cathy's depressed state of mind is again succinctly conveyed earlier in the novel when Lockwood tells us that though he has not been invited to tea, she is 'the proper person to ask [him]'. She then resumes her chair 'in a pet, her forehead corrugated, and her red under-lip pushed out, like a child's, ready to cry'.[65]

It is, however, Hareton's sensitive awareness of Cathy's tears, that almost certainly helps to bring about their eventual reconciliation and betrothal. Such awareness is already apparent on the day of their very first meeting at the Heights. Thus, having seen Cathy bitterly crying at the thought that he is her cousin — and notwithstanding that he has by then been incensed by her for treating him like a servant — Hareton nevertheless 'seemed moved by her distress' enough to offer her 'a fine crooked-legged terrier whelp' only to have her flatly reject this 'peace-offering'.[66] This sensitive awareness we note again later when, having forbidden Cathy to read the note Lockwood has brought her from Nelly, but then noticed that she 'drew out her pocket-handkerchief and applied it to her eyes', Hareton, we are told, 'pulled out the letter and flung it on the floor beside her as ungraciously as he could', and that 'after struggling a while to keep down his softer feelings'.[67] That Hareton's tendency to be moved by the sufferings of others seems to be innate is evidenced in his early childhood when, on seeing Nelly's 'tears' after Catherine has ordered her to leave 'the house' during her troubled rendezvous with Edgar, he 'commenced crying himself, and sobbed out complaints against "wicked aunt Cathy"',[68] only to be as roughly treated by the latter as Nelly was. All such episodes in turn seem forcibly linked with those in which Cathy shows the same sort of sympathy at the sight of someone crying. Thus, when, for example, having seen that Linton Heathcliff, who has only shortly beforehand arrived at the Grange from the South and soon afterwards asked to be allowed to go to bed, 'put his fingers to his eyes to remove incipient tears', Nelly recalls being prompted to say this to the boy: 'Come, come, there's a good child. [...] You'll make [Cathy] weep too — see how sorry she is for you!'[69] — words that somehow point forward to the essential selflessness she is soon to evince in her love relationship with Linton. And so it is through these and other episodes in which Cathy and Hareton are notable for their compassionate attitudes towards others, whether in a state of tears or not, that we may perhaps wonder whether Emily Brontë has not done well to invest these two characters with a certain heroic status at the end of her novel.[70]

Brontë Studies, 47/3 (2022)

Notes

1 Although tears are referred to now and then in critical writings on *Wuthering Heights*, no scholar appears to have yet published a monograph on the subject I have chosen here.

2 Emily Brontë, *Wuthering Heights*, ed. by Ian Jack and Patsy Stoneman (Oxford: Oxford University Press, 1998), 142.

3 For the sake of convenience, the first Catherine will be referred to as 'Catherine', the second as 'Cathy'.

4 Brontë, 57.

5 Brontë, 32.

6 See Brontë, 18, 37, 38.

7 See Brontë, 41.

8 Brontë, 75.

9 Brontë, 211.

10 See Brontë, 211.

11 See Brontë, 224.

12 Brontë, 63.

13 Brontë, 63.

14 Brontë, 79.

15 Brontë, 79.

16 See Brontë, 110, 111, 119.

17 Brontë, 51.

18 Brontë, 123.

19 Brontë, 153-154.

20 Brontë, 151.

21 Brontë, 152.

22 Brontë, 151.

23 Brontë, 153.

24 See Brontë, 153.

25 Brontë, 52.

26 Brontë, 86.

27 Brontë, 240.

28 Brontë, 249.

29 See Brontë, 38, 77, 163.

30 Brontë, 24.

31 See Brontë, 49.

32 Brontë, 32.

33 Brontë, 34.

34 Brontë, 42.

35 Brontë, 132.

36 Brontë, 102.

37 Brontë, 183.

38 See Brontë, 233, 235, 236, 237.

39 Brontë, 237.

40 Brontë, 242.

41 Brontë, 244.

42 Brontë, 146.

43 The name 'Penistone Craggs' is spelt 'Craggs' on p. 168 and 'Crags' on p. 175 in Brontë 1998.

44 Brontë, 211.

45 Brontë, 211.

46 Brontë, 212.

47 Brontë, 212.

48 See Brontë, 40.

49 Brontë, 50.

50 Brontë, 50.

51 Brontë, 197.

52 Brontë, 197.

53 Brontë, 186.

54 Brontë, 203.

55 Brontë, 203.

56 Brontë, 202.

57 Brontë, 207.

58 Brontë, 251.

59 Brontë, 243.

60 Brontë, 254.

61 See Brontë, 173.

62 Brontë, 222.

63 Brontë, 277.

64 Brontë, 278.

65 Brontë, 8.

66 Brontë, 173.

67 Brontë, 266.

68 Brontë, 63.

69 Brontë, 177.

70 For references to Cathy's and Hareton's compassionate attitudes towards others, see Graeme Tytler, 'The Presentation of Hareton Earnshaw in *Wuthering Heights*', *Brontë Studies* 39(2) (2014): 118-129; and idem, 'The Presentation of the Second Catherine in *Wuthering Heights*', *Brontë Studies* 42(1) (2017): 126-136.

Violence in *Wuthering Heights*

Readers of *Wuthering Heights* (1847) can scarcely have failed to notice how much the novel is permeated by various kinds of violence.[1] It is, moreover, the very violence of its content that has put a good many people off the book, including academics devoted to the study of English literature. No doubt, living as we do in a society, at least here in Britain, where an act of physical violence wrought by one person against another is in many cases against the law, not a few of us admirers of Emily Brontë's masterpiece have been similarly perturbed, and principally so by sundry acts of violence as inflicted by her characters on one another, whether by hand, fist, foot, fingernails, teeth, iron weight or knife. Thus we may mention Hindley's physical violence to Heathcliff in chapter 4; Heathcliff's to Edgar in chapter 7; Catherine's to Nelly, Edgar and Hareton in chapter 8; Catherine's and Isabella's to each other in chapter 10; Heathcliff's to Cathy and Nelly in chapter 13; Heathcliff's and Hindley's to each other, and Heathcliff's and Isabella's to each other in chapter 17; Heathcliff's to Cathy and Nelly Dean in chapter 27; and Hareton's to Cathy in chapter 31, to cite the most glaring instances.[2] However, for those readers who love animals, and perhaps even set store by animal rights, the physical violence perpetrated against dogs, horses and birds in the narrative may be just as perturbing. Indeed, those very readers may well take umbrage at Heathcliff's tendency in boyhood to shoot and trap birds, and in adulthood to hit or kick dogs and horses, to say nothing of his hanging of Isabella's springer spaniel.[3] Some such readers might go even further, not only by denouncing Catherine for asking her father to bring her a whip from Liverpool, or for 'cutting the wing of a goose' (*WH*, p. 52) at the Christmas dinner in chapter 7, but also by condemning outright Heathcliff's, Hareton's and Lockwood's practice of hunting game in the Yorkshire countryside.[4]

It is nevertheless obvious that animals are, in turn, now and again physically violent towards human beings in Emily's novel.[5] We see early examples of this when Lockwood is attacked by the dogs in chapter 1 and when Joseph sets those same dogs on to Lockwood for seizing his lantern in chapter 2. As at Wuthering Heights, dogs at Thrushcross Grange are evidently trained to assault outsiders, especially intrusive outsiders. In this connection, it is noteworthy that Heathcliff and Catherine's illicit visit to the Grange one Sunday evening, for which the latter is savagely bitten on the ankle by a bulldog, happens to take place at a well-appointed house owned by the local magistrate, who, overseeing as he does court cases and other legal matters, is perhaps understandably ever on the alert for criminals of any and every stamp.[6] This is amply suggested when, perhaps prompted by his servant Robert's having presumed that Heathcliff and Catherine are members of a gang intent on murdering the inmates of the Grange, and even having assured Heathcliff that he 'shall go to the gallows for this' (*WH*, p. 43), Mr Linton, while examining the latter's personal appearance, says this to his wife: 'Oh, my dear Mary, look here! Don't be afraid, it is but a boy — yet the villain scowls so plainly in his face, would it not be a kindness to the country to hang him at once, before he shows his nature in acts, as well as features?' (*WH*, p. 43). That the idea of this extreme form of punishment seems to be deeply ingrained in the minds of the Linton family as a whole is plain enough when, for example, Isabella relates that, in the aftermath of Heathcliff's fight with Hindley in chapter 17, she felt 'as reckless as some malefactors show themselves at the foot of the gallows' (*WH*, p. 157); and when Cathy, fearing violence from Hareton at the very moment he is, ironically enough, about to apologize to her for evicting her and Linton Heathcliff from 'the house', 'frightened' him off, as she informs Nelly, 'by [her] assertions that [she] would tell papa, and that he should be put in prison and hanged' (*WH*, p. 222).

Since this punitive ethos appears to be tacitly accepted by those who constitute the inherently patriarchal society portrayed in the novel, it is easy to see why punishment in general and corporal punishment in particular should be regarded as something to be readily resorted to in the upbringing and education of children. Not surprisingly, therefore, one may draw a plausible link between the physical acts of violence perpetrated by Heathcliff, Hindley and Catherine and the fact that they have each been subjected to corporal punishment during childhood. Thus we are told, for example, that Catherine, having been caught 'grinning and spitting' at the foundling brought home by Mr Earnshaw, is given 'a sound blow from her father to teach her cleaner manners' (*WH*, p. 32). That Mr Earnshaw is even more inclined to mete out corporal punishment to Hindley is already obvious enough when Heathcliff, who has been thrashed by the latter three times one week, gives him the following warning: 'if I speak of these blows [to Mr Earnshaw], you'll get them again with interest' (*WH*, p. 33).[7] It is, therefore, little wonder that Hindley, who feels painfully deprived of his father's love, should not only thrash Heathcliff to make up for this lack of affection, but that, after taking over the mastership of the Heights on his father's death, he should also assume the latter's role as punisher, doing so partly by delegating to Joseph the authority to thrash Heathcliff or to box Catherine's ears for their sundry acts of insubordination.[8]

It is, accordingly, not difficult to see why Heathcliff, beaten up or whipped as he has so often been by Hindley and Joseph in his youth, should as an adult now and again deem physical punishment a suitable way of dealing with those who have in some way offended or angered him. Thus, for example, we may refer to the occasion when, having hit Cathy hard for trying to wrest the house key from his grasp, Heathcliff says this to her: 'I know how to *chastise* children, you see' (*WH*, p. 239; emphasis added). It is also interesting to note the extent to which Catherine, too, shares Heathcliff's outlook in this respect. One example may be seen when, in her annoyance with Edgar and Isabella in the early part of her married life, Catherine says this to Nelly: 'though I humour both, I think *a smart chastisement* might improve them, all the same' (*WH*, p. 87; emphasis added).[9] Later, Catherine says this to Edgar in response to the accusation he has unfairly made against her: 'I wish Heathcliff *may flog you sick*, for daring to think an evil thought of me!' (*WH*, p. 102; emphasis added). Nelly, too, seems conscious of the effectiveness of corporal punishment when, for example, in her rage at having been trapped with Cathy inside the Heights by Heathcliff, she says this to his son Linton: 'You *want whipping* for bringing us in here at all, with your dastardly, puling tricks' (*WH*, p. 240-41; emphasis added).

Nelly's aforementioned words remind us of the frequency with which some of the main characters are prone to threatening one another with various kinds of physical violence, many of which threats are expressions of anger for what someone has said or done. The character most given to making such threats is undoubtedly Heathcliff, one memorable instance among several being his threat to detain Nelly at the Heights unless she agrees to arrange a meeting between him and Catherine at the Grange and, in the event of her refusal to do so, his warning her that he will 'fight [his] way to Catherine over Linton and his footmen', and that 'if Edgar Linton meets [him, he would] not hesitate to knock him down, and give him enough to ensure his quiescence while [he stays]', adding, 'If his servants oppose me, I shall threaten them off with these pistols' (*WH*, p. 135). Some of Heathcliff's physical threats are almost too brutal to be practicable, such as the one that Nelly learns about when, having asked young Hareton whether the curate teaches him to 'read and write', she sums up the boy's answer thus: 'No, I was told the curate should have his — teeth dashed down his — throat, if he stepped over the threshold — Heathcliff had promised that!' (*WH*, p. 98). What is especially interesting about all these threats is that not one of them is ever carried out by Heathcliff.[10]

The same is true of the physical threats voiced on occasion by Hindley, and nowhere more grotesquely than in chapter 9 when, in his drunken state, he utters the most improbable threats to Nelly and an infant Hareton. Yet though Hindley is by then especially memorable for his various physical threats to Heathcliff, both during Mr Earnshaw's lifetime and after he has taken over the mastership of the Heights, no such threat is ever actually fulfilled. Indeed, it is curious to note how well the author brings out Hindley's essential fecklessness through the outrageous threats he fails to realize. Accordingly, it comes as no surprise to the reader when Hindley says this to Nelly in his drunken state in the Heights kitchen: 'with the help of Satan, I shall make you swallow the carving knife, Nelly!', and then even gone so far as to push the point of that instrument between her teeth, she tells of being 'never much afraid of his vagaries', and that she 'spat out, and affirmed it tasted detestably' (*WH*, p. 65). Hardly less vicious in the same context is Hindley's following verbal response to his son's frightened reactions to his behaviour: 'As sure as I'm living, I'll break the brat's neck' (*WH*, p. 66), not to mention the threat he has made only moments earlier: 'I want to kill some of you, I shall have no rest till I do!' (*WH*, p. 65). What is notable about the latter threat is the way in which it ironically foreshadows his telling Isabella of his daily intention to murder Heathcliff should he find his bedroom door unlocked. Yet when he later reassures Isabella that he is about to kill Heathcliff, we sense much the same inability on his part to honour such a resolution.[11]

The foregoing detail forms part of several references in the text to killing or murder as an idea which, oddly enough, now and again weighs on the minds of the characters.[12] Thus, for example, when called upon by Isabella to see to a seriously injured Hindley, Joseph instantly says: 'Und soa, yah been murthering on him?' (*WH*, p. 157), with much the same emotion as that with which Zillah, on catching sight of Lockwood lying on the floor, taunts Hareton with this rhetorical question: 'Are we going to murder folk on our very door-stones?' (*WH*, p. 14). Such metaphors are, to be sure, not unrelated to the threats made by some of the characters to kill someone who has angered them. A flagrant example of this may be noted when, just after being violently turned out of 'the house' with Cathy by Hareton, Linton Heathcliff threatens the latter as follows: 'I'll kill you! [...] Devil! devil! I'll kill you, I'll kill you!' (*WH*, p. 221). That detail, which forms part of Cathy's confession to Nelly about her illicit visits to the Heights, is, ironically enough, followed up when, alluding to Linton's having coughed up blood as a consequence of the eviction, Cathy tells Nelly of her own reaction to Hareton's forbidding her to visit Linton upstairs: 'I exclaimed that he had killed Linton and I *would* enter' (*WH*, p. 222). The rage underlying these threats to kill, or accusations of killing, is especially linked with those contexts in which Heathcliff threatens to kill Cathy in much the same spirit with which, in his rage at having been struck on the throat by Edgar, he earlier threatened to 'murder him some time' (*WH*, p. 103). This we note when, for example, he reacts to Cathy's vituperation of him in chapter 33 with these words: 'Fling her into the kitchen! I'll kill her, Ellen Dean, if you let her come into my sight again!' (*WH*, p. 284). This threat is presently supplemented when, suddenly relaxing his tight hold on Cathy, Heathcliff addresses her thus: 'You must learn to avoid putting me in a passion, or I shall really murder you, some time!' (*WH*, p. 285).[13] In this connection, it is interesting to recall how much at their last tryst Catherine and Heathcliff accuse each other of murder or self-murder in their love relationship.[14] Even just after Catherine's passing Heathcliff is overheard by Nelly uttering these words: 'You said I killed you — haunt me, then! The murdered *do* haunt their murderers' (*WH*, p. 148). Moreover, later in a long confession to Nelly, Heathcliff describes Catherine's haunting of him for eighteen years as tantamount to being 'a strange way of killing, not by inches, but by fractions of hair-breadths, to beguile me with the spectre of a hope, through eighteen years!' (*WH*, p. 257).

The irony of all those references to killing and murder — and here we might include remarks that various other characters sometimes make about themselves or about someone else being killed or murdered or nearly so — lies in our eventually learning that nobody is actually killed or murdered at any time in the narrative.[15] Even Isabella, notwithstanding her murderous thoughts against Heathcliff, shows that she would not go so far as to kill him, much as she would at the same time be content to imagine his being killed by someone other than herself.[16] The fact that all threats to kill or murder, as with other threats of physical violence, including, most notably, the threats of suicide uttered by Heathcliff, Catherine and Hindley, are never executed, may help us to understand why so much physical violence in Emily's novel happens to take place almost entirely within the boundaries of the mind and the tongue.[17] And, as the author suggests, it is already in childhood that mental violence of all kinds seems to take root. Certainly, the mental violence that Catherine shows as an adult appears to have something to do with her tendency as a young girl both to be physically violent towards, and domineering over, her peers and to be generally rebellious towards her parents.[18] This may in part explain her aggressive attitudes not only towards Edgar, Isabella and Nelly in the early months of her married life, but even towards Heathcliff after his return to Gimmerton, as may be seen, for example, when, still mentally unstable after the brain fever she is convalescing from, she says this to him during their final meeting: 'I shouldn't care what you suffered. I care nothing for your sufferings. Why shouldn't you suffer? I do!' (*WH*, p. 140).

Catherine's mental violence is, to be sure, hardly as intense or as extreme as Heathcliff's, which, not unlike Catherine's, seems to be rooted in unpleasant childhood experiences. Indeed, no character in the novel has a more brutal mentality than that which Heathcliff already displays in boyhood, as is quite evident, for example, when, having assured Nelly in the account of his and Catherine's illicit visit to the Grange that he would not exchange his condition at the Heights for Edgar Linton's, he goes on to say: 'not if I might have the privilege of flinging Joseph off the highest gable, and painting the house-front with Hindley's blood!' (*WH*, p. 42). Much of Heathcliff's mental violence, especially after his return to Gimmerton, is of an essentially prospective nature. Thus to Catherine's having warned him about the fingernails by which Isabella has just managed to release herself from her sister-in-law's tight grasp, Heathcliff replies: 'I'd wrench them off her fingers, if they ever menaced me' (*WH*, p. 94). And it is in much the same vein that he presently goes on to tell Catherine what he would do to Isabella if she were living with him: 'You'd hear of odd things, if I lived alone with that mawkish, waxen face; the most ordinary would be painting on its white the colours of the rainbow, and turning the blue eyes black, every day or two' (*WH*, p. 94). It is, however, noteworthy that Heathcliff never once treats Isabella to such brutal acts, and that, even after he has been viciously struck on the throat by Edgar in the Grange kitchen, he simply addresses the latter as follows: 'By God, Mr Linton, I'm mortally sorry that you are not worth knocking down!' (*WH*, p. 101) — words that, incidentally, are surely more insulting than any physical violence he might have resorted to in retaliation. Still, Heathcliff seems none the less anxious to make up for this desistence by imagining how he would deal with Edgar physically in some future context when he presently says this to Catherine: 'I would not strike him with my fist, but I'd kick him with my foot, and experience considerable satisfaction' (*WH*, p. 102). Moreover, having shortly afterwards been warned by Catherine that, just after going out of the kitchen to the front entrance, Edgar will 'return with a brace of pistols, and half-a-dozen assistants', Heathcliff angrily puts this rhetorical question to her: 'Do you suppose I'm going with that blow burning in my gullet?', supplementing it with the following vow: 'By Hell, no! I'll crush his ribs in like a rotten hazel-nut, before I cross the threshold! If I don't floor him now, I shall murder him some time, so, as you value his existence, let me get at him!' (*WH*, p. 103). Such resolutions are, however, not realized once Heathcliff has presently decided to 'avoid a struggle against three underlings [of Edgar]' (*WH*, p. 103) who have just entered the court.

Even more gruesome in content is the imaginary scenario that Heathcliff relates to Nelly after dismissing Isabella from 'the house' in chapter 14: 'I have no pity! I have no pity! The worms writhe, the more I yearn to crush out their entrails! It is a moral teething, and I grind with greater energy, in proportion to the increase of pain' (*WH*, p. 134). Such a sentiment is forcibly linked with those that Heathcliff conveys to Nelly moments after locking Nelly and Cathy in the Heights in preparation for the latter's marriage to his son: 'How she does stare! It's odd what a savage feeling I have to anything that seems afraid of me! Had I been born where laws are less strict, and tastes less dainty, I should treat myself to a slow vivisection of those two, as an evening's amusement' (*WH*, p. 238). Yet, as is made perfectly plain, never once does Heathcliff injure Cathy or his son Linton, or, for that matter, Isabella or Edgar, with any one of those physical acts of brutality he so gloatingly imagines.[19]

If Heathcliff's mental violence seems to have its origins partly in the traumas of his childhood both before and after he was picked up by Mr Earnshaw in Liverpool, the reader may well consider why it is that Lockwood and Nelly Dean, about whom next to nothing is known about their early lives, should also be conspicuous from time to time for the violence of their minds. To be sure, neither of them uses any physical violence to speak of, even while clearly disposed to do so on occasion, as, for example, when, mistakenly presuming that he has just been insulted by Joseph, a 'sufficiently enraged' Lockwood 'stepped towards the aged rascal with an intention of kicking him out of the door' (*WH*, p. 11), but is prevented from doing so at the last minute on realizing that the insult was directed at Cathy. Such desistence on Lockwood's part may help to account for his compensating himself, not unlike Nelly, with physical violence at a purely mental level as a means of coping with his feelings of anger.[20] Perhaps the most striking example of this is provided by the two ghastly nightmares, in which, through the verbal violence of the Rvd Jabes Branderham and the physical violence of the members of his congregation towards one another, as well as through his own excessive cruelty to the waif child, Lockwood doubtless achieves a cathartic release of the anger induced in him by the unpleasantness of his experiences at the Heights in the first two chapters.

Nelly's mental violence, on the other hand, seems due generally to her experiences of the rough-and-tumble of everyday life since she became part of Mr Earnshaw's household as a youngster. This is somewhat suggested by Nelly's generally hostile attitude towards Catherine — an attitude by which she betrays a curiously tough mentality, not to say a certain hardness of heart, as is especially apparent when, having noticed towards the end of Catherine's tryst with Heathcliff that her mistress's arms 'had fallen relaxed, and her head hung down', Nelly reacts with this thought: 'She's fainted or dead, […] so much the better. Far better that she should be dead, than lingering a burden and a misery-maker to all about her' (*WH*, p. 143).[21] Such toughness of outlook has already been manifested when in an attempt to help Heathcliff to recover his self-respect on the Christmas morning after he asked her to 'make [him] decent' because he is 'going to be good', she includes this flattering comparison between himself and Edgar Linton: 'You are younger, and yet, I'll be bound, you are taller and twice as broad across the shoulders — you could knock him down in a twinkling; don't you feel that you could?' (*WH*, pp. 49-50). Nelly's image of Heathcliff is clearly that of someone capable of vicariously carrying out the kind of physical violence which, being a woman, she is reluctant to carry out herself. Yet it seems as if the violence Nelly thus imagines is the product of her own mind rather than the violence she somewhat unfairly imagines Heathcliff being disposed to perpetrate. A blatant example of this may be noted just after Heathcliff has by pure chance saved Hareton from certain death. Thus Nelly imagines what Heathcliff would probably have done if he had known that the child had been dropped over the banister by Hindley: 'Had it been dark, I dare say, he would have tried to remedy the mistake by smashing Hareton's skull on the steps' (*WH*, p. 66). Nor should we forget that Nelly later goes so far as to imagine the following scenario unless Cathy is released by Heathcliff from her imprisonment at the Heights in time to visit her dying father: 'Her father *shall* see her, I vowed, and vowed again, if that devil be killed on his own door-stones in trying to prevent it!' (*WH*, p. 250). Such thoughts on Nelly's part, and, indeed, similarly violent ones of hers in other contexts, should remind us that, despite nowhere using any kind of vicious physical violence to speak of, she scarcely deserves to be looked on merely as the level-headed, easy-going 'good sort' she has so often been taken for.

One by-product of a mind given to violent images and attitudes is undoubtedly a similarly violent figurative language.[22] We note, for example, how readily the genteel Lockwood in his fits of anger or frustration falls back on extravagant similes and metaphors to convey the unpleasantness of his experiences at the Heights. Thus as well as using conventional ones such as 'storm', 'tempest' and 'high wind' when referring to various stages of his fight with the dogs, he seems to give fullest vent to his anger when he says this to Heathcliff about their behaviour: 'The herd of possessed swine could have had no worse spirits in them than those animals of yours, sir' before further exaggerating the danger of the dogs to an absurd degree by adding: 'You might as well leave a stranger with a brood of tigers!' (*WH*, p. 5). Such a comparison surely betokens the violence of Lockwood's mind rather than the violence of the dogs, and is a notable instance of his tendency to suggest that certain physical acts or situations are far more violent than they are in reality. For example, when describing Cathy's angry response to his offering to reach the tea-canisters on the chimney piece, he does so with this comparison: 'she turned upon me as a miser might turn, if any one attempted to assist him in counting his gold' (*WH*, p. 8). There is little doubt that such a comparison is far grimmer than the reality of Cathy's conduct towards him.[23]

Nelly's comparisons also tend to have a similarly violent quality. Thus it is obvious that her deep dislike of Joseph accounts for the hyperbolic language with which she rather fallaciously sums him up as a human being, thereby suggesting that he is far worse than he is in reality: 'the wearisomest, self-righteous pharisee that ever *ransacked* a Bible to rake the promises to himself and *fling the curses* on his neighbours' (*WH*, p. 35; emphasis added). Noteworthy, too, is Nelly's practice of imparting the idea of a certain kind of behaviour or a certain relationship or even a look with images which, entailing animals or plants, seem somewhat excessive.[24] For example, to convey the nature of Heathcliff's utterly hostile manner of staring at Isabella, she does so by suggesting 'as one might do at a strange repulsive animal, a centipede from the Indies, for instance' (*WH*, p. 93). It goes without saying that Nelly has probably never had first-hand knowledge of such an exotic creature but, rather, has come across a description of one in one of the many books she has read. Not surprising, therefore, is the occasional image she draws from the Bible, with which she is evidently quite familiar. Thus, when alluding to Heathcliff's nefarious influence on Hindley during the time he has been lodging at the Heights since his return to Gimmerton, Nelly says this to Lockwood: 'I felt that God had forsaken the stray sheep there to its own wicked wanderings, and an evil beast prowled between it and the fold, waiting his time to spring and destroy' (*WH*, p, 95). Although the image is not altogether inappropriate, it is none the less shot through with Nelly's incurably superstitious attitude towards Heathcliff, which is especially apparent in contexts where she refers to him as a ghoul, a vampire, a goblin, a monster, and other fanciful creatures, thereby virtually dehumanizing him altogether.[25] It is, then, little wonder that Heathcliff has so often been viewed by many a reader not as the natural human being, as he is surely meant to be understood, but as some preternatural creature of extra-terrestrial substance and origin.

There are, to be sure, various other forms of violence in *Wuthering Heights* that might be said to deserve our critical attention. Thus we might refer to violence of speech, examples of which abound in the narrative, and perhaps most noticeably in the vituperative language that Isabella suffers from both Heathcliff and Joseph; to the violence of hostile looks and even of laughter that Lockwood has to put up with from Heathcliff, Hareton and Cathy in the first two chapters, and which other characters have to endure elsewhere; to the violence directed at man-made objects, memorable instances being not only Catherine's throwing the Grange kitchen-door key into the fire or

Isabella's stamping on her wedding ring and then casting it into the Grange parlour fire, but the remarkably detailed description of the much damaged state of Hindley's bedroom as shown to Isabella by Joseph shortly after her arrival at the Heights as Heathcliff's bride.[26] We might also mention the violence of nature, as already suggested by the epithet used in the title of the novel, and borne out by references to plants and fir trees stunted by what Lockwood designates as 'the power of the north wind' (*WH*, p. 2), and by references to storms, one of which destroys 'a portion of the east chimney-stack' (*WH*, p. 75) on the night of Heathcliff's disappearance, as well as the reference to the autumnal storms that Lockwood expects to erode further the largely slateless roof of the long-disused 'kirk' (*WH*, p. 300). Finally, it is interesting to note how often words such as 'fling', 'strike', 'hit', 'throw', 'wrench', 'thrust', 'catch', 'grasp', 'pull', 'push', 'arrest', and similar verbs indicative of physical violence are used with figurative as well as concrete meaning.[27]

Yet, for all that *Wuthering Heights* is conspicuous for violence of various kinds, it is useful to remember that, as has already been shown above, the most serious forms of violence, that is to say, the physical violence exerted by one person on another, happens far less often in the narrative than some readers might be inclined to suppose or to recall. As we have already seen, the most heinous acts of physical violence are but figments of heated imaginations, and, like threats of physical violence, remain safely within the confines of the human mind as well as within those of the tongue. In that respect, *Wuthering Heights* may be said to be, psychologically speaking, a remarkably modern novel. All this may, nevertheless, seem rather surprising in a narrative where, for example, revenge is such a prominent theme.[28] It is, however, worth bearing in mind that even Heathcliff, the character most committed to the idea of revenge, finds himself, owing to the effects of his mental illness, ultimately unable to wreak the vengeance which, as he himself admits, he could so easily have done during the last days of his life against the youngest generation of Lintons and Earnshaws, and that notwithstanding his having always been careful not to commit specific criminal offences of any kind through his constant concern to keep on the right side of the law.[29]

If, however, such knowledge would still do little to assuage the unease of those unconscionably disturbed by the violence of the book, especially readers who regard the violence as often seemingly gratuitous, one might perhaps do well to point out that the author is by no means intent on bringing violence into her book for its own sake; on the contrary, her many references to violence are but testimonies to the remarkable realism of her novel. Yet, at the same time as she is perfectly aware that a proclivity to violence is an inherent trait of human nature, and, as we have seen, one latent even in the most respectable of people, she is no less concerned to remind her readers that there is a way out of violence that is within the power of us all. This she does pre-eminently through her presentation of Hareton Earnshaw, who, though reminding us somewhat of Heathcliff with his occasional acts or threats of physical violence, is nevertheless notable for being the only character not only to show remorse for his violence to others but also to exercise self-control in the very moment when he bids fair to hit someone for antagonizing him in some way or other, be it Lockwood, Linton Heathcliff or even Cathy herself.[30] Indeed, it is through his exceptional capacity for self-restraint that Hareton, brought up though he has been in rough-and-ready fashion, may surely be said to have deservedly become the hero (or anti-hero) of the second half of *Wuthering Heights*, and the more so as his intrinsically compassionate awareness of his fellow creatures, as manifest on and off throughout the narrative, has somehow adumbrated the markedly benign, not to say non-violent, atmosphere that has begun to prevail towards the end of the novel.[31]

Brontë Studies, 46/3 (2021)

Notes

1 Among several works that discuss violence in *Wuthering Heights*, we may refer especially to Wade Thompson, 'Infanticide and Sadness in *Wuthering Heights*', *Publications of the Modern Language Association of America*, 78 (1963), 69-74; N. M. Jacobs, 'Gender and Layered Narrative in *Wuthering Heights* and *The Tenant of Wildfell Hall*', *The Journal of Narrative Technique*, 16 (1986), 204-19; Patricia Yaeger, 'Violence in the Sitting Room: *Wuthering Heights* and the Woman's Novel', *Genre*, 21 (1988), 203-29; Robin DeRosa, 'To Save the Life of the Novel: Sadomasochism and Representation in *Wuthering Heights*', *Rocky Mountain Review of Language and Literature*, 52 (1998), 27-43; Lisa Surridge, 'Animals and Violence in *Wuthering Heights*', *Brontë Society Transactions*, 24 (1999), 161-73; Judith E. Pike, '"My name *was* Isabella Linton": Coverture, Domestic Violence, and Mrs. Heathcliff's Narrative in *Wuthering Heights*', *Nineteenth-Century Literature*, 64.3 (2009), 347-83.

2 For references to, or quotations from, the novel, see Emily Brontë, *Wuthering Heights*, ed by Ian Jack and Patsy Stoneman (Oxford: Oxford University Press, 1998); hereafter *WH*. For the sake of convenience, the first Catherine is referred to as 'Catherine', the second as 'Cathy'. For Emily Brontë's use of the words 'violence' and 'violent' in the text, see *Wuthering Heights*, pp. 23, 62-63, 75, 104, 108, 114-15, 140, 155, 211, 213, 283.

3 For references to Heathcliff's mistreatment of animals, see *Wuthering Heights*, pp. 4, 42-43, 108, 114, 248. Noteworthy, too, is Hindley Earnshaw's cruelty to the bulldog Throttler: see *Wuthering Heights*, p. 127.

4 For references or allusions to game-hunting, see *Wuthering Heights*,

pp. 80, 210, 218, 271. No less a probable cause for alarm among certain animal lovers would surely be Lockwood's reference to the 'clusters of legs of beef, mutton and ham' displayed in 'a vast oak dresser' (*WH*, pp. 2-3).

5   For violence of dogs to one another, see *Wuthering Heights*, pp. 171, 175.

6   This is partly suggested by Mr Linton's pompous words: 'To beard a magistrate in his strong-hold, and on the Sabbath, too!', (*WH*, p. 43).

7   Mr Earnshaw's punitive practices are nostalgically recalled by Joseph when, exasperated at Heathcliff and Catherine's violent treatment of his theological books, he calls out to Hindley, saying: 'It's fair flaysome ut yah let 'em goa on this gait. Ech! th'owd man ud uh laced 'em properly — bud he's goan!' (*WH*, p. 17).

8   See *Wuthering Heights*, pp. 16, 17.

9   See also *Wuthering Heights*, pp. 94, 205.

10 For Heathcliff's other physical threats, see *Wuthering Heights*, pp. 22, 44, 132, 135, 161, 236, 239, 243, 255, 284.

11 For Hindley's talk about killing Heathcliff, see *Wuthering Heights*, pp. 67, 123, 124, 155, 159-60.

12 For such references, see *Wuthering Heights*, pp. 22, 29, 31, 57, 60, 65, 66, 87, 96, 131, 134, 160, 170, 186, 191, 196, 204, 235, 296.

13 For Heathcliff's other physical threats to Cathy, see *Wuthering Heights*, pp. 239, 243, 255.

14 See *Wuthering Heights*, pp. 100, 115, 139, 140, 142, 143. Relevant here are Heathcliff's and Catherine's frequent references to death: see *Wuthering Heights*, pp. 19, 20, 87, 105, 106, 108, 110-11, 113, 140, 164, 236, 237, 240, 247.

15 See *Wuthering Heights*, pp. 22, 28, 29, 31, 57, 60, 65, 66, 87, 96, 170, 186, 191, 204, 235.

16 See *Wuthering Heights*, pp. 153-56. Not without relevance here is Heathcliff's following comment on Isabella as imparted to Nelly in the latter's presence: 'But no brutality disgusted her — I suppose she has an innate admiration of it, if only her precious person were secure from injury!' (*WH*, p. 133).

17 For references or allusions to suicide, see *Wuthering Heights*, pp. 67, 78, 85, 100, 104, 106, 107, 113, 140, 153, 155, 156, 164, 297. Somewhat related to Heathcliff's and Catherine's talk of suicide are references to their moments of self-harm: see *Wuthering Heights*, pp. 12, 23, 69, 70, 105, 106, 109-10, 147, 148. In this connection, Heathcliff's assumption that Hindley deliberately committed suicide is something of an exaggeration. Indeed, it appears that the latter's heavy drinking on the last night of his life was no more than one of his usual attempts to forget his troubles: see *Wuthering Heights*, pp. 164, 165.

18 See *Wuthering Heights*, pp. 36, 37, 104, 105.

19 Heathcliff's violence towards Isabella — and even to their son Linton — seems to have been mainly, if not entirely,

psychological: see especially *Wuthering Heights*, pp. 134, 187, 229, 254.

20 For Nelly's comparatively minor acts of violence, see *Wuthering Heights*, pp. 32, 51, 73, 199, 241. For Nelly's occasional threats of physical violence to Linton Heathcliff, see *Wuthering Heights*, pp. 240, 247.

21 See also *Wuthering Heights*, pp. 58, 59, 68, 81, 104, 105.

22 Conspicuous among violent similes are those involving knives and arrows: see *Wuthering Heights*, pp. 42, 81, 93, 265.

23 This tendency on Lockwood's part may also be sensed in his use of military metaphors when referring to matters of everyday life: see *Wuthering Heights*, pp. 2, 4, 5, 25, 28, 80. Such metaphors seem to have some bearing on the fact that both Lockwood and Nelly wonder whether Heathcliff spent some time as a soldier while abroad: see *Wuthering Heights*, pp. 80, 82, 84.

24 See *Wuthering Heights*, pp. 30, 64, 68, 81, 241, 296.

25 See *Wuthering Heights*, pp. 98, 293.

26 For examples of violent speech, which includes scolding, cursing and name-calling, see *Wuthering Heights*, pp. 10, 24, 25, 42, 44, 56, 57, 65, 67, 70, 74, 75, 77, 83, 97, 122, 127, 132, 134, 142, 155, 156, 157, 158, 160, 172, 182, 183, 184, 191, 192, 194, 201, 221, 222, 237, 238, 243, 255, 260, 262, 267, 278, 283, 285; for examples of hostile looks and scornful laughter, see *Wuthering Heights*, pp. 2, 7, 9, 10, 12, 13, 14, 47, 57, 59, 67, 71, 90, 92, 101, 120, 124, 125, 147, 182, 183, 191, 195, 220, 224; for examples of violence to

man-made objects, see *Wuthering Heights*, pp. 15, 16, 17, 32, 103, 105, 108, 126, 154, 200, 238, 244, 268.

27 See *Wuthering Heights*, pp. 1, 4, 6, 8, 10, 13, 14, 17, 20, 21, 22, 25, 26, 31, 34, 35, 41, 42, 47, 51, 56, 62, 63, 65, 66, 67, 72, 73, 76, 78, 83, 84, 85, 86, 88, 97, 100, 102, 111, 112, 115, 116, 123, 127, 128, 130, 131, 138, 139, 142, 143, 152, 153, 157, 169, 179, 187, 191, 197, 198, 206, 211, 221, 238, 258, 263, 270, 271.

28 For references to revenge, retaliation and paying back, see *Wuthering Heights*, pp. 5, 8, 14, 22, 28, 34, 40, 53, 69, 88, 98, 99, 100, 103, 107, 153, 155, 159, 196, 241, 248, 254, 287.

29 See *Wuthering Heights*, pp. 133, 134, 158, 287.

30 See *Wuthering Heights*, pp. 10, 194, 279.

31 For references to Hareton's sensitive awareness of others, see *Wuthering Heights*, pp. 13, 63, 171, 173, 186, 211, 222, 262, 283, 291, 298-99. For a discussion on Hareton's inherently compassionate nature, see Graeme Tytler, 'The Presentation of Hareton Earnshaw in *Wuthering Heights*', *Brontë Studies*, 39.2 (2014), 126-27.

Thematic Functions of Fire
in *Wuthering Heights*

Conspicuous among Lockwood's observations on Wuthering Heights and Thrushcross Grange are his references to fires and fireplaces, some of these references indicating no little familiarity on his part with northern domestic life.[1] Thus, having already noticed 'the huge fireplace' in 'the house' on his first visit to the Heights, he finds on his second visit there the following afternoon that that same room 'glowed delightfully in the radiance of an immense fire compounded of coal, peat and wood' (*WH*, p. 7).[2] Lockwood's knowledge of the very fuel being burnt in that fire is later matched by the following documentary detail he gives on his final visit to the Heights in September 1802, amid very warm weather: 'Both doors and lattices were open; and yet, *as is usually the case in a coal district*, a fine, red fire illumined the chimney; the comfort which the eye derives from it, renders the extra heat endurable' (*WH*, p. 273; italics mine). But if Lockwood's interest in fires and fireplaces is partly aesthetic, his concern with them is, understandably enough, mainly due to his strong need for physical comfort, especially during cold weather.[3] For example, it is because the afternoon of the day after his first visit to Heights 'set in misty and cold' that he has 'half a mind to spend it by [his] study fire, instead of wading through heath and mud to Wuthering Heights' (*WH*, p. 6); and it is only on finding a servant-girl putting out his study fire that Lockwood determines on the latter course of action. Other instances of Lockwood's attachment to fires may be noted on the morning after his night in the oak-panelled room: his enticing a 'little flame' to 'play between the ribs' (*WH*, p. 24) of the back-kitchen hearth so that he may doze on a bench nearby; his watching Zillah 'urging flakes of flame up the chimney with a colossal bellows' (*WH*, p. 25) in 'the house'; and his remarking on the 'cheerful fire' (*WH*, p. 27) in his study at the Grange on arriving there after his laborious walk through the snow. It is also interesting to note that, on his return to Gimmerton in September 1802, Lockwood not only makes a point of telling the old woman looking after the Grange that all that is 'necessary' for his accommodation are 'good fires and dry sheets', but also mentions her bungling work at 'the grates' and even her 'skurrying away with a pan of hot cinders' (*WH*, p. 272). Finally, it is worth keeping in mind that Lockwood hears the first part of Nelly's narrative (from Chapter 4 to Chapter 9) while enduring the onset of a bad cold by his study fire.

Constituting as they do part of the realism of the novel, Lockwood's references to fires and fireplaces are more or less linked with similar references made both by Nelly Dean and by some of the other characters in their respective narratives. Thus as well as being apprised of the presence of a fireplace in a kitchen, a back-kitchen, a living-room, a drawing-room, a parlour, a library, a bedroom, whether at the Heights or at the Grange, we are now and again informed of the nature or state of a fuel or of a relevant adjunct or appurtenance — coal-hole, coal-scuttle, coal, cinders, ashes, embers, ribs, grates, shovel, poker, hearth, hearthstone, hearthbrush, hob, fender, oven, chimney, chimneypiece, chimney stack, chimney corner, and so on. We are also made aware that, whatever the function of fires, whether for heating or cooking, or even for providing light, their setting or extinguishing is almost entirely the responsibility of servants. Noteworthy, too, as an aspect of realism is the presence of a fireplace as a background to those at leisure, as is touchingly illustrated by Nelly's remarking on the fact that, during Mr Earnshaw's mastership of the Heights, he and his family would spend their evenings together with the servants round the fireplace in 'the house'. In this connection, mention should also be made of the inordinate importance of fireplaces and hearths in Joseph's everyday life, more especially when he is not working.[4] Also illustrative of realism are episodes in which characters are described seeking or being taken to a fireplace for relief from the cold they have been exposed to out of doors. Thus Nelly relates that, having arrived at the Heights after church on Christmas morning, Catherine 'took a hand of each of the [Linton] children, and brought them into the house and set them before the fire, which quickly put colour into their white faces' (*WH*, p. 51). Such a quest for a fireplace is as normal as when, having entered the Heights kitchen after walking all the way with Nelly from the Grange in very wet and frosty weather, Cathy 'ran to the hearth to warm herself' (*WH*, p. 208).

But whereas Cathy is here described going to a fireplace as she is in other contexts simply in order to recover her bodily heat, it is noteworthy how often a fireplace is resorted to in the novel for psychological reasons rather than for mere physical comfort. We see this, for example, in Hareton during the period of tension and hostility between himself and Cathy consequent upon his burning of the books. It is no doubt natural that after a long day of hard manual work Hareton should spend some of his evenings by the kitchen fire and, like Joseph, even smoke a pipe. Certainly that same hearth seems a suitable place for him to convalesce by after having accidentally wounded himself with his gun. For Cathy, on the other hand, anxious as she is, despite her constant teasing of Hareton at this time, to re-establish her friendship with him, it is puzzling 'how he could sit a whole evening staring into the fire, and dozing' (*WH*, p. 276). Even on the Easter Monday, shortly before he will be reconciled with Cathy, Hareton's uncomfortable state of mind is still evident from Nelly's significantly remarking that he 'sat, morose as usual, at the chimney corner' (*WH*, p. 277).[5] And yet Hareton's sitting by fires and staring into them, as recounted by Nelly in Chapter 32, marks but a brief unhappy phase in his otherwise contented way of life and is certainly not to be compared to, say, Linton Heathcliff's inveterate habit of hugging fireplaces. That Linton's dependency on fires seems to compensate him for the lack of love he thinks he suffers from is amply suggested by Heathcliff's unnamed housekeeper's following complaint about his selfish demands at the Heights: 'And he must have a fire in the middle of summer; [...] there he'll sit, wrapped in his furred cloak in his chair by the fire' (*WH*, p. 186). It is, moreover, through his chronic attachment to fireplaces that Linton Heathcliff proves to be temperamentally the very antithesis of Cathy. Indeed, when asked by Linton, at their first reunion, whether, instead of being shown the garden and the stable, she would not prefer to keep him company by the fire, Cathy's response is to cast 'a longing look to the door' (*WH*, p. 192). In view of what we already know about Linton, we are not surprised to learn that he 'kept his seat, and shrank closer to the fire' (*WH*, p. 192). The fact that Cathy's encounters with Linton at the Heights, both pleasant and unpleasant, occur for the most part at a hearth or on a hearthstone is ironically corroborated by her when, at their first official reunion on the heath, she rebukes him thus for his eccentric behaviour towards her: 'Get off! I shall return home — *it is folly dragging you from the hearth-stone*, and pretending — what do we pretend?' (*WH*, p. 235; italics mine).[6]

Linton Heathcliff's self-indulgent attitude to fireplaces seems scarcely different in kind from that which Hindley and Frances Earnshaw have evinced in earlier episodes of the novel. No doubt their fondness for fires in part derives from the fact that, on her arrival at the Heights for the first time, Frances 'expressed such pleasure at the white floor, and huge glowing fire-place' (*WH*, p. 39). Not to be wondered at, therefore, especially in view of the couple's exclusive devotion to each other, is Catherine's mentioning in her diary that, during Joseph's three-hour religious service, which she and Heathcliff had to endure in a cold garret one Sunday, 'Hindley and his wife basked down stairs before a comfortable fire' (*WH*, p. 16). Indeed, Heathcliff's own awareness of this incongruity serves as the reason he gives Nelly for the illicit visit that he and Catherine have paid to the Grange later that day: '[…] we thought we would just go and see whether the Lintons passed their Sunday evenings standing shivering in corners, while their father and mother sat eating and drinking, and singing and laughing, and *burning their eyes out before the fire*' (*WH*, p. 41; italics mine). Interesting, too, for signalling Hindley's mental and moral decline after Frances's death are accounts of his presence at fireplaces. For example, on the morning after the storm described in Chapter 9, Nelly notes that Hindley 'had come out, and stood on the kitchen hearth, haggard and drowsy' (*WH*, p. 76) — a detail that aptly evokes the pathos of a man only dimly aware of what is going on in the household of which he is master. A similar pathos is to be felt in Isabella's observation of Hindley's eccentric demeanour relative to fireplaces during her short-lived sojourn at the Heights as Heathcliff's bride. For example, in the immediate wake of his fight with Heathcliff, Isabella observes that, instead of acting on the latter's advice to go to bed, Hindley merely 'stretched himself on the hearthstone' (*WH*, p.

158), such a posture being almost caricatural of much the same need for the psychological comfort of a fireplace we have noted in Linton Heathcliff. Not surprising, therefore, is the fact that on the following morning Isabella finds Hindley 'sitting by the fire, deadly sick' (*WH*, p. 158). Another instance of Hindley's dependency on fireplaces, brought about this time, ironically enough, by his misguided resolve to remain sober for Catherine's funeral, has been exemplified a day or two earlier in Isabella's following account: 'Consequently, he rose, in suicidal low spirits, as fit for the church as for a dance; and *instead, he sat down by the fire,* and swallowed gin or brandy by tumblerfuls' (*WH*, p. 153; italics mine). Still, it should be said to Hindley's credit that it is at a fireplace that he appears to have saved Isabella from possible death at the hands of Heathcliff in pursuit of her. As she says to Nelly Dean: 'The last glimpse I caught of [Heathcliff] was a furious rush on his part, checked by the embrace of his host; and both fell locked together on the hearth' (*WH*, p. 161).

The fact that Isabella manages to escape from her unhappy marriage and lead a life of her own in London for some twelve years afterwards might seem unimaginable during her early presentation as a highly-strung young woman. And yet in spite of her restricted circumstances and the indifference or hostility of her fellow residents, Isabella shows a strong spirit of independence while living at the Heights. For example, having told Nelly in her letter that, after a futile search with Joseph for a bedroom on the night of her arrival there, she was eventually assured by the latter that she could have 'the house' all to herself, Isabella continues: 'Gladly did I take advantage of this intimation; and the minute I flung myself into a chair, *by the fire,* I nodded, and slept' (*WH*, p. 128; italics mine). (This is, ironically enough, precisely what Lockwood himself would also have gladly done had Heathcliff not forbidden it.) Isabella's reference here exemplifies one of her very practical uses of fireplaces. Indeed, the fireplace proves to be an ideal setting for Isabella, given her lonely and loveless existence in her new home. As she says to Nelly: 'When Heathcliff is in, I'm often obliged to seek the kitchen, and [Joseph's and Hareton's] society, or starve among the damp, uninhabited chambers; when he is not, as was the case this week, I *establish a table and chair at one corner of the house fire*' (*WH*, p. 154; italics mine). The idea of the fireplace as Isabella's habitual setting in the Heights is soon afterwards confirmed when, having warned Heathcliff not to enter the building on account of Hindley's threat to kill him, she recalls this detail: 'With that I shut the window, and *returned to my place by the fire*' (*WH*, p. 156; italics mine). Again, noticing Heathcliff and Hindley by the fireplace in 'the house' on the morning after their fight, and finding that, of all three of them, she is to dine alone, at the same time as, casting 'a look towards [her] silent companions', she both 'experienced a certain sense of satisfaction and superiority' and 'felt the comfort of a quiet conscience within [her]', Isabella goes on to say: 'After I had done, I *ventured on the unusual liberty of drawing near the fire*, going round Earnshaw's seat, and kneeling in the corner beside him' (*WH*, p. 158; italics mine).[7] Moreover, it is on the strength of that mood of almost overweening self-sufficiency that, while looking up from the fireplace at Heathcliff, who is himself, significantly, 'leant against the chimney' (*WH*, p. 158), Isabella will become bold enough to taunt and humiliate him both for his physical violence towards Hindley the day before and for his probable maltreatment of Catherine had she been his wife, thereby provoking him into a near-fatal pursuit of her that will end their relationship once and for all.

What we have seen in the foregoing, then, is that fires and fireplaces are practically indispensable in the everyday life of the two northern households portrayed, and that irrespective of times of the year or even weather conditions. The realism of such references is further pronounced by the different ways in which some of the characters disclose their psychology, their moral disposition or their personal circumstances through their relationship with fires and fireplaces. And yet it would appear that a good many such references are also invested with an essentially symbolic or thematic function. This is eminently true of references that are made to Heathcliff's movements towards, his postures at, or his gazing into, fires and fireplaces. For example, on his first visit to the Heights, Lockwood relates that he 'took a seat at the end of the hearthstone opposite that towards which [his] landlord advanced' (*WH*, p. 4). This detail in some sense foreshadows the idea of fireplaces as normal settings for social intercourse in the novel. Yet there is a grimness about the word 'advanced' here, suggestive as it is of the psychological tension Heathcliff has usually manifested in earlier contexts when moving towards, sitting at, or even standing on a hearth.[8] Thus we note that it is while seated in front of the kitchen fire, after his release from the garret, that Heathcliff thinks up ways in which he hopes to wreak vengeance on Hindley. Later, when Heathcliff suspects one afternoon that Catherine has dressed up in preparation for a visit from Edgar Linton, and, since Hindley and Joseph are absent, is therefore disinclined to work any longer, Nelly observes that he '*lounged to the fire*, and sat down' (*WH*, p. 60; italics mine).

Like the words just quoted, others concerning Heathcliff and fireplaces seem symbolically to mark stages in his problematic relationship with Catherine, even beyond her death. For example, after being scolded by the latter in the Grange kitchen for making advances to Isabella, Heathcliff, we are told, 'stood on the hearth, with folded arms, brooding on his evil thoughts' (*WH*, p. 100). Again, momentarily unable to look Catherine in the face at their tryst in Chapter 15, Heathcliff 'walked to the fire-place, where he stood, silent, with his back towards us' (*WH*, p.141).[9] Several years later, when, having come to the Grange to fetch Cathy home, Heathcliff asks Nelly to have Catherine's portrait delivered to the Heights, it is obvious from his elliptical utterance, 'Not because I need it, but

—', that he is by then badly suffering from visual hallucinations of Catherine. Heathcliff's tension at this point is further underlined when he presently 'turned abruptly to the fire' (*WH*, p. 255), words that form a kind of prelude to his long account of his visit to Catherine's grave. That the tension is by no means over at the end of his account is evident from Nelly's following detail: 'Mr Heathcliff paused and wiped his forehead — his hair clung to it, wet with perspiration; *his eyes were fixed on the red embers of the fire*' (*WH*, p. 257; italics mine). Nor is that detail unrelated to the moment when, suddenly reminded of Catherine by the resemblance borne to her separately by Cathy and Hareton, both of whom can, incidentally, be clearly seen because '[t]he red firelight glowed on their two bonny heads, and revealed their faces' (*WH*, p. 286), Heathcliff reacts thus according to Nelly: 'I suppose this resemblance disarmed Mr Heathcliff: he walked to the hearth in evident agitation' (*WH*, p. 287).

Fewer, but no less important, are references to Catherine's approaching or sitting at fireplaces as movements or postures somehow pertinent to her relationship with Heathcliff. We note, for example, that just before her long dialogue with Nelly about Edgar's proposal of marriage and about the distinction she will draw between her love for Edgar and her love for Heathcliff, Catherine is described coming into the Heights kitchen thus: 'She entered and approached the hearth' (*WH*, p. 68). Such a movement is no doubt natural, given that Nelly is supposedly sitting by the fire with baby Hareton in her lap. Yet it can also be understood as symbolically prefiguring the content of the dialogue that is about to take place. Certainly Catherine's distraught mental state is hinted at when, in reaction to Nelly's asking her to give reasons why she loves Edgar, she complains that her interlocutor is 'making a jest of it' and being 'exceedingly ill-natured', at the same time as Nelly describes her at that moment 'scowling, and *turning her face to the fire*' (*WH*, p. 69; italics mine). It is, moreover, at the very same fireplace that, on the morning after the storm, Nelly will find Catherine still seated in damp clothes, presently noting that 'her teeth chattered as she shrunk closer to the almost extinguished embers' (*WH*, p. 77), as if the girl were seeking consolation for the loss of Heathcliff as much as she needs physical comfort. Significant, too, on the occasion of Heathcliff's sudden arrival at the Grange, after a three-year absence from Gimmerton, is Catherine's reaction to Edgar's suggesting that the guest be shown to the kitchen rather than the parlour. Thus having accordingly asked Nelly with no little sardonic humour to set two separate tables in the parlour, one for Edgar and Isabella, 'being gentry', and the other for herself and Heathcliff, 'being of the lower orders', Catherine then asks Edgar: 'Or must I have a fire lighted elsewhere?' (*WH*, p. 84). Although with this snide rhetorical question Catherine implies that going to another room perforce means lighting a fire there, her words are of interest chiefly for symbolically portending the revival of her relationship with Heathcliff. And yet, even as in this context, comments made about Catherine relative to fireplaces practically all pertain to her problematic friendship with Heathcliff. One striking example may be noted when, intent on humiliating Isabella in Heathcliff's presence for her infatuation with him, she 'gaily' welcomes his sudden arrival in the Grange library, at the same time as she is described by Nelly 'pulling a chair to the fire' (*WH*, p. 92). That Catherine will have doubtless rued her careless divulgence of Isabella's talk is suggested by the virulent altercation she soon afterwards has with Heathcliff in the kitchen, at the end of which she warns him of the danger of not leaving Isabella alone. Significant, at this point, then, is Nelly's following observation: 'The conversation ceased — Mrs Linton sat down by the fire, flushed and gloomy' (*WH*, p. 100).

It is interesting to note one particular reference to fire made at a climactic moment in Catherine's dilemma between her two men.

Thus, shortly after Edgar has ordered Heathcliff to leave the Grange, Catherine locks the kitchen door so as to prevent the latter's being evicted by some menservants, and then foils Edgar's attempt to wrest the key from her grasp by flinging it 'into the hottest part of the fire' (*WH*, p. 102). Here fire as a destructive force seems as symbolically apt in this episode as Heathcliff's presently making his timely escape by smashing the kitchen-door lock with a fireside appurtenance, namely, a poker. Appropriately symbolic, too, of problematic love, though in a quite different way, is Isabella's own use of a poker when, in her mixed feelings about Heathcliff, she tries to destroy her wedding ring, first by smashing it with one and then by dropping 'the misused article among the coals' (*WH*, p. 151) of the Grange parlour fireplace. But perhaps the most memorable instance of the destructiveness of fire as symbolic of problematic love or, as in this case, of frustrated love, happens when, humiliated for his illiteracy by the young woman to whom he is already attached, Hareton hurls 'on the [house] fire' (*WH*, p. 268) the books by which he has been teaching himself to read. Nor should we overlook the relevance of a like symbolism in Nelly's burning of the love letters that Cathy has received from Linton Heathcliff.

What is, however, striking about the acts of burning referred to above is that some of them are performed by those in a frame of mind that seems more or less bordering on insanity. This is perhaps hardly surprising when we reflect that the figurative language in the novel entailing the nature and effects of fire is sometimes resorted to by one or two characters in an extreme emotional state. Consider, for example, Catherine's utterances both just before and during her delirium, later to be diagnosed as 'a brain fever' (*WH*, p. 118). Thus, having gone up to the parlour immediately after the showdown between Heathcliff and Edgar in the Grange kitchen, and amid much rambling talk, Catherine says this to Nelly about the latter: 'To this point he has been discreet in dreading to provoke me; you must represent the peril of quitting that policy, and remind him of my passionate temper, verging, *when kindled*, on frenzy —' (*WH*, p. 104; italics mine). Again, after telling Nelly of her subsequent blackout and, on awakening from it, of her painful realization of her present situation in life, she suddenly says: 'Oh, *I'm burning*! I wish I were out of doors —' (*WH*, p. 111; italics mine). Of like interest here is Nelly's recourse to fire in descriptions of Catherine's delirious talk and behaviour at this time. Thus at one point Nelly says: '[…] our *fiery* Catherine was no better than a wailing child!' (*WH*, p. 110; italics mine). Similarly, while vituperating Nelly for sneaking on her to Edgar about her conduct in the past several minutes, Catherine is described as follows: 'A maniac's fury *kindled* under her brows' (*WH*, p. 114; italics mine). Nor without relevance here are Nelly's references to Heathcliff's eyes after his return to Gimmerton. For example, part of his physical appearance as depicted at the Grange on his unexpected arrival there includes these details: 'A half-civilized ferocity lurked yet in the depressed brows and eyes *full of black fire*' (*WH*, p. 84f; italics mine). Nelly also notes Heathcliff's shocked reaction to the sight of Catherine's facial appearance soon after he has arrived in her bedroom for the tryst in Chapter 15: 'And now he stared at her so earnestly that I thought the very intensity of his gaze would bring tears into his eyes; but they *burned with anguish*, they did not melt' (*WH*, p. 139; italics mine).[10]

That Heathcliff's association with fire is, symbolically speaking, almost invariably negative is corroborated by references to candles and candlelight as made in contexts involving his physical presence or bespeaking his influence on events. Consider, for instance, how in her bewilderment at Heathcliff's sudden appearance at the Grange after his three-year absence, Nelly at first hesitates to announce his arrival to Catherine and Edgar, until, in the end, she 'resolved on making an excuse to ask if they would have the candles lighted' before opening the parlour door. Nelly's quandary is momentarily worsened by the fact that she nevertheless 'shrank reluctantly from performing [her] errand' and that she was 'actually going away, leaving [the announcement] unsaid, after having put [her] question about the candles' (*WH*, p. 83). Again, consider the reference made to candlelight (and to fire) by Isabella one night at the Heights as an eerie portent both for Hindley's imminent disclosure to her of his plan to kill Heathcliff and for the subsequent fight between both men: 'There was no sound through the house but the moaning wind which shook the windows every now and then, the faint crackling of the coals, *and the click of my snuffers as I removed at intervals the long wick of the candle*' (*WH*, p. 154; italics mine). No less interesting here is Nelly's recalling that, having already put Linton Heathcliff to bed on the night of his arrival at the Grange, she 'had come down, and was standing by the table in the hall, *lighting a bed-room candle for Mr Edgar*' (*WH*, p. 178; italics mine) when a maid announces the unexpected advent of Joseph, who has been sent by Heathcliff to take the boy with him back to the Heights. Also symbolically portentous of Heathcliff's appearance at the Grange to fetch Cathy home to the Heights is Nelly's following detail about the moon shining into the library: '*We had not yet lighted a candle*, but all the apartment was visible, even to the portraits [of Catherine and Edgar] on the wall' (*WH*, p. 253; italics mine).

More obviously symbolic, on the other hand, are references to candlelight in descriptions of Heathcliff's personal appearance and demeanour. Take, for example, the sentence with which Nelly prefaces her detailed depiction of Heathcliff's physicality as observed by her in the Grange parlour in Chapter 10: '*Now fully revealed by the fire and candlelight*, I was amazed, more than ever, to behold the transformation of Heathcliff' (*WH*, p. 84; italics mine). Significant, too, it seems, are several references to candlelight and fire in Heathcliff's pathetic dependency on these two sources of heat and light during the last few days of his life. Especially memorable among such references is one whereby, in timid reaction to Heathcliff's grim facial appearance, Nelly accidentally lets the candle she has just brought in to him 'bend towards the wall' (*WH*, p. 293), thereby extinguishing it. Such a curious detail is somewhat redolent of Heathcliff's own behaviour in Chapter 3, in so far as, having been aroused by Lockwood's scream, he enters the oak-panelled room '*with a candle dripping over his fingers*, and his face as white as the wall behind him' (*WH*, p. 21; italics mine), and is presently observed by Lockwood '*setting the candle on a chair*, because he found it impossible to hold it steady' (*WH*, p. 22; italics mine). Tragically revelatory as they are of Heathcliff's acute mental disorder, both details also have their comical counterparts in Lockwood's own problems with candles. We see this first at the moment he discovers that the candle by which he has been able to read texts whose content will have partly determined his two nightmares has 'roasted' (*WH*, p. 15) a calf-skin book cover; and then again when, having groped his way downstairs in the dark, he reaches the back-kitchen, from whose 'gleam of fire' he manages to 'rekindle [his] candle', which, given to him by Heathcliff, has been blown out upstairs by 'the snow and wind' (*WH*, p. 24).[11]

As we have seen in the foregoing, a good many references made to fire in its various forms and manifestations have largely negative implications in *Wuthering Heights*, notably when they are considered from a symbolic perspective. Such an aesthetic treatment of fire is to some extent comprehensible enough when we are reminded now and again in the narrative of the hazards and dangers of fire to persons and property alike.[12] Yet as in accordance with the principle of contrast inherent in the structure of her novel, Emily also makes references to fires and fireplaces that have utterly affirmative, not to say lyrical, connotations. This is especially true of Nelly's account of Cathy's relationship with Hareton. We note, for instance, that after her long search for Cathy (in Chapter 18), Nelly finds her at the Heights '*seated on the hearth*' where, with 'her hat [...] hung against the wall', she 'seemed perfectly at home, laughing and chattering, in the best spirits imaginable, to Hareton, now a grand, strong lad of eighteen' (*WH*, p. 170f; italics mine). And though, as we saw above, Cathy will shortly afterwards find herself in conflict with Hareton, and will remain in conflict with him for some time to come, the passage just quoted already prefigures in somewhat poetic fashion a happy ending for both of them. Noteworthy among episodes leading up to that happy ending are those in which they are observed at varying distances from each other in relation to a fireplace. Thus after having spent several days in a cold garret in the wake of Linton Heathcliff's death, and, prompted by Heathcliff's absence from the Heights, having now come down to 'the house', Cathy is invited by Hareton to 'come to the settle, and sit close by the fire', for he 'was sure she was starved [frozen]' (*WH*, p. 262). Instead of accepting such a thoughtful offer, however, Cathy gets 'a chair for herself' and places it 'at a distance' (*WH*, p. 262) from Hareton and Zillah. But though, after Nelly's return to the Heights as Heathcliff's housekeeper, Cathy is in a good position to maintain her detachment from Hareton through being allowed to use the parlour as a sitting-room, she soon prefers to be in the kitchen where, like Hareton himself, she finds herself disposed, even compelled, to live out her everyday life. Moreover, it is, ironically enough, the more or less forced proximity of the cousins to each other in the Heights kitchen, and not, say, the unrestricted freedom offered by natural surroundings outside, that helps to bring about their eventual reconciliation. At the same time, it is above all at the kitchen fireside where, despite Hareton's dogged resistance to Cathy's blandishments at first, and amid her nervous movements to and from that same hearth, that the cousins will renew their friendship, just as it is 'upon the chimney-piece' (*WH*, p. 280) that Cathy will leave the book which Hareton has unwrapped as a gift from her only a few moments earlier.

We have seen, then, some of the principal ways in which the author enhances both the realism and the symbolism in *Wuthering Heights* through her sundry references or allusions to fire. We have also seen that, far from being mere aspects of 'local colour' arbitrarily placed here and there in the text, such references practically always serve some thematic function. This is no less true when the references seem purely incidental. Thus when in Chapter 7 Nelly Dean tells of 'making the house and kitchen cheerful with great fires befitting Christmas eve' (*WH*, p. 48), or when on entering the Heights kitchen with Cathy at the beginning of Chapter 25, she notices that Joseph 'seemed sitting in a sort of elysium alone, beside a roaring fire' (*WH*, p. 208), it should be obvious, if only in retrospect, that both statements are meant to have some ironic pertinence to Heathcliff's presentation or situation at the time they are each made. Even references to something as mundane as pipe-smoking, however minor they might appear to the reader, seem to have a particular thematic significance. For example, whereas, on the one hand, pipe-smoking seems symbolically to bespeak the gloomy atmosphere of the Heights under Heathcliff's dominance, it seems, on the other hand, to betoken a new and happier era for both households when, on his return to Gimmerton in September 1802, Lockwood observes that an old woman, presently to be identified as the person keeping house at the Grange, 'reclined on the horse-steps, smoking a meditative pipe' (*WH*, p. 272). It is this sort of detail about a seemingly casual aspect of fire which, all too easily overlooked in our concern with the famous love story, helps to make us aware of the consummate art with which, word by word, Emily Brontë constructed her masterpiece. If, however, there still remain things to be said about our chosen topic, then perhaps a start might be made with the contention that, notwithstanding popular notions about the setting of *Wuthering Heights* as sustained in part by reproductions of paintings or photographs of landscapes on the covers of its paperback editions, the most important phases of the action take place much less often on the Yorkshire moors than within the four walls of a fire-lit room.

Brontë Studies, 38/2 (2013)

Notes

1 Although some Brontë scholars have now and again remarked on Emily's treatment of fire in *Wuthering Heights*, no detailed study has, to my knowledge, been published on this topic hitherto.

2 For quotations from the novel, see Emily Brontë, *Wuthering Heights*, ed. by Ian Jack and Helen Small (Oxford: Oxford University Press, 2009); hereafter *WH*. For the sake of convenience, the first Catherine will be referred to as 'Catherine', the second as 'Cathy'.

3 See *Wuthering Heights*, pp. 7, 11, 30, 54.

4 See *Wuthering Heights*, pp. 24, 208, 221, 277, 283, 299. The importance of fires in everyday life is tellingly corroborated by Isabella's following allusion to Hareton on her arrival at the Heights as Heathcliff's bride: 'By the fire stood a ruffianly child, strong in limb and dirty in garb' (*WH*, p. 121).

5 This reference is ironically foreshadowed in Nelly Dean's account of Mr Earnshaw's physical decline, whereby she recalls that 'when he was confined to the chimney-corner he grew grievously irritable' (*WH*, p. 35). It is, incidentally, 'by the fire-side' that Mr Earnshaw 'died quietly in his chair one October evening' (*WH*, p. 37).

6 For other references to Linton Heathcliff's proximity to fireplaces, see *Wuthering Heights*, pp. 190, 194, 212, 218, 223.

7 For other links between Isabella and fireplaces, see *Wuthering Heights*, p. 150f.

8   Consider, for example, the similarity borne to that sentence by the one used by Nelly in Chapter 29, just after Heathcliff has unexpectedly turned up in the Grange library to fetch Cathy back to the Heights: 'Heathcliff advanced to the hearth' (*WH*, p. 253). Of like interest here is Nelly's recalling an earlier occasion when, having locked Cathy and herself in the Heights, Heathcliff 'approached the fire, where my mistress and I stood silent' (*WH*, p. 241).

9   This detail is somewhat foreshadowed when, on the morning after his night in the oak-panelled room, Lockwood notices, on entering 'the house', that Heathcliff 'stood by the fire, his back towards me, just finishing a stormy scene to poor Zillah' (*WH*, p. 25).

10 Interesting by way of contrast is the affirmatively metaphorical use of 'sparkle' and its cognates with respect to both Catherine and Isabella. See *Wuthering Heights*, pp. 40, 44, 182, 190.

11 The negative symbolism of candlelight (including lanterns) is manifest chiefly in contexts of hostility, dissipation, mental illness, and even death. See *Wuthering Heights*, pp. 21, 37, 41, 44, 92, 109, 111, 120.

12 For references to such hazards and dangers, see *Wuthering Heights*, pp. 65, 67, 81, 153, 241, 274.

Weather in *Wuthering Heights*

Readers coming to *Wuthering Heights* for the first time are hardly likely to know the meaning of the epithet in its title until Lockwood has defined it shortly after starting his diary in Chapter 1. And no doubt, once defined, the word 'wuthering', which Lockwood designates 'a significant provincial adjective' and which he illustrates by referring to the 'atmospheric tumult' that the building and its grounds are subjected to in 'stormy weather' (*WH*, p. 2), gives some readers the impression that they are about to peruse some Gothic novel.[1] Such an impression will, however, soon prove to have been quite as mistaken as, say, the idea now and then indirectly promoted by cinema and television adaptations of the book, namely, that nature in Emily Brontë's novel is made up almost entirely of the Yorkshire moors. And though the term 'wuthering' may seem appropriate enough to those readers who assume northern weather to be predominantly bleak, it needs to be emphasized at the outset that the actions and events of the narrative occur in all kinds of weather, ranging from the bitterest cold to the intensest heat. It is also necessary to stress that, as in every temperate climate, weather in northern England is in no small measure contingent upon, even determined by, the seasons, all four of which play their part in the novel. Especially interesting in this respect are references to summer and winter, sometimes in sentences where the sharp contrast between those two seasons is implicit.[2] But whatever may be said about weather in *Wuthering Heights* from a purely meteorological viewpoint, my main concern here will be to show some of the ways in which Emily's treatment of weather is integral to her novel as a work of art.[3]

Let me, first of all, consider how far Lockwood's presentation is determined by the comments he makes about weather and seasons during his two sojourns in Yorkshire. As someone supposedly accustomed to the generally milder climate in southern England, Lockwood is, as has been suggested above, perhaps inevitably inclined while visiting the north to make some note or other about local weather, and the more so as it affects his movements or excursions. Thus, for example, sentences such as 'Yesterday afternoon set in misty and cold' (*WH*, p. 6) and 'Yesterday was bright, calm, and frosty' (*WH*, p. 265) are evidently written as reasons as to whether he should go out or stay indoors. Sometimes, too, Lockwood will make a matter-of-fact reference to a season, as, for example, when, having taken a diversion on his walk back to Thrushcross Grange from the Heights during his final visit to Gimmerton in order to give the 'kirk' one last look, and then noticed its slates jutting off 'beyond the right line of the roof', he confidently deduces that they will be 'gradually worked off in coming autumn storms' (*WH*, p. 300). Nevertheless, despite the meteorological knowledge he amply displays already in Chapter 1, Lockwood is soon made to feel a kind of greenhorn as regards northern weather and seasons when, on his second visit to the Heights, he is sardonically rebuffed by Heathcliff for fearing that, thanks to the snow he can see falling outside, he will be 'weather-bound' for but 'half an hour' (*WH*, p. 8). And though as a southerner Lockwood can hardly have been expected to allow for the snowstorm about to afflict Gimmerton already before winter has officially set in, his presumptuousness about the duration of the snowfall may be understood as being essential to his portrayal as a somewhat pretentious dilettante who, as may be gathered from his strained conversation with Heathcliff during the evening meal in Chapter 2, is much given to drawing hasty conclusions from questionable premisses.

More interesting perhaps are the ways in which Lockwood shows himself to be physically affected by weather and seasons. Thus in Chapter 2 we surmise how much he feels the cold when, in an attempt to engage Cathy in conversation with him in 'the house', he 'drew closer to the hearth, repeating [his] comment on the wildness of the evening' (*WH*, p. 7). A similarly 'normal' reaction is registered in the apparent glee with which, after a long period of illness amid cold weather, he records this detail in his diary at the beginning of Chapter 15: 'Another week over — and I am so many days nearer health, and spring!' (*WH*, p. 137). And yet there are times when Lockwood seems unduly fastidious about wintry conditions, as, for example, when, in spite of being adequately shielded from them in his sick bed, he laments thus about them at the beginning of Chapter 10: 'Oh, these bleak winds and bitter, northern skies, and impassable roads [...]!' (*WH*, p. 80); or when, at the end of Chapter 30, he asserts that he 'would not pass another winter here, for much' (*WH*, p. 264). In view of such sentiments, it is not surprising that, when referring to benign or bracing weather, he should imply how important such weather is for his sense of well-being. This is suggested when, for example, he prefaces the story of his encounter with a beautiful young woman with the words '[w]hile enjoying a month of fine weather at the sea-coast' (*WH*, p. 3); or when, in the wake of his uncomfortable night at the Heights and of the tension in 'the house' the following morning, he recalls that 'at the first gleam of dawn, [he] took an opportunity of escaping into the free air, now clear, and still, and cold as impalpable ice' (*WH*, p. 26). It is, however, not until his second visit to Gimmerton in September 1802 that Lockwood finds himself walking amid weather the very opposite of what he had to put up with about a year earlier; a conjuncture that doubtless explains the detail with which he writes about it in his diary as follows: 'It was sweet, warm weather — too warm for travelling; but the heat did not hinder me from enjoying the delightful scenery above and below; had I seen it nearer August, I'm sure it would have tempted me to waste a month among its solitudes' (*WH*, p. 271). What is striking about this passage is its suggesting the idea of Lockwood as someone who, sensitive to extreme heat as much as he is to extreme cold, comes across to the reader as the leisured aesthete par excellence, and who as such reminds one of those well-to-do early Romantics that were drawn much like him to an outdoor life amid nature in fine weather.

It is, then, easy to understand why, amid his preoccupation with weather, not to mention his strong cultural background and his excellent command of English, Lockwood should now and again resort to meteorological metaphors in the first four chapters — 'cloud', 'storm', 'stormy' and 'tempest', words that he uses negatively with respect to his conflict with the dogs, the tense atmosphere during high tea, Hareton's anger towards him, and Heathcliff's scolding of Zillah.[4] Especially interesting about such metaphors is the degree to which, not unlike his richly figurative language in general, they each bespeak Lockwood's tendency to gloss over unpleasant realities; or, in other words, to avoid calling a spade a spade.[5] More varied, on the other hand, is Nelly Dean's own recourse to meteorological metaphors, reflecting as they probably do her memories of all manner of weather patterns she has experienced over the years. Take, for example, her figurative uses of 'cloud' and its cognate forms, a term to which she invariably attaches a pejorative meaning.[6] Thus, when alluding to Cathy's educational influence on Hareton, Nelly recalls this about the latter: 'His honest, warm, and intelligent nature shook off rapidly the clouds of ignorance and degradation in which it had been bred' (*WH*, p. 286). However, when describing agreeable human situations, Nelly makes appropriate use of references to sunshine. Here, for example, is a passage about the benefits to the Grange household of Catherine's reconciliation with Edgar on the day after their disaccord over the newly-returned Heathcliff: '[S]he rewarded him with such a summer of sweetness and affection [...] as made the house a paradise for several days; both master and servants profiting from the perpetual sunshine' (*WH*, p. 88). Another example is Nelly's summary account of young Cathy's wholesome influence on the same household some years later: 'She was the most winning thing that ever brought sunshine into a desolate house' (*WH*, p. 167).[7]

Such images forcibly remind us of Nelly's affirmative comments about sunshine which, in real life, she tends to associate with summer, as we see exemplified when, referring to the guide-post where she and Hindley used to play some twenty years earlier, she recalls that '[t]he sun shone yellow on its grey head, reminding me of summer' (*WH*, p. 96).[8] That Nelly is also quite conscious of the beneficial effects of the sun is apparent when, having been instructed by Edgar to set 'an easy-chair in the sunshine by the [parlour] window' for his convalescent wife, she recalls the latter sitting 'a long while enjoying *the genial heat*' (*WH*, p. 119; italics mine); and, later, when at her first reunion with Linton Heathcliff at the Heights, Nelly notices that his eye and complexion are 'brighter than [she] remembered them, though with merely temporary lustre borrowed from the salubrious air and *genial sun*' (*WH*, p. 190; italics mine). These affirmative references to the sun may in turn explain Nelly's acute awareness of bad weather and its dangers to human health, as is plainly suggested when she tries in vain to discourage a delirious Catherine from opening her bedroom window because, as she recollects, they were 'in the middle of winter' and 'the wind blew strong from the north-east' (*WH*, p. 108); or, again, when she later advises Heathcliff a few days before his death against his nocturnal walks in April, adding that 'it is not wise, at any rate, this moist season' (*WH*, p. 291). The interest of such details derives for us not a little from their underlining Nelly's presentation as an utterly conventional and fastidiously practical person, yet one who, notwithstanding her worthy concern for the health of her social superiors or her usefulness to them through her ability to read clouds, seems at times to be all too judgemental and opinionated about weather to the point where she betrays a quite egotistical disregard for other people's feelings.[9] This may be seen more particularly in contexts where she is expressing her delight in fine weather.

Consider, for example, how in the account of the morning after Heathcliff's disappearance Nelly seems somewhat indifferent to a rain-drenched Catherine's plight when, having noticed 'by the sunbeams piercing the chinks of the shutters, Miss Catherine still seated near the fire-place', she goes on to say this: 'The morning was fresh and cool; I threw back the lattice, and presently the room filled with the sweet scents from the garden', only to hear Catherine 'peevishly' calling to her to 'shut the window' (*WH*, p. 76) because she is 'starving', i.e. very cold. Such unconcern on Nelly's part can also be sensed when, on the very morning after Linton Heathcliff's arrival at the Grange from the south she is due to take him to the Heights, she finds the boy recalcitrant enough for her to fall back on this fallacious comparison in order to get him out of bed: 'An early ride on *such a beautiful morning* is much preferable to an hour's more sleep' (*WH*, p. 180; italics mine). That fair weather sometimes even distracts Nelly from the tragic implications of a particular human situation is evident enough from her description of Catherine on the day after her death: 'Next morning — bright and cheerful out of doors — stole softened in through the blinds of the silent room, and suffused the couch and its occupant with a mellow, tender glow' (*WH*, p. 145). For alive as Nelly then is to the 'exhausted anguish' of Edgar's facial features as he lies beside his deceased wife, the reader cannot but feel that there is something slightly tasteless about Nelly's evident enjoyment of the 'bright and cheerful' weather outside. Furthermore, Nelly's mentioning shortly afterwards, on discovering that Edgar has fallen asleep on that bed, that she 'ventured soon after sunrise to quit the room and steal out to the pure, refreshing air' (*WH*, p. 146) would suggest how short-winded she is when involved in a woeful state of affairs. Certainly, good weather can so enthuse Nelly as to make her momentarily quite unmindful of those less fortunate in health than her. One memorable example of this may be noted when, alluding to Cathy's second 'official' meeting with Linton Heathcliff, she says: 'We deferred our excursion till the afternoon; a golden afternoon of August — every breath from the hills so full of life, that it seemed whoever respired it, though dying, might revive' (*WH*, p. 234). Such words prove to have been ironically sentimental in retrospect, chiefly because Nelly seems at this stage to have forgotten that Edgar, though himself among the dying, would not after all revive.

If Nelly's delight in warm weather sometimes seems untimely or out of place, it might nevertheless be excused to some extent for being at worst one of the few pleasures available to her in her austere mode of life. The same, however, can scarcely be said of those contexts where an affirmative reference to weather is clearly intended to distract her momentarily from the enormity of her disloyalty to Edgar. Consider, for instance, the quasi-idyllic atmosphere Nelly evokes one Sunday morning just after describing a moribund-looking Catherine sitting at her bedroom window and just before giving her Heathcliff's note: 'A book lay spread on the sill before her, and the scarcely perceptible wind fluttered its leaves at intervals' (*WH*, p. 138). On that same Sunday, moreover, while Edgar is attending church, Nelly relates that, though they 'generally made a practice of locking the doors during the hours of service', the weather was 'so warm and pleasant that [she] set them wide open' (*WH*, p. 137). Yet the more important reason for opening the doors is, of course, that she is expecting Heathcliff's arrival at the Grange at any moment. Noteworthy, too, is that while witnessing Heathcliff's tryst with Catherine, Nelly makes two seemingly gratuitous references to the sun. The first occurs when she realises that the church service is over: 'I could distinguish, *by the shine of the westering sun up the valley*, a concourse thickening outside Gimmerton chapel porch' (*WH*, p. 142; italics mine). The second reference, which is made shortly afterwards, seems intended, as it were, to shield her briefly from the thought of the possibly dire consequences for her of Edgar's likely encounter with Heathcliff. Thus not far behind the servants passing towards the kitchen wing is Edgar, who, as Nelly observes, 'opened the gate himself, and sauntered slowly up, *probably enjoying the lovely afternoon that breathed as soft as summer*' (*WH*, p. 142f.; italics mine). Such references can be said to be thematically linked with other contexts where sunny weather, welcome though it usually is to Nelly, forms an ironic background to a fateful incident or episode, whether it be the 'fine summer morning' (*WH*, p. 30) when Mr Earnshaw sets out on his sixty-mile walk to Liverpool; or 'the July sun' (*WH*, p. 169) shining on the morning Cathy illicitly rides off to Penistone Craggs and discovers Wuthering Heights for the first time; or the occasion when, having perceived the main sitting-room at the Heights to be 'filled with sunshine' (*WH*, p. 247) after her release from her five-day imprisonment in Zillah's room, Nelly presently finds herself pleading in vain with Linton Heathcliff to be kind to his new wife Cathy.

At this juncture it is perhaps worth noting that, unlike Lockwood's comments on weather, almost all of which have to do with observations he has made only a day or two beforehand, Nelly's references to weather are usually based on memories of happenings dating back several years earlier. How far her memory of particular weather has been determined by a particular episode or event amid such weather, or vice versa, is probably impossible to ascertain. Indeed, we might ask in vain why it is that Nelly remembers that Heathcliff's unexpected return to the Grange after a three-year absence happened '[o]n a mellow evening in September' (*WH*, p. 81); that Isabella's sudden appearance in the Grange parlour after her snowbound flight from the Heights occurred as she (Nelly) was sitting there with baby Cathy on her knee, 'watching […] the still driving flakes build up the uncurtained window' (*WH*, p. 150); or that she caught Cathy returning from an illicit visit to her cousin Linton on the night 'a sprinkling of snow covered the ground' (*WH*, p. 216). No doubt, the memory of a particular kind of weather is easy to sustain if it has a strongly personal significance, as, for example, when Nelly recalls that, despite deeming futile Joseph's ordering her to run to Gimmerton 'for the doctor and the parson' in the wake of Mr Earnshaw's sudden death, she nevertheless did so, as she says, 'through wind and rain' (*WH*, p. 38); or when she prefaces her memory of being Edgar's confidante on the occasion he tenderly expressed his thoughts about his late wife and about his daughter Cathy with this detail: 'It was a misty afternoon, but the February sun shone dimly' (*WH*, p. 226); or when she remembers the weather on the day she set out on horseback with Cathy for the latter's first 'official' meeting with Linton Heathcliff: 'It was a close, sultry day; devoid of sunshine, but with a sky too dappled and hazy to threaten rain' (*WH*, p. 230).

It is, however, Nelly's extraordinarily detailed description of the sudden change in the weather on the evening of Catherine's funeral which, perhaps more than any other weather reference, seems to bespeak an unwonted intensity of emotion in Nelly such as to suggest that she may still be feeling uneasy about having herself contributed to her mistress's untimely death. Thus, after recalling that 'the wind shifted from south to north east and brought rain first, and then sleet and snow', Nelly continues as follows: 'On the morrow one could hardly imagine that there had been three weeks of summer: the primroses and the crocuses were hidden under wintry drifts: the larks were silent, and the young leaves of the early trees smitten and blackened — And dreary, and chill, and dismal that morrow did creep over!' (*WH*, p. 150). That Nelly's memory of weathers may not, however, be altogether reliable is to some extent suggested by her words 'three weeks of summer', for, as is obvious, what she really means here is that there was continual sunshine during the last three weeks of winter, that is, the winter of 1783/84. Similarly, when by way of alluding to the account she has just given of Cathy's illicit visits to her cousin Linton, she says this to Lockwood: 'These things happened last winter, sir, […] hardly more than a year ago' (*WH*, p. 226), apparently unaware that 'these things' actually happened in the autumn. Nevertheless, it might be asserted that Nelly's occasional confusion between weather and seasons serves but to confirm the remarkable realism of Emily Brontë's treatment of the elements in much the same way as does Nelly's very plausible memory of the calm, sunny morning which, as so often happens, followed the terrible storm that had raged over the Heights the night before.

Yet for all that Emily makes use of weather in order to characterize her two principal narrators, it is none the less necessary here to point up some of the ways in which she also lets weather play its part in the structure of her novel. For example, Lockwood's unpleasant experiences of snow and wind in Chapter 3, whether undergone within the Heights, or on his walk back to the Grange, or even in his two dreams, may be understood as being partly intended not only to adumbrate Isabella's account (in Chapter 13) of the wintry conditions prevailing at the Heights during her brief sojourn there as a hapless bride, as well as her account (in Chapter 17) of her own snowbound return to the Grange, but to serve as a brilliant means of foreshadowing Catherine's presentation as a fundamentally tragic figure. We also note how weather can have a certain influence on the plot. Thus we may reflect whether Cathy's first meeting with Hareton at the Heights would have happened had she not been prompted, as she appears to have been, by the hot weather one July morning to ride off on her illicit excursion to Penistone Craggs in the first place. That bad weather, too, can affect the plot is evident not only when Catherine is stricken with a delirious fever by dint of spending the night in rain-drenched clothes, but when, thanks to nursing the latter during her convalescence at the Grange, Mrs Linton brings about her own death and that of her husband. Again, it is owing to the 'rainy night' referred to at the beginning of Chapter 23 that Nelly gets her feet 'thoroughly wetted' on her walk to the Heights with Cathy the following morning, just as it is chiefly through sitting there 'such a while' in 'soaked shoes and stockings' (*WH*, p. 214) that Nelly is 'laid up' for three weeks, thereby enabling Cathy to pay illicit visits to her cousin Linton. Finally, it is without doubt the bad cold Lockwood catches as a consequence of his wintry journey back to the Grange that renders this somewhat restless man immobile enough for him to be disposed to hear most of 'Heathcliff's history' on and off during the time he is confined to study or bedroom.

But if, as we have just seen, bad weather can deter the movements of the characters and, as we may further see, when, for example, on Cathy's seventeenth birthday, Edgar 'did not visit the churchyard [to see Catherine's grave]: it was raining' (*WH*, p. 227), there are occasions when such weather is by no means a deterrent to outdoor activity, as on the Sunday evening Catherine and Heathcliff pay their delinquent visit to the Grange, or, again, when on the night of Heathcliff's disappearance Nelly cherishes the mistaken assumption that 'the approaching rain would be certain to bring him home without further trouble' (*WH*, p. 75). The idea that rain is normally a good reason for not venturing abroad is, however, cunningly exploited by Catherine as one way of propitiating a suspicious Heathcliff on the afternoon she is expecting Edgar Linton to visit her at the Heights. Thus when, on seeing her wearing a 'silk frock', Heathcliff has asked her if she is 'going anywhere', she replies: 'No, it is raining' (*WH*, p. 60). Such an answer is, of course, a prevarication much like the one with which she will soon afterwards seek to placate him further: 'Isabella and Edgar Linton talked of calling this afternoon. [...] As it rains, I hardly expect them' (*WH*, p. 61). A like example of deceit may be sensed, albeit in retrospect, in the play-acting by which, at his first 'official' meeting with Cathy on the heath, Linton Heathcliff hopes eventually to lure her into the Heights for their fateful union in marriage, when, having already told her that 'it's too hot for walking', he presently adds that 'it is the heavy weather and heat that make [him] dull' (*WH*, p. 231).

Yet over and above Emily Brontë's uses of weather for structural purposes, the question perhaps inevitably arises as to how far and in what ways weather is also meant to serve some sort of symbolic function. Thus it might be said, for example, that Lockwood's detailed account of the snowstorm in Chapters 2 and 3 is partly intended to underline symbolically the low morale of the Heights household under Heathcliff's rigid jurisdiction. Again, it would be hard to deny that, like some of her predecessors in the epic genre since time immemorial, Emily makes use of weather here and there in order to draw our attention to a significant moment in the portrayal of her characters. Among notable examples may be mentioned Nelly's reference to 'the westering sun' (*WH*, p. 142) as a portent for Catherine's imminent death, or Lockwood's noting, on his walk to the Heights, 'a beamless, amber light along the west' (*WH*, p. 272) shortly before he is to learn of Heathcliff's demise. In some contexts the symbolism may seem all too obvious, not to say ingenuous. Take, for example, Nelly's account of the weather immediately after she has told Lockwood that Mr Earnshaw 'died quietly in his chair one October evening, seated by the fire-side'. Thus she recalls: 'A high wind blustered round the house, and roared in the chimney: it sounded wild and stormy, yet it was not cold' (*WH*, p. 37). We might, then, consider whether this quite realistic meteorological detail is a mere coincidence or is meant to represent a certain attitude on the part of nature, not unlike that which might be also ascribed to it through the violent storm that breaks out over the Heights on the night of Heathcliff's flight. Interestingly enough, Joseph and Nelly both go so far as to regard that storm as a kind of judgement on their household, thereby suggesting that some such interpretations of overwhelming acts of nature are partly rooted in superstition. Still, the reader might well wonder whether or not the violent storm is meant to be a symbolic expression of sympathy with Heathcliff. Whatever the answer to that question, it may not be entirely fortuitous that rainy weather goes hand in hand with other important stages of Heathcliff's presentation. Thus as well as the rainy night on which he pays an illicit visit to the Grange with Catherine, we may point to the rain that 'began to drive through the moaning branches of the trees' (*WH*, p. 206) just after his second fateful encounter with Cathy outside Thrushcross park; to 'the rain driving straight in' (*WH*, p. 298) in his bedroom on the morning he is found dead; and to the fact that, 'on every rainy night since [Heathcliff's] death', Joseph affirms that he has seen 'two on 'em' from his 'chamber window' (*WH*, p. 299), presumably the ghosts of Heathcliff and Catherine.

To what extent the aforementioned references to rain, or indeed any references to weather, have a symbolic meaning may be thought ultimately a matter for readers to decide. No doubt, some readers might be disposed, as earlier readers have been, to interpret weather symbolism as a device whereby Emily Brontë seems to be indirectly expressing her views on, say, a particular character or a particular human situation. Such an interpretative approach might be adjudged by other readers to be unduly bold, if only because they believe the author to be completely hidden behind her text. At the same time, it might even be asked by more practical-minded readers whether references to weather are necessary in a work of fiction unless they have a more or less direct effect on the movements or actions of the characters. Yet though, as has been suggested above, Emily goes well beyond fulfilling such a basic requirement, it is evident that she does not make use of weather as extensively or, for that matter, as liberally as some of her contemporaries may be seen to have done, notably her sister Charlotte.[10] Certainly, apart from, say, the violent storm overwhelming the Heights in Chapter 9 or the lyrical comments on spring wind and sunshine uttered in Edgar's conversation with a convalescent Catherine at the beginning of Chapter 13, or Nelly's elaborate description of the change of weather on the evening of Catherine's funeral in Chapter 17, Emily's references to weather can otherwise scarcely be said to leap to the eye. Be that as it may, what matters most about *Wuthering Heights* on that head is the essential realism of Emily's treatment of weather, manifest as such realism is both in the variety of weathers depicted here, usually with a seeming touch of meteorological authenticity, and in the contradictions and incongruities she shows us to exist between weather and seasons in a northern climate. Finally, in view of my primary concern with the aesthetic scope of my chosen topic, mention should be made not only of the dexterity with which Emily Brontë enlightens us further about some of her characters through her ingenious uses of weather, but of the admirable economy with which she has, whether structurally or thematically, integrated all such uses into the fabric of her masterpiece.

Brontë Studies, 41/1 (2016)

Notes

1   For quotations from the novel, see Emily Brontë, *Wuthering Heights*, ed. by Ian Jack and Patsy Stoneman (Oxford: Oxford University Press, 1998); hereafter *WH*. For the sake of convenience, the elder Catherine will be referred to as 'Catherine', the younger as 'Cathy'.

2   For similar contrasts, see *Wuthering Heights*, p. 168, 227.

3   Although no published monograph has, to my knowledge, yet been entirely devoted to weather in *Wuthering Heights*, discussions of varying length and quality on this topic may be found in the following essays: Wilson Midgley, 'Sunshine on Haworth Moor', *Brontë Society Transactions*, Vol. 11, no. 5, pt. 60 (1950), 309-326; Jacquetta Hawkes, 'Emily Brontë in the Natural Scene', *Brontë Society Transactions*, Vol. 12, no. 3, pt. 63 (1953), 173-186; Margaret Homans, 'Repression and Sublimation of Nature in *Wuthering Heights*', *PMLA*, 93.1 (1978), 9-19; Steven Vine, 'The Wuther of the Other in *Wuthering Heights*', *Nineteenth-Century Literature*, 49.3 (1994), 339-359; Miho Katayama, 'Longing for the World of Sounds: The Battle of Nature against Civilization in *Wuthering Heights*', *Osaka Literary Review*, 37 (1998), 67-82; Laura Gruber Godfrey, '"That Quiet Earth": Tourism, Cultural Geography, and the Misreading of Landscape in *Wuthering Heights*', *Interdisciplinary Literary Studies*, 12.2 (2011), 1-15. Special mention should also be made here of Rebecca Chesney, 'The Brontë Weather Project 2011-2012', *Brontë Studies*, 39.1 (2014), 14-31 for providing an immensely useful biographical background to the treatment of weather in the novels of the Brontë sisters.

4   The same is true to a much lesser extent of Heathcliff, Catherine and Isabella, all of whom occasionally resort to meteorological

metaphors, though invariably those with negative connotations. See *Wuthering Heights*, pp. 88, 92, 104, 160, 165.

5   See *Wuthering Heights*, pp. 4, 5, 6, 9, 10, 25, 28.

6   For Nelly's other metaphorical uses of 'cloud' and its cognates, see *Wuthering Heights*, pp. 47, 81, 139, 188, 203, 206, 279. Noteworthy, too, are Nelly's metaphorical uses of such words as 'storm' and 'tempest' to mean anger or conflict, and always with respect to Catherine. See *Wuthering Heights*, pp. 48, 115.

7   For Nelly's other metaphorical uses of 'sunshine', see *Wuthering Heights*, pp. 80, 204, 234. Nelly also makes metaphorical use of 'weather' (as a verb) and of 'season'. See *Wuthering Heights*, pp. 78, 81.

8   The idea of summer as *the* season for outdoor activities of all kinds is suggested now and again in the narrative. See *Wuthering Heights*, pp. 82, 203, 218, 228, 234.

9   For allusions to Nelly's weather expertise, see *Wuthering Heights*, pp. 75, 202f, 209.

10 Here I am thinking in particular of *Jane Eyre*, where elaborate descriptions of all kinds of weather serve to enhance the dramatic or psychological interest of many a moment or episode in the narrative.

Gimmerton in
Wuthering Heights

It is interesting to note the prominent role played by Gimmerton in *Wuthering Heights*.[1] As well as being referred to now and again as 'the village', it is also understood to be 'the parish' or 'the neighbourhood'. Gimmerton itself is scarcely described physically other than with fitful mention of its hilly landscapes, its marshy terrain and its moorlands. It is evidently quite extensive in area in that its cottages are often separated from one another by a distance of 'two or three miles' (Brontë 1998, 78). A number of very minor characters mentioned in the narrative may be assumed to be, or to have been, residents there, such as 'the mourners' (Brontë 1998, 39) at Mr Earnshaw's funeral, the midwife 'Dame Archer' (Brontë 1998, 56), Hindley Earnshaw's 'companions' (Brontë 1998, 58, 78), 'a milk-fetcher who came from the village' (Brontë 1998, 198), 'a little herd-boy' (Brontë 1998, 230), the 'old woman' and 'a girl of nine or ten' (Brontë 1998, 271-272) looking after Thrushcross Grange, 'the sexton' (Brontë 1998, 255, 293, 297,

299) and Heathcliff's unnamed housekeeper who, according to Nelly Dean, 'formerly lived at Gimmerton' (Brontë 1998, 170). Gimmerton's special importance in the novel is also suggested when, for example, Nelly details all the musical instruments of the Gimmerton band, which 'go the rounds of all the respectable houses' (Brontë 1998, 52-53) during Christmas, as it is also hinted at when, in order to underline the second Catherine's sheltered childhood at Thrushcross Grange, Nelly tells Lockwood that 'Gimmerton was an unsubstantial name in her ears' (Brontë 1998, 167).[2] The prestige of Gimmerton is also underlined when, in her description of the first Catherine as a youngster, Nelly speaks of her having 'the bonniest eye, the sweetest smile, and lightest foot *in the parish*' (Brontë 1998, 36; italics mine). Catherine herself evokes this prestige when she tells Nelly that by marrying Edgar she will 'like to be the greatest woman *of the neighbourhood*' (Brontë 1998, 69; italics mine). Gimmerton is also notable as a place to visit people for professional services such as the local doctor, parson and lawyer, or for commercial transactions. Thus Mr Earnshaw buys 'a couple of colts at the parish fair' (Brontë 1998, 33) to give to Heathcliff and Hindley; and on an Easter Monday several years later Joseph is mentioned going to 'Gimmerton fair with some cattle' (Brontë 1998, 277) and, later, overlaying his Bible with 'dirty bank-notes from his pocket-book, the produce of the day's transactions' (Brontë 1998, 280).

Of somewhat greater interest are some of Nelly's own visits to Gimmerton, especially for their relevance to the development of the plot. It is true that some such visits prove to be not altogether necessary. Thus on the night of Mr Earnshaw's sudden death in Chapter 5, Nelly is ordered by Joseph to 'put on [her] cloak and run to Gimmerton for the doctor and the parson' (Brontë 1998, 38) but manages only to bring back the doctor. Again, having much later obtained Edgar's permission to find out how, on his death,

Hindley's 'property was left' (Brontë 1998, 164), Nelly calls 'at the village', ultimately to find her master's lawyer seemingly reluctant to accompany her to Thrushcross Grange; for, as she adds, the lawyer 'shook his head, and advised that Heathcliff should be let alone; affirming, if the truth were known, Hareton would be found little else than a beggar' (Brontë 1998, 164). On the other hand, it is on visits paid to Gimmerton of her own accord that Nelly obtains information about some of the characters with whom she is no longer in direct contact. Thus it is by meeting Heathcliff 'one day in the village' that Nelly is advised by him that his estranged wife Isabella 'must beware of coming to her brother; she should not be with him, if he had to keep her himself' and later, that Heathcliff 'often asked about the infant [his son], when he saw [her]', at one point saying, 'But I'll have it [...] when I want it. They may reckon on that!' (Brontë 1998, 161-162). Later still, 'in paying business-visits to Gimmerton' (Brontë 1998, 186), Nelly encounters Heathcliff's unnamed housekeeper, whose disparaging account of Linton Heathcliff's behaviour at Wuthering Heights is enough to turn her against the boy and henceforth to harbour a continually negative attitude towards him, especially during his early relationship with Cathy. There are also occasions when, as housekeeper of Thrushcross Grange, Nelly sends servants to Gimmerton, two of whose commissions turn out to be either fruitless or morally questionable. Thus in accordance with Edgar's wish to alter his will to the benefit of Cathy, Nelly 'despatched a man to fetch the attorney', namely, Mr Green, who not only does not come to Thrushcross Grange because he 'had a little business in the village' (Brontë 1998, 250) but turns out in the end to have 'sold himself to Mr Heathcliff' (Brontë 1998, 251). Nor should we forget that earlier still, in order to clear the way for Heathcliff's secret visit to Catherine, Nelly dishonestly tells 'a man servant left to keep the house with [her]' during Edgar's absence at church that 'the mistress wished very much for some oranges, and he must run over to the village and get a few, to be paid for on the morrow' (Brontë 1998, 137).

What is particularly memorable about Nelly's visits to Gimmerton is the fact that she is often made aware how much members of the two households she has served are the subject of malicious gossip in the village. This we gather already in Volume 1 Chapter 4 when Nelly alludes to Hareton's lowly position at Wuthering Heights by saying: 'The unfortunate lad is the only one, *in all this parish*, that does not guess how he has been cheated!' (Brontë 1998, 30; italics mine). Soon afterwards Nelly relates that when Hindley has returned to the Heights on the death of his father, his bringing 'a wife with him' set 'the neighbours gossiping right and left' (Brontë 1998, 39). Again, after Heathcliff has become master of Wuthering Heights, he clearly enjoys a certain notoriety in Gimmerton inasmuch as '[t]he villagers affirmed Mr Heathcliff was *near* [stingy; original italics], and a cruel hard landlord to his tenants' (Brontë 1998, 174). Similarly, when referring to Heathcliff's funeral, Nelly makes a point of saying this: 'We buried him, to the scandal of the whole neighbourhood, as he had wished' (Brontë 1998, 299), that is to say, next to Catherine's grave on the green slope of Gimmerton chapel kirkyard. The fact that Gimmerton is a place much given to gossip, manifest enough as that is from references to hearsay, rumour and the imparting of messages here and there in the narrative, is sometimes a matter of serious concern for Nelly.[3] Thus it is doubtless through her connections with people living in the village that she is prompted to consider it a duty to warn Hindley 'how people talked regarding his ways' (Brontë 1998, 96). Accordingly, it is when 'on a journey to Gimmerton' (Brontë 1998, 96) that Nelly happens to pass Wuthering Heights gate, through which she catches sight of young Hareton. Having presently asked the boy to tell his father to come and speak to her, but then, on seeing Heathcliff instead of Hindley appear 'on the door-stones' (Brontë 1998, 98), she runs away in terror, thereby failing, albeit rather comically, to carry out her original intention, while reminding us how often her journeys to Gimmerton prove disappointing or fruitless.

Much more constructive, and indeed more important for the plot, is the visit Nelly pays to Mr Kenneth in Gimmerton in order to get him to attend to Catherine in her second delirium. For it is on seeing him by chance 'issuing from his house to see a patient in the village as [she] came up the street' (Brontë 1998, 114) that Nelly is to discover how much this village doctor has an ear for gossip. This we gather when he first asks her: 'What has there been to do at the Grange? We've odd reports up here' (Brontë 1998, 114) and then goes on to tell her that, according to 'good authority', namely, an 'informant' (Brontë 1998, 115), Isabella is likely to elope with Heathcliff. Such information proves, however, to have been provided too late for anything to be done by the time Nelly has hurriedly returned to Wuthering Heights. The elopement is finally confirmed thanks to the report given by a maid who, as Nelly recalls, had been 'on an early errand to Gimmerton' (Brontë 1998, 116) and 'met on the road a lad that fetches milk' (Brontë 1998, 117) from Thrushcross Grange. Such news has been made available because the daughter of the local blacksmith, whose shop is 'two miles out of Gimmerton', saw and recognized the elopers who stopped there in the middle of the night to 'have a horse's shoe fastened', and then, without saying a word to her father, 'told it all over Gimmerton' (Brontë 1998, 117) in the morning.

Just as Brontë uses gossip in Gimmerton for distinctly dramatic, not to say tragic, purposes, at the same time as she makes plain that practically nobody in the village is entirely immune to it, so she shows it in a marvellously comic light through her portrayal of Heathcliff's second housekeeper Zillah. That Zillah appears to have a close association with the village may be gathered partly from Linton Heathcliff's complaint to Cathy that, since his father has been absent from Wuthering Heights, she has been 'constantly gadding off to

Gimmerton' (Brontë 1998, 209). And it will be later, because she and Joseph have been sent off 'on a journey of pleasure' (Brontë 1998, 238) so that they may be out of the way both before and after Heathcliff has had his son married to Cathy, that Zillah hears about Nelly's having been rescued by her master from 'Blackhorse marsh' (Brontë 1998, 246). Thus Zillah says to Nelly on entering her bedroom, where the latter has been locked up for some five days: 'Eh, dear, Mrs Dean, [...] Well! there is a talk about you at Gimmerton'; but in spite of Nelly's outright denial of Heathcliff's 'tale', Zillah stubbornly retorts: 'What do you mean? [...] It's not his tale — they tell that in the village — about your being lost in the marsh' (Brontë 1998, 246). Such ironically humorous treatment of the paludal soil of Gimmerton has already been shown when, for example, on the night of Heathcliff's disappearance from Wuthering Heights. Joseph counters Nelly's claim that the boy will simply 'be gone to Gimmerton' by retorting: 'Nay, nay, he's noan at Gimmerton! [...] Aw's niver wonder, bud he's at t' bothom uf a bog-hoile' (Brontë 1998, 76). This detail is somewhat linked with Hindley's drunken talk in Volume 1 Chapter 9, in which he responds to Nelly's light-hearted reaction to his threat to make her 'swallow the carving knife', by saying: 'You needn't laugh; for I've just crammed Kenneth, head-downmost, in the Blackhorse marsh; and two is the same as one — and I want to kill some of you, I shall have no rest till I do!' (Brontë 1998, 65).

The foregoing comic and essentially fantastical references may be said to have been adumbrated somewhat seriously in Volume 1 Chapter 3, when Lockwood interrupts his account of his first nightmare about Gimmerton chapel, formerly known as 'the Chapel of Gimmerden Sough', by saying that he has 'passed it really in [his] walks, twice or thrice', adding that it 'lies in a hollow between two hills [...] near a swamp, whose peaty moisture is said to answer all the purposes of embalming on the few corpses deposited there' (Brontë 1998, 18-19) — a detail that points forward to Heathcliff's discovering Catherine's own well-preserved corpse some eighteen years after her burial, as much as it indicates how familiar Lockwood is with Gimmerton by now. Already in Volume 1 Chapter 1 we gather how well he has become acquainted with local life. This is exemplified when in his description of Heathcliff's 'apartment and furniture' he writes: 'Such an individual, seated in his armchair, his mug of ale frothing on the round table before him, is to be seen in any circuit of five or six miles among these hills, if you go at the right time, after dinner' (Brontë 1998, 3). Yet it is Gimmerton Kirk that is the primary focus of this cultured and history-minded tourist from the South. Indeed, before he visits Wuthering Heights for the first time he has already learnt enough about the chapel and its pastor even to know that, although its roof has been kept whole hitherto, 'it is currently reported that his flock would rather let him starve than increase the living by one penny from their own pockets' (Brontë 1998, 19). Lockwood's interest in Gimmerton Kirk is confirmed once and for all on his fourth and final visit to Wuthering Heights, when, on his way back to Thrushcross Grange, he notices that the chapel has further decayed through its many broken windows and missing slates.

Lockwood's exceptional interest in Gimmerton Kirk is forcibly associated with the part played by the chapel in Catherine's relationship with Heathcliff as well as with Edgar over the years. Thus we may refer to the time of Catherine's second delirium in Volume 1 Chapter 12 in which she has hallucinations based on memories of her childhood and, in a mixture of soliloquy and dialogue, alludes to one of the journeys that she and Heathcliff made to Wuthering Heights late at night, during which, as she says, they 'must pass by Gimmerton Kirk, to go that journey! We've braved its ghosts often together, and dared each other to stand among the graves and ask them to come' (Brontë 1998, 111). All these and similar utterances of the delirious Catherine can be linked both with Heathcliff's continual visits to her grave and with the fact that he will ultimately be buried side-by-side with her in Gimmerton Kirkyard. Reference should, however, also be made to Edgar's regular visits to Catherine's grave either early in the morning or late in the evening, 'before other wanderers were abroad' (Brontë 1998, 162). Noteworthy in this connection is Edgar's anxiety about his daughter Cathy's future in Volume 2 Chapter 11, whereby, despite having longed for his own death, he has now begun 'to shrink, and fear it' (Brontë 1998, 227). Such thoughts seem to have been prompted partly by his looking out from a window at Thrushcross Grange 'towards Gimmerton Kirk' (Brontë 1998, 226). Moreover, it is when Edgar presently refers to 'the hour [he] came down that glen a bridegroom' (Brontë 1998, 227) that we may be reminded of Nelly's having recalled Edgar's believing himself 'the happiest man alive on the day he led [Catherine] to Gimmerton chapel' (Brontë 1998, 79) as his bride.

Gimmerton *qua* village also features now and again in the author's treatment of the love relationships of the main characters. We note, for example, that, on his arrival at Thrushcross Grange after a three-year absence, Heathcliff insists on Nelly's announcing his presence to Catherine as 'some person from Gimmerton' (Brontë 1998, 82), doubtless not so much to prevent her being unduly taken aback as to make his visit sound respectable. And though the newly-returned Heathcliff would have had to reside somewhere in the village, he is spared that obligation by Hindley's having invited him to lodge at Wuthering Heights, whereby, as Catherine herself hopes, she will 'have more opportunities of seeing him there than [she] could have if he settled in Gimmerton' (Brontë 1998, 88). Gimmerton is again mentioned by name, and ironically so at the time Heathcliff is waiting in Thrushcross Grange grounds for news of Catherine since her collapse at the end of their tryst in Volume 2 Chapter 1. And though, as Nelly recalls, Heathcliff 'would have heard nothing of the stir at the Grange', she nevertheless supposes that he might have caught 'the gallop of the messenger going to

Gimmerton' (Brontë 1998, 146) to suspect the worst, the very word 'Gimmerton' being enough here to underline the urgency of the message conveyed. We have already seen a reference to the village in the account of the first stage of Heathcliff's elopement with Isabella at a blacksmith's shop outside Gimmerton. Accordingly, there is a certain irony when Isabella, having later escaped from Wuthering Heights and arrived at Thrushcross Grange, almost instantly asks Nelly to 'have the goodness to step out and order the carriage to take [her] on to Gimmerton' (Brontë 1998, 150), resisting as she firmly does Nelly's reluctance to do so by saying: 'Certainly, I shall, [...] walking or riding' (Brontë 1998, 151). This may be seen as foreshadowing Lockwood's final visit to Gimmerton from London in so far as it is *to* London that she has presumably decided to go from there to start a new life. At the same time, Isabella's express use of 'Gimmerton' may be said to suggest a kind of nostalgia for her elopement with Heathcliff, all the more as it is clear from her subsequent conversation with Nelly that she still has very mixed feelings about him.[4]

It is also interesting to note how certain references to Gimmerton point forward to the problem that Heathcliff's unexpected return is to have on the marriage of Catherine and Edgar. That Nelly herself senses this already is evident when she is hesitant about announcing Heathcliff's arrival from this description of the couple together in the Thrushcross Grange parlour:

> They sat together in a window whose lattice lay back against the wall, and displayed, beyond the garden trees and the wild green park, the valley of Gimmerton, with a long line of mist winding nearly to its top (for very soon after you pass the chapel, as you may have noticed, the sough that runs from the marshes joins a beck which follows the bend of the glen). Wuthering Heights rose above this silvery vapour; but our old house was invisible — it rather dips down on the other side. (Brontë 1998, 83)

Apart from doubtless reminding Lockwood, through the bracketed interpolation, of what he has already written in his diary about the environs of Gimmerton Kirk, this passage is one of a handful in the narrative that are remarkable for their poetic quality. It is, therefore, little wonder that, when Nelly has noted that '[b]oth the room, and its occupants, and the scene they gazed on, looked wondrously peaceful', she at first 'shrank reluctantly from performing [her] errand' (Brontë 1998, 83), namely, to announce Heathcliff's arrival. Indeed, it would seem largely due to this somewhat sentimental aesthetic response to the nearby landscape that Nelly fears for Catherine and Edgar's apparent marital happiness being disturbed by the return of Heathcliff.

A similar sentimentality may be felt in Nelly's following pastoral description, made as it is at a time when Heathcliff is about to come to Thrushcross Grange for his illicit tryst with Catherine while Edgar is away attending a service in Gimmerton Kirk:

> Gimmerton chapel bells were still ringing; and the full, mellow flow of the beck in the valley came soothingly on the ear. It was a sweet substitute for the yet absent murmur of the summer foliage, which drowned that music about the Grange when the trees were in leaf. At Wuthering Heights it always sounded on quiet days, following a great thaw, or a season of steady rain — and of Wuthering Heights Catherine was thinking as she listened; that is, if she thought, or listened, at all; but she had the vague, distant look I mentioned before, which expressed no recognition of material things either by ear or eye. (Brontë 1998, 138)

The fact that Nelly readily attributes such physical reactions to a convalescent, not to say moribund, Catherine sitting at her bedroom window makes Nelly's rather lyrical description seem none the less a vain attempt on her part to mask the guilt she once felt, and perhaps continues to feel, about the illicit meeting she has made possible to take place. The foregoing passage may also be said to point forward to a much later one also entailing a reference to the beck, whose sound Nelly can hear from Wuthering Heights while Heathcliff is presumably at a sort of climax of his monomaniacal obsession with Catherine's ghost some three days before his death. Thus, having brought his supper into 'the house' at eight o'clock in the evening, Nelly observes Heathcliff as follows:

> He was leaning against the ledge of an open lattice, but not looking out; his face was turned to the interior gloom. The fire had smouldered to ashes; the room was filled with the damp, mild air of the cloudy evening, and so still, that not only the murmur of the beck down Gimmerton was distinguishable, but its ripples and its gurgling over the pebbles, or through the large stones which it could not cover. (Brontë 1998, 292)

Through this passage, then, taken in conjunction with the preceding two concerning the Gimmerton countryside, the author succeeds in poetically marking an important stage of Heathcliff's tragic love relationship with Catherine since his return from abroad, thereby showing us one of the ways in which she has carefully constructed her novel.

Yet it is at this stage that, concerned as we may still be with the role of Gimmerton in the novel, we shall shortly afterwards read about the ghosts of Heathcliff and Catherine, references to which may have led many a reader of the novel to assume that both figures have been united in death. Thus, for example, Nelly says this to Lockwood about the late Heathcliff: '[T]he country folks, if you asked them, would swear on their Bible that he *walks*. There are those who speak to having met him near the church, and on the moor, and even within this house [Thrushcross Grange]' (Brontë 1998, 299; original italics). And though the hard-headed Joseph, too, affirms that 'he has seen two on 'em looking out of his chamber window, on every rainy night since [Heathcliff's] death' (Brontë 1998, 299),

Nelly presumes that Lockwood will dismiss such talk or experiences as 'idle tales' as much as she does, just as she has already dismissed the claim made by 'a little boy with a sheep and two lambs before him' that he has seen 'Heathcliff and a woman, yonder, under t' Nab' — words which Nelly interprets as the consequence of the lad's thinking 'on the nonsense he had heard his parents and companions repeat' (Brontë 1998, 299). And though Nelly admits that she does not like being 'out in the dark' (Brontë 1998, 299), her evaluation of those who claim to have seen Heathcliff's and Catherine's ghosts may be deemed a sort of critique of the commonplace minds of the inhabitants of Gimmerton. Further, Nelly and Lockwood may, in their intrinsic scepticism, be thought to be speaking not only for the rational reader but for the author herself. Perhaps that is why the concluding sentence of Lockwood's narrative, in which he wonders 'how any one could ever imagine unquiet slumbers for the sleepers in that quiet earth' (Brontë 1998, 300), may be said to constitute a much more satisfactory means of settling the matter of Heathcliff's and Catherine's fate after death once and for all.

In this connection, it is useful to consider how the author prepares to round off her treatment of Gimmerton just before Lockwood pays his final visit there. As we have already seen by then, Gimmerton is, on the one hand, a Yorkshire village which is visited for professional or commercial facilities and serves as a centre for travel to other parts of England or elsewhere, and all that in a region delightful enough for Lockwood to sum it up as 'a beautiful country' (Brontë 1998, 1). On the other hand, it is scarcely a place to write home about as concerns its residents, a good many of whom are given to gossip, credulity and superstition, as well as being notorious for their comparative indifference to religion, as manifest both by their reluctance to support the local pastor and by their wilful desistence from stemming the continuous deterioration and decay of Gimmerton Kirk.[5] By now, too, we have seen how many disappointments and embarrassments have been experienced in Gimmerton by those living in Wuthering Heights or in Thrushcross Grange. Nevertheless, it is noteworthy that for Lockwood, who has a sound knowledge of the topography and the history of the village, 'Gimmerton' turns out, not surprisingly, to be the one word but for which he might have remained utterly oblivious of his experiences of Wuthering Heights and Thrushcross Grange in 1801. Indeed, had he not heard the name of the village uttered by the hostler of a roadside public-house while on his journey 'to devastate the moors of a friend, in the North' (Brontë 1998, 271) in September 1802, it is almost certain that not only would his diary have been incomplete, but Brontë's masterpiece would not have existed.

Brontë Studies, 48/1-2 (2023)

References

Adams, Ruth M. 1958. "*Wuthering Heights:* The Land East of Eden." *Nineteenth-Century Fiction* 13 (1): 58-62.

Brontë, Emily. 1998. *Wuthering Heights*. Edited by Ian Jack and Patsy Stoneman. Oxford: Oxford University Press.

Flintoff, Everard. 2006. "The Geography of *Wuthering Heights*." *Brontë Studies* 31 (1): 37-52.

Marsden, Hilda. 1957. "The Scenic Background of *Wuthering Heights*." *Brontë Society Transactions* 13 (2): 111-130.

Marsden, Hilda. 1990. "The Moorlands: The Timeless Contemporary." *Brontë Society Transactions* 20 (1): 25-34.

Notes

1   Although no study appears to have been devoted entirely to the subject of Gimmerton, the following articles are interesting for their pertinence to my chosen topic: Adams (1958), Marsden (1957, 1990), Flintoff (2006).

2   For the sake of convenience, the elder Catherine will hereafter be referred to as 'Catherine', the younger as 'Cathy'.

3   For references to rumour, hearsay and message-carrying, see especially Brontë (1998, 85, 91, 119, 161, 236).

4   See Brontë (1998, 151).

5   Here it is necessary to note that whereas several Gimmertonians are conspicuous for their indifference to orthodox Anglican Christianity, some villagers, including Joseph and Zillah, nevertheless attend the local Dissenters' chapel. As Nelly explains to Lockwood: '[T]he Kirk, you know, has no minister now, […] and they call the Methodists' or Baptists' place, I can't say which it is, at Gimmerton, a chapel' (Brontë 1998, 261). Whether this detail is meant to represent a negative aspect of the Gimmertonian way of life rather than, say, an indirect attack on backsliding orthodox Christians, must needs remain an open question.

Rooms in *Wuthering Heights*

A mid our absorption in Emily Brontë's masterpiece for
its sundry plots and happenings, we might yet remain
comparatively unaware of the ingenious ways in which the author
makes use of rooms as settings for, or backgrounds to, the actions
or situations depicted therein.[1] The fact that Emily's novel is
entitled *Wuthering Heights* should remind us that this eponymous
domicile, and indeed Thrushcross Grange itself, constitute the
only dwellings in whose rooms almost all the significant episodes
occur. Moreover, notwithstanding the impression that seems
to have been created over the years by pictures of landscapes
on the covers of various editions of this book, to say nothing
of filmed adaptations thereof, namely, that the Yorkshire moors
are where everything takes place, it is worth pointing out that,
though now and then referred or alluded to in the narrative, they
serve principally as a means of signalling a particular geographical
area as a background to a particular story.[2] Certainly, where it is
a question of settings, the moors can hardly be said to play as
important a part as that assigned to certain rooms both in the

Heights and in the Grange, as I hope to show in my ensuing discussion.

First of all, it is interesting to note how the social differences between the two houses are suggested by references to some of the rooms or buildings they are each made up of. Thus whereas, for example, 'garret', 'wash-house' and 'pigeon cote' are peculiar to the Heights, 'library', 'hall' and 'drawing-room' are exclusively associated with the Grange. The social significance of the Grange drawing room is first brought to our attention by a young Heathcliff's rapturous description of its elegant furniture and furnishings as seen by him through a window from outside. And since it is also the room in which he will shortly afterwards be humiliated by the Lintons, and will later observe Catherine being fussed over by them, it is doubtless an early source of inspiration behind his subsequent quest to better himself.[3] Curiously enough, the Grange drawing-room is mentioned only twice more in the narrative, each time with negative implications: as the setting for Catherine's coffin and as the room through whose 'casement-window' Nelly sees Cathy returning from an illicit outing.[4] Another room with somewhat negative implications is the garret, of which there seem to be more than one at the top of the Heights. Such a room is first referred to in Catherine's diary as the place where she and Heathcliff were compelled to sit while Joseph held a religious service lasting three hours. Whether this is also the garret in which Heathcliff is locked up by Hindley on Christmas Day and from which he is rescued by Catherine is not made clear, though it is unlikely to be the one that Lockwood and Isabella designate as Joseph's bedroom in Chapters 3 and 13 respectively.[5] Several other bedrooms or chambers are also mentioned, most often in connection with unpleasant moments or periods in the narrative.[6] Noteworthy in this connection is that Catherine's bedroom in the Grange is the setting not only of her three-night sequestration from Edgar and Nelly Dean in Chapter

12, but also that of her final tryst with Heathcliff in Chapter 15.[7] Also deserving of mention here is the oak-panelled closet where Lockwood undergoes his nightmare of the waif girl; where, as if symbolically foreshadowed by that nightmare, the ghostly Catherine constantly haunts Heathcliff, as we learn in Chapter 29; and where the latter is eventually found dead.[8] Yet none of the rooms singled out so far plays as frequent a structural role in the novel as any of the following four rooms: the sitting room at the Heights, the library at the Grange, and the parlour and the kitchen in both households.

Perhaps the most memorable room is 'the family sitting-room' known as 'the house' (*WH*, p. 2), being the only one described in some detail by Lockwood, as if he, a southerner, were as much taken with its 'exoticism' as Hindley's wife Frances was on her arrival at the Heights some twenty-four years earlier.[9] And though very occasionally a setting for pleasant gatherings and activities, 'the house' is interesting mainly as a room in which a number of unhappy incidents occur: Mr Earnshaw's death; Catherine's vicious behaviour during Edgar's visit to her; Heathcliff's humiliation of Isabella in Nelly's presence; Heathcliff's trapping of Nelly and Cathy on the eve of the latter's marriage to his son; and Hareton's burning of the books, to give but a few striking examples.[10] References to 'the house' are especially notable for marking stages in the history of the Heights from the time of Mr Earnshaw's mastership, that is to say, when it was a place of leisure shared by family and servants alike, until the day when, on his final visit to the Heights, Lockwood witnesses a betrothed Cathy and Hareton there in the midst of a reading lesson. Thus we may recall how, on returning home after his father's death, Hindley insists on 'the house' being a place of leisure for himself and Frances to the exclusion of everybody else. Soon after Hindley has been widowed and begun leading a dissipated life, however, 'the house' falls into conspicuous deterioration, especially by the time Isabella has arrived at the Heights as Heathcliff's bride. As she says in her letter to Nelly: 'There was a great fire, and that was all the light in the huge apartment, whose floor had grown a uniform grey; and the once brilliant pewter dishes which used to attract my gaze when I was a girl partook of a similar obscurity, created by tarnish and dust' (*WH*, p. 122), a description confirmed by Nelly when, on coming to the Heights shortly afterwards, she finds that '[t]here never was such a dreary, dismal scene as the formerly cheerful house presented!' (*WH*, p. 129). Moreover, part of the grimness of Isabella's brief sojourn at the Heights is due to her spending most of her time in that 'dreary, dismal scene.' The grimness of 'the house' is, however, more particularly to be felt when it has become the place that Heathcliff occupies while at leisure, and that practically to the detriment of other members of his household. And though Hareton tends to sit in 'the house' when he, too, is at leisure, he finds himself more and more excluded from it once Heathcliff has begun to want the place entirely to himself. Indeed, by the end of his life, Heathcliff has become the sole occupant of 'the house', even though he once or twice asks Nelly and Cathy, albeit in vain, to keep him company there. But if in the last stages of Heathcliff's acute mental illness 'the house' has become as isolated a room as it was when Hindley and Frances were in charge of the household, it is obvious that, by the time of Lockwood's final visit to the Heights, that room has once again become the normal place of leisure it used to be during Mr Earnshaw's lifetime.

At the Grange, on the other hand, the sitting room is not the drawing room, as some readers might have expected, but the library or, as we shall see later, the parlour. During Lockwood's tenancy there, it would appear that the library is his study; it is also the room where Nelly brings him his supper in Chapter 4, and where he gets her to tell him the first part of Heathcliff's history until the end of Chapter 9.[11] Although Nelly alludes to the primary function of the Grange library when she tells Lockwood that he 'could not open a book in this library that [she has] not looked into' (*WH*, p. 55),

Lockwood, by contrast, will suggest in his conversation with the bibliophile Cathy in Chapter 31 that, though provided with 'a large library', he is 'frequently very dull at the Grange' (*WH*, p. 266). Such a confession is a poignant reminder of what Nelly has already told Lockwood, namely, that while Catherine was sequestered in her bedroom for three nights, Edgar 'did not inquire concerning his wife's occupations' (*WH*, p. 105), later somewhat presumptuously adding that he 'shut himself up among books that he never opened' (*WH*, p. 106); in which connection, it is perhaps little wonder that Catherine herself, on learning to her dismay that Edgar is 'continually among his books, since he has no other society' (*WH*, p. 107), should jump to the conclusion that her husband prefers books to any concern for her well-being. Hence, no doubt, the irony of Nelly's later recalling that, on every anniversary of Catherine's death, Edgar 'spent that day alone in the library' (*WH*, p. 187). With such details in mind, and notwithstanding the affirmation of books and reading to be sensed by the end of the novel, we should be hardly surprised to find that the Grange library is usually referred to in somewhat unfavourable contexts, all of which seem foreshadowed by our realization that, while Lockwood is listening to Nelly's narrative in that very room, he is already badly suffering from the cold that will keep him laid up for several weeks. Consider, too, that in the wake of Catherine's taunting of Isabella for her infatuation with Heathcliff, both women are described by Nelly as 'sitting in the library, on hostile terms, but silent' (*WH*, p. 92), the library being also the room where Catherine will soon afterwards humiliate Isabella in Heathcliff's presence and where the latter, on learning of Isabella's love for him, presently seems intent on taking full advantage of such news. Again, after Edgar has gone down south to visit Isabella, Nelly recalls that 'the first day or two, [Cathy] sat in a corner of the library, too sad for either reading or playing' (*WH*, p. 169). The library is also the first room Linton Heathcliff is shown into shortly after his arrival at the

Grange, and yet a place where he will behave rather neurotically while he is having tea with Edgar and Cathy. And it is in the library where Edgar will very shortly afterwards find himself confronted by a very aggressive Joseph, who has come, albeit in vain, to take the newly-arrived Linton immediately back with him to the Heights.

The library also happens to be the room where Cathy keeps Linton Heathcliff's love letters to her in a cabinet drawer, whose lock Nelly manages to prise open, thereby succeeding in presently putting an end to the cousins' correspondence. It will also be the place where, in the wake of her fateful encounter with Heathcliff outside the Thrushcross Park door in Chapter 22, Cathy will ask Nelly to 'sit with her' (*WH*, p. 207). And it is while pretending to read a book there that Nelly, having noticed Cathy 'silently weeping' (*WH*, p. 207), will proceed to pooh-pooh Heathcliff's talk about his dying son in a futile attempt to distract Cathy from her concern over the latter, but will nevertheless find herself obliged to accompany her young mistress to the Heights the following morning. There is also a certain irony about the fact that, though deeply grateful to Cathy for nursing her through her three-week cold and, therefore, inclined to ascribe the best motives to the girl's somewhat enigmatic behaviour at the time, Nelly will attribute the 'fresh colour' in Cathy's cheeks 'to the charge of a hot fire in the library' (*WH*, p. 215) and not, as she is later to discover, to the cold rides the girl has been making across the moor after visiting Linton at the Heights. For it is in the library where, during her convalescence, Nelly gets Cathy to read to her at night, albeit much to the inconvenience of the latter in her concern to keep her illicit appointments with her cousin. Later we learn that the library, where her fatally ill father 'stopped a short time daily — the brief period he could bear to sit up', together with his 'chamber', had become Cathy's 'whole world' (*WH*, p. 234). And it is probably in the library that Nelly 'obtained permission to order her out of doors' (*WH*, p. 234) so that the latter might attend her second 'official' meeting with Linton on the heath, an occasion that will, of course, have unpleasant consequences for both women on the day before Cathy's marriage to Linton. The final reference to the library is as the room in which, on the evening of Edgar's funeral, Cathy and Nelly 'were seated' and where they both agree that staying on at the Grange would be 'the best destiny which could await Catherine' (*WH*, p. 253). Such optimism is, however, soon rendered useless by the sudden appearance of Heathcliff in the library, which, oddly enough, Nelly designates as 'the same room in which he had been ushered, as a guest, eighteen years before' (*WH*, p. 253). Yet Nelly, it would appear, has forgotten that Heathcliff was actually ushered into the parlour; indeed, it is likely that Nelly means the parlour after all, for it is in that very room where Isabella, just before her departure for the south, kissed the portraits of Edgar and Catherine, the latter's portrait being the one that Heathcliff, after making his long confession to Nelly about being haunted by Catherine's ghost, 'took [...] down and leant [...] against the sofa to contemplate [...] at better advantage', and then asked Nelly to '[s]end that over [to the Heights] to-morrow' (*WH*, p. 257), just before ordering Cathy to get ready to return with him to the Heights.[12]

Nelly's aforementioned factual error is perhaps understandable in view of the fact that the library and the parlour seem practically interchangeable as rooms for leisure and social gatherings. That a parlour, not unlike a library, is a room peculiar to upper-class houses such as the Grange is made obvious enough when, for example, Joseph rather sardonically informs Isabella that there is no such space in the Heights as a parlour in which she hopes to eat her porridge in privacy.[13] In this connection, it is noteworthy that, but for Frances' delighting in 'the house' on first coming to the Heights, Hindley would have 'carpeted and papered a small spare room for a parlour' (*WH*, p. 39), as if perhaps aware that she has been used to upper-class dwellings. The earliest reference to the Grange parlour is made on the evening of Heathcliff's return to Gimmerton after a three-year absence, the function of that room as a tranquil place of leisure being never more patently suggested than when Nelly explains why on entering that room she was at first reluctant to announce Heathcliff's arrival to Edgar and Catherine: 'Both the room, and its occupants, and the scene they gazed on, looked wondrously peaceful' (*WH*, p. 83). Moreover, at no time is the idea of the social prestige of that room indicated more clearly than when Edgar presently suggests that Catherine entertain the visitor whom he remembers as 'the gipsy — the plough-boy' (*WH*, p. 83) in the kitchen rather than in the parlour. And though, thanks to Catherine's insistence, Heathcliff is after all invited into the parlour to partake of tea, it is evident that, by the time the meal is over, that room has ceased to be the idyllic setting it was not long beforehand, being henceforth referred to in essentially negative contexts. Thus, for example, Isabella, amid her infatuation with Heathcliff soon afterwards, complains that people at the Grange, among other things, 'let the parlour fire go out on purpose to vex her' (*WH*, p. 89). The parlour is also the room into which a 'desperate' (*WH*, p. 110) Catherine runs after the showdown between Edgar and Heathcliff in the Grange kitchen, as well as the room where she will have her blackout and where she will be in fresh conflict with Edgar for having asked her to choose between himself and Heathcliff.[14] Again, when Catherine is convalescing from her brain fever, that room is described as 'the many-weeks-deserted parlour' in which Edgar asks Nelly to 'light a fire', and whose sofa Catherine uses as a bed 'till another room could be prepared' (*WH*, p. 119). After Catherine's death, however, it would appear that Edgar no longer uses the parlour for recreation. As Nelly relates on the day after Catherine's funeral: 'I took possession of the lonely parlour, converting it into a nursery' (*WH*, p. 150) for the newborn Cathy, it being also the room which, by now seemingly much reduced in status, a snow-drenched Isabella suddenly enters after her flight from the Heights and from which she will leave the Grange for good.

The only references to a parlour thereafter have to do entirely with the one originally set up at the Heights for Linton Heathcliff. And in view of Edgar's having suggested that Catherine entertain her unexpected visitor in the kitchen rather than in the parlour, it is somewhat ironic that, on the morning Nelly has brought his son to the Heights, Heathcliff should inform her that he has 'a room upstairs, furnished for him in handsome style' as one means by which to 'preserve the superior and the gentleman in him, above his associates' (*WH*, p. 184), that is, a room later referred to by the unnamed Heights housekeeper as 'a small apartment they called the parlour' in which Linton 'learnt his lessons and spent his evenings' (*WH*, p. 186). The parlour is, however, a room which, as the housekeeper adds, Heathcliff not only 'never enters', but to which Linton is sent off if he behaves badly 'in the house' (*WH*, p. 187). That this parlour nevertheless has its drawbacks is obvious enough not only because Linton often feels lonely there, but because, as he tells Nelly and Cathy, the servants 'resolved never to hear him upstairs' (*WH*, p. 209). Further, Linton's parlour is clearly a source of resentment for some members of Heathcliff's household. Thus, for example, one reason why Hareton, angered as he is by Cathy's having humiliated him a second time for his illiteracy, turns her and Linton out of 'the house' is that the latter has a room in which to entertain his guests. As Hareton says to Linton in his rage: 'Get to thy own room! [...] Take her there if she comes to see thee — thou shalln't keep me out of this. Begone, wi' ye both!' (*WH*, p. 221). When Cathy visits Linton again a few days later, she is shown by Zillah into his parlour for the first time, namely, 'a small, tidy, carpeted apartment' (*WH*, p. 223). But because Linton blames Cathy for Hareton's violent behaviour towards them, she walks out of the room, returning to the Heights a few days later to find Linton not in the parlour, as she had expected, but in 'the house.' It is only when Heathcliff is on the premises during her illicit visits that Cathy has 'always gone to [Linton's] little parlour' (*WH*, p. 224). That Linton's parlour is, as we have seen, a fundamentally problematic room, is finally confirmed when, having asked Nelly to return to the Heights as his housekeeper, Heathcliff instructs her to make that room her 'sitting room' and to 'keep [Cathy] with [her]' there because he has grown 'tired of seeing [her]' (*WH*, p. 275). Yet, like her late husband, Cathy finds the parlour an inconvenient place in which to spend all her time, preferring as she does 'quarrelling with Joseph in the kitchen, to sitting at peace in her solitude' (*WH*, p. 276).

The foregoing quoted reference to the kitchen is one of a large number through which that room, whether at the Heights or at the Grange, turns out to be the one most often mentioned in the novel. Part of the interest of the Heights kitchen derives from its being a room whose particular state, like that of 'the house' itself, seems at any one time to mark a significant phase in the recent history of that household. Thus Nelly Dean's lyrical description of the kitchen in Chapter 7 with, among other things, its 'shining kitchen utensils, the polished clock, [...] and, above all, the speckless purity of [her] particular care — the scoured and well-swept floor' (*WH*, p. 48), suggests a household being as well run under Hindley and Frances as it had been in Mr Earnshaw's days. That the same kitchen will, however, have considerably deteriorated in the years since Hindley has been widowed and, more especially, since Nelly has been housekeeper of the Grange, is evident from the description that Isabella, barely arrived at the Heights as Heathcliff's bride, gives of the place in her letter to Nelly: 'a dingy, untidy hole; I dare say you would not know it, it is so changed since it was in your charge' (*WH*, pp. 120-21). After the death of Hindley, however, the kitchen, like other parts of the Heights, recovers its orderliness, thanks chiefly to Heathcliff's efficiency as master of that household. This is somewhat confirmed when, at the beginning of Chapter 23, Nelly observes Joseph there on the morning she and Cathy have arrived at the Heights. And no doubt it is due to Heathcliff's week-long absence that Joseph 'seemed sitting in a sort of elysium alone, beside a roaring fire; a quart of ale on the table near him, bristling with large pieces of toasted oat cake; and his black, short pipe in his mouth' (*WH*, p. 208). It is also interesting to note at the end of the narrative that, once the newly-wed Cathy and Hareton have moved to the Grange with Nelly, Joseph will stay behind at the Heights and that, with 'a lad to keep him company', he will 'live in the kitchen, and the rest will be shut up' (*WH*, p. 300) — a detail that somehow points up the idea that as well as being the room most often referred to, the kitchen is, despite its low standing, the most resilient room in the Heights.

Mentioned only three times as a room in which a culinary activity takes place, most notably Isabella's bungled cooking of porridge in Chapter 13, the kitchen functions otherwise principally as the setting for servants, especially those employed at the Heights, whether they be at work or at leisure, and where, when sought, they are almost always to be found.[15] It is, nevertheless, interesting to note the Heights kitchen sometimes fulfilling a certain ominous function, as, for example, when it is the room where Catherine consults Nelly about Edgar's proposal of marriage; where Heathcliff overhears Catherine rejecting the idea of him as a possible husband and, accordingly, takes flight; and where Catherine, having long waited in the rain for Heathcliff to return, spends the night in drenched clothes and thus falls ill with delirium.[16] A similarly ominous function can certainly be ascribed to all references to the kitchen at the Grange, the earliest such reference occurring when, one September evening, Nelly sets a basket of apples 'on the house steps by the kitchen door' (*WH*, p. 82) just before being surprised by the sudden appearance of Heathcliff after a three-year absence. The Grange kitchen is also the room where, as well as catching Cathy out for her illicit correspondence with Linton Heathcliff, Nelly observes people's movements and behaviour through its window, as she once did at the Heights, and most memorably so when she spots Heathcliff amorously approaching Isabella; and where, because immediately voicing her disapproval thereof loud enough for Catherine to overhear her, she sets off a train of events that will eventually lead to the showdown between Edgar and Heathcliff in the same room.[17] At this point, the reader might be reminded by Edgar's having advised Catherine to entertain the newly-returned Heathcliff in the kitchen rather than in the parlour that the kitchen is, socially speaking, the humblest, not to say the lowest room, in both households. Thus, for example, on his return to the Heights as master thereof, Hindley tells Nelly and Joseph that they 'must thenceforth quarter [themselves] in the back-kitchen, and leave the house for him' (*WH*, p. 39), the back-kitchen being that space in the kitchen that supposedly comprises the scullery as well as an area set aside for non-culinary or leisure purposes. Yet it is also a kind of punishment room, for it is 'into the back-kitchen' that Hindley 'hurled' (*WH*, p. 17) Catherine and Heathcliff for their bad behaviour in 'the house' one Sunday evening. The idea of the kitchen as a place for those in disgrace is somewhat hinted at when Cathy tells Nelly of Hareton's 'nearly throwing [Linton] into the kitchen' (*WH*, p. 221) just after he has evicted them both from 'the house.' This idea seems corroborated at the time the recently widowed Cathy is still in conflict with Hareton. Thus Lockwood, on his third visit to the Heights, notices that although Cathy, while 'preparing some vegetables for the approaching meal', is ordered by Hareton to 'remove her things to the kitchen' (*WH*, p. 265), she moves instead to a window in 'the house'. Soon afterwards, however, when Lockwood has been invited to partake of the 'midday meal', Heathcliff tells Cathy, who has just come into 'the house' bearing 'a tray of knives and forks', to 'get [her] dinner with Joseph [...] and remain in the kitchen till [Lockwood] is gone' (*WH*, p. 269).[18]

Nevertheless, the kitchen from time to time serves as a sort of refuge in sundry ways. For example, it is the room through whose outer door some characters make — or try to make — their exits or entrances, especially in moments of uncertainty or crisis.[19] Thus it is through that door that Isabella will eventually take flight from Heathcliff once and for all. The Heights kitchen is also now and then a place to go to when one has had trouble in another part of the household. For example, it is the room to which Nelly, conscious as she is of young Heathcliff's unease over Catherine since her return from the Grange, invites him on Christmas Eve, albeit in vain, to partake of 'a little cake,' having already assured him that 'the kitchen is so comfortable' (*WH*, p. 48); where, after he has been released from the garret on Christmas Day, she, once more in vain, 'offered him a quantity of good things' (*WH*, p. 53); and where a little earlier she has given him advice in answer to his request to her to 'make [him] decent' (*WH*, p. 49). Nelly herself, too, sometimes turns to the kitchen for refuge, as when, having been injured and humiliated by Catherine for doing housework in 'the house' in the presence of herself and Edgar, she 'lifted Hareton in [her] arms, and walked off to the kitchen with him' (*WH*, p. 63). Similarly, in the wake of the incident in which Hareton has been saved from certain death by Heathcliff as well as in that of Hindley's drunken talk and behaviour both before and after that incident, Nelly relates that she 'went into the kitchen and sat down to lull [her] little lamb [Hareton] to sleep' (*WH*, p. 67). Here we may be reminded that Isabella, puzzled by Hindley's strange demeanour and utterances in 'the house' shortly after arriving at the Heights as Heathcliff's bride, 'raised the latch, and *escaped* into the kitchen' (*WH*, p. 124; italics mine). Noteworthy, too, is the following detail from Isabella's oral account to Nelly about her sojourn at the Heights: 'When Heathcliff is in, I'm often obliged to seek the kitchen, and [Joseph and Hareton's] society, or starve among the damp, uninhabited chambers' (*WH*, p. 154). The same kitchen is much later the room for Cathy to resort to when 'all wildered like, and looked as if she would fain beg assistance' (*WH*, p. 260) from Zillah for her fatally ill husband Linton, albeit to no avail, but also a room to which, as Lockwood observes, she 'escaped' (*WH*, p. 269) on seeing Heathcliff return to the Heights. The importance of the Heights kitchen as a place of refuge is, however, nowhere more tellingly underscored than at the time Cathy and Hareton find themselves more or less compelled to occupy that space in proximity to each other, Cathy because she has become bored with sitting in the parlour assigned to her by Heathcliff, and Hareton, who as well as having to recuperate there after accidentally injuring himself with his gun was, as Nelly recalls, 'often obliged to seek the kitchen also, when the master wanted to have the house to himself' (*WH*, p. 276). Yet, notwithstanding Cathy's initially rather bumbling attempts to regain Hareton's friendship, it is in the Heights kitchen where, because almost inescapably thrown into each other's company, they will both be ultimately reconciled.

The thematic significance of the Heights kitchen as both the 'lowest' room in that household, a place of refuge and a means of escape is at once foreshadowed and confirmed in Lockwood's presentation. Thus, it is 'an inhabitant of the kitchen' (*WH*, p. 5), namely Zillah, who manages to put an end to his fight with the dogs, just as it is that same 'inhabitant' who, after Lockwood has been knocked down by the dogs next day, will come to his rescue for his nosebleed when she 'suddenly splashed a pint of icy water down [his] neck, and pulled [him] into the kitchen' (*WH*, p. 14). Again, after having woken Heathcliff later that night with a loud yell, a somewhat embarrassed Lockwood leaves the room with the oak-panelled closet and 'descended cautiously to the lower regions and landed in the back-kitchen' (*WH*, p. 24), as if, not unlike some of the youngsters in the novel, he were himself in disgrace, especially through feeling somewhat out of place in that area once he has been joined there by a silent and surly Joseph.[20] It is, however, on his final visit to the Heights that the kitchen will become for Lockwood both a refuge and a means of exit in perhaps the most ridiculously shameful way shown in the narrative. Thus, having observed Cathy and Hareton's reading lesson in 'the house' he has quietly entered, Lockwood in his inveterate vanity presumes, as he notices them about to go out, that he would be 'condemned in Hareton Earnshaw's heart, if not by his mouth, to the lowest pit in the infernal regions if [he] showed [his] unfortunate person in his neighbourhood then' (*WH*, p. 273). Accordingly, instead of, say, bravely confronting the couple and maturely wishing them well, a 'very mean and malignant' feeling Lockwood 'skulked round to seek refuge in the kitchen' (*WH*, p. 273). Later, having been told the last part of Heathcliff's history by Nelly in 'the house', Lockwood will betray his vanity once again when, 'disregarding [Nelly's] expostulation at [his] rudeness', he 'vanished through the kitchen' as Cathy and Hareton, back from their nocturnal ramble, 'opened the house-door' (*WH*, p. 300), concerned as he also is on his way out to drop a sovereign at Joseph's feet in an attempt to assure him that his meeting with Nelly has been utterly respectable. Still, as we saw above, it is this lowest of all rooms that will have none the less proved its durability at the end of the novel as practically the only habitable one in an otherwise shut-up Wuthering Heights.

Notes

1   Although references have been made now and again to certain rooms at the Heights or at the Grange in descriptions in Emily's novel, no scholar has, to my knowledge, yet written exclusively on the topic I have chosen to consider here. For quotations from the text, see Emily Brontë, *Wuthering Heights*, ed. by Ian Jack and Patsy Stoneman (Oxford: Oxford University Press, 1998), hereafter *WH*. For the sake of convenience, the first Catherine will be referred to as 'Catherine', the second as 'Cathy'.

2   It is true that some important episodes take place on the moors. Thus, for example, it happens to be the setting of Cathy's first meeting with Heathcliff in Chapter 21, just as it is on the 'heath' that she will have her two 'official' meetings with Linton Heathcliff in Chapters 26 and 27. The only description of the moors to speak of, however, is the one given by Lockwood on his return to Gimmerton. See *WH*, p. 271. For references to 'moor', 'moors' and 'heath', see *WH*, pp. 20, 40, 49, 168, 210, 218, 228, 230, 231, 234, 240, 257, 259, 299, 300.

3   See *WH*, pp. 41-44.

4   See *WH*, pp. 145, 217.

5   See *WH*, pp. 24, 216.

6   For references to 'bedroom' or 'chamber' and, synonymously, to 'room' or 'apartment', see *WH*, pp. 32, 35, 38, 48, 51, 77, 78, 86, 115, 117, 119, 123, 127, 145, 150, 153, 176, 180-81, 195, 197-201, 216, 224-25, 244-46, 250-52, 260, 261, 293. Hindley's bedroom is the only one described in detail: see *WH*, p. 126. It is

also interesting to note that Lockwood hears the second part of Nelly's narrative while he is laid up in his bedroom, that is, from Chapter 10 to Chapter 26.

7   See *WH*, pp. 106-14, 116, 139-41.

8   For references or allusions to the oak-panelled closet, see *WH*, pp. 20, 21, 110, 257, 293, 298.

9   See *WH*, pp. 39, 40.

10 See *WH*, pp. 37, 62, 63, 132-34, 238-44, 268. For similar examples, see *WH*, pp. 7-13, 25, 27, 31, 40, 46-48, 60, 61, 75-76, 130-36, 172-73, 210-11, 259, 261-66, 283-85, 287-89, 291-95.

11 Although Lockwood does not say which room he is in at the beginning of Chapter 4, we may assume it to be the Grange library, at least to judge by Nelly's reference, during a break in her narrative, to 'this library' (*WH*, p. 55). For Lockwood's references to his study, see *WH*, pp. 6, 27.

12 For relevant references to Isabella's visit to the Grange parlour before her final departure, see *WH*, pp. 150, 161.

13 See *WH*, p. 125.

14 See *WH*, pp. 103-05.

15 For references to cooking in the Heights kitchen, see *WH*, pp. 2, 73, 124, 125.

16 See *WH*, pp. 68-78.

17 See *WH*, pp. 98-103, 198-99.

18 For other ominous implications in references to the kitchen, whether at the Heights or at the Grange, see *WH*, pp. 51, 65, 178, 244, 297.

19 See *WH*, pp. 154, 156, 208, 300.

20 See *WH*, p. 24.

Clothes in *Wuthering Heights*

One subject that appears to have received comparatively little attention from Brontë scholars is the part played by clothes in *Wuthering Heights*.[1] Not that this is to be wondered at if we reflect that Emily Brontë's references to clothes are somewhat minimal, even though she was writing in an era when, owing mainly to the influence of Sir Walter Scott, clothes tend to figure quite prominently in nineteenth-century character description in much the same way as they had done in various continental European romances and comic novels of the seventeenth and eighteenth centuries.[2] Nevertheless it is through those few references to clothes, whether in general terms or as individual items, that we at least gain some idea of the mores of the England of the last quarter of the eighteenth century and beyond, such references ranging from, say, the wearing of black during a period of mourning to a housekeeper's or nursemaid's helping their masters and mistresses both young and old to dress or undress themselves.[3] But though clothes are by no means as conspicuous in Emily's book as they are in a good many other contemporary works of fiction, their modest presence therein is nonetheless important enough to serve as so many testimonies to her remarkable versatility as a novelist. Indeed, I hope to show that, as well as performing sundry structural and thematic functions, clothes are used by the author in a number of ways that help both to sustain and to enhance the essential realism of her narrative.

Any consideration of the uses of clothes in *Wuthering Heights* cannot but entail a keen awareness of their significance in what we are shown here to be an intrinsically hierarchical society. For example, we are made aware of the upper-class implications of Edgar Linton's 'cambric pocket-handkerchief' (*WH*, p. 52) and Isabella's 'frock [...] of light silk' (*WH*, p. 150), as we are of the 'cloaks and furs' that the Linton children are 'smothered' in on their arrival at the Heights 'in the family carriage' (*WH*, p. 51) on Christmas morning, or, later, of the 'warm, fur-lined cloak' (*WH*, p. 177) wrapped round Linton Heathcliff on his arrival at the Grange in a similar vehicle, to say nothing of the 'feathered beaver', the 'long cloth habit', the 'grand plaid silk frock', the 'white trousers', the 'burnished shoes' (*WH*, p. 46), all of which, worn by Catherine on her return to the Heights from Thrushcross Grange, the aristocratic Mrs Linton has presumably decreed as appropriate attire for someone whom she evidently looks upon already as a prospective daughter-in-law. By the same token, Nelly's description of Hareton, whom she encounters on the moors (in Heathcliff's company) several months after Cathy's first meeting with him at the Heights is notable for confirming his lowly status in that she observes him attired in 'garments befitting his daily occupations of working on the farm, and lounging among the moors after rabbits and game' (*WH*, p. 173), just as Lockwood's remarking on an as yet unidentified Zillah, who in Chapter 1 comes from the kitchen to rescue him from the Heights dogs, as 'a lusty dame, with tucked-up gown' (*WH*, p. 5) effectively substantiates her menial position in the household. Such indeed is Lockwood's tendency to comment on clothing that, having by his yell induced

Heathcliff to come to the room containing the oak-panelled closet, he amply suggests the latter's evident haste in doing so by describing him standing 'near the entrance, in his shirt and trousers' (*WH*, p. 21).

The irony of the above-quoted detail derives from its contrasting markedly with Lockwood's earlier impression of Heathcliff's attire in Chapter 1. In this connection, it is perhaps hardly surprising that, presented as he is as a gentleman of leisure and alluded to as such by his reference to his 'coat-laps' (WH, p. 4), Lockwood should be much given to remarking on clothes in the first two chapters, doing so not without obvious social implications. Thus having deemed the interior of the Heights appropriate to a 'homely, northern farmer' wearing 'knee-breeches and gaiters', Lockwood notes that, despite being 'a dark-skinned gypsy in aspect', Heathcliff is 'in dress and manners a gentleman — that is, as much a gentleman as many a country squire' (*WH*, p. 3). Yet unperturbed as Lockwood seems to be by the incongruities in Heathcliff's physical appearance, his description of it nevertheless betokens something of that snobbery which will be more overt in Chapter 2, when, for example, he refers to the 'decidedly shabby upper garment' (*WH*, p. 8) that Hareton Earnshaw puts on shortly after they have both entered 'the house', the enormity of such snobbery being confirmed when Lockwood presently labels Hareton as 'he of the shabby coat' (*WH*, p. 9). And though uncertain whether or not Hareton is a servant, Lockwood makes no bones about the latter's 'dress and speech' being 'both rude, entirely devoid of the superiority observable in Mr and Mrs Heathcliff' (*WH*, p. 8).

As well as showing Lockwood in a ridiculous light, and that partly through his presumptuously taking Heathcliff and Cathy for man and wife at first, the arrantly class-conscious judgement just quoted above may be seen as a caricatural foreshadowing of, say, Isabella's contemptuous comments in her letter to Nelly about the clothes worn by Hindley, Hareton and Joseph.[4] More importantly, however, Lockwood's class-conscious judgement in some sense also adumbrates the fact that on the day after Catherine's return to the Heights from Thrushcross Grange and, because presumably still afflicted by the memory of her elegant outfit, therefore induced to ask Nelly to 'make [him] decent' (*WH*, p. 49), Heathcliff is so influenced by her advice to him about improving his facial appearance as naively to conclude that all he needs is to look exactly like Edgar Linton. Indeed, notwithstanding his having told Nelly on his return from his illicit visit to the Grange with Catherine that he would 'not exchange, for a thousand lives, [his] condition [at the Heights], for Edgar Linton's at Thrushcross Grange —' (*WH*, p. 42), Heathcliff forcibly betrays a patent class-consciousness through his deep-seated envy of Edgar's personal qualities when, as he says to Nelly, he wishes, among other things, that he 'was dressed and behaved as well' (*WH*, p. 50). Such envy is surely one of the principal roots of Heathcliff's social rise, as already suggested on his return to Gimmerton after his three-year absence when, though not yet quite recognized by Nelly, he is described by her as 'a tall man dressed in dark clothes' (*WH*, p. 82).

Class consciousness with regard to clothes may, nevertheless, be just as strongly sensed in the servants portrayed in the novel. Take, for instance, the inverted snobbery with which Joseph reacts to Isabella's personal appearance shortly after her arrival at the Heights with Heathcliff, first, when she notices him 'surveying [her] dress and countenance (the former a great deal too fine, but the latter [...] as sad as he could desire) with sovereign contempt' (*WH*, p. 121); and, later, when, while showing her rooms at the top of the house, he sardonically advises her to spread her handkerchief over a pack of corn if, as he says, 'yah're feared uh muckying yer grand silk cloes' (*WH*, p. 125). Hardly less snobbishly hierarchical in her attitude to clothes is Nelly Dean herself, her awareness of the social implications of dress having been early suggested when, for example, she notices a change in Hindley's person on his return to the Heights after his father's death by observing that he 'dressed quite differently' (*WH*, p. 39). It is, however, more particularly through her detailed description of Catherine's attire on the day of her return to the Heights from her five-week sojourn at the Grange that Nelly seems to disclose much the same snobbery that Hindley and Frances plainly evince on the same occasion. Nelly's snobbery is further manifested when, having already described Heathcliff's scruffy appearance in some detail, she says this about his response to the sight of the newly-arrived Catherine: 'He might well skulk behind the settle, on beholding such a bright, graceful damsel enter the house, instead of a rough-headed counterpart to himself, as he expected' (*WH*, p. 47). And in spite of her attempt the following morning to persuade Heathcliff to be reconciled with Catherine, Nelly still betrays her class-conscious attitude to clothes when, having advised him to approach the girl with some show of affection, she adds: 'only, do it heartily, and not as if you thought her converted into a stranger by her grand dress' (*WH*, p. 49). A more glaring example of this attitude may, however, be sensed in the way in which, while conscious from Isabella's letter of how unhappy she is as Heathcliff's bride, Nelly seems unduly preoccupied, on arriving at the Heights, with Isabella's ill-kempt appearance, assuming as she does, among other things, that '[p]robably she had not touched her dress since yester evening' (*WH*, p. 129), and then going on to maintain that Heathcliff 'would certainly have struck a stranger as a born and bred gentleman, and his wife as a thorough little slattern!' (*WH*, p. 130).

Nelly's concern with clothes is, to be sure, due not only to their decorative qualities or their social implications but to their practicality in everyday life. Accordingly, it is understandable that, in her position as housekeeper or nursemaid, she should sometimes be distressed by the state of the clothes of her masters or mistresses, especially when they have been adversely affected by the elements.[5] One early example of this occurs when, noticing Catherine lying on the settle in drenched clothes because she has long been waiting in the rain for Heathcliff to return to the Heights, Nelly 'vainly begged the wilful girl to rise and remove her wet things' (*WH*, p. 76). Nelly elicits much the same negative reaction to a similar piece of advice on her part when, on seeing Isabella suddenly appear in the Grange parlour after her snowbound flight from the Heights, she has said this to the latter: 'I'll stir nowhere, and hear nothing, till you have removed every article of your clothes, and put on dry things' (*WH*, p. 151). On this occasion, Nelly is disobeyed outright until she has carried out Isabella's instructions concerning her imminent departure from the Grange. What is, however, significant about both these episodes is the way in which Nelly's conventional wisdom seems mediocre by comparison with the heroic indifference exhibited by her social superiors towards her practical advice. All the same, the danger of wearing wet clothes is evidenced not only because Catherine will soon afterwards go down with a bout of delirious fever but because Nelly herself, as a consequence of accompanying Cathy to the Heights in order to visit Linton Heathcliff at his father's instigation, will be laid up with a bad cold for three weeks through 'sitting such a while' there in 'soaked shoes and stockings' (*WH*, p. 214).

In view of the fact that clothes are sometimes exposed to the hazards of weather, it is only to be expected that in a novel where journeys of varying length are now and then undertaken, references should sometimes be made to outdoor wear. Such references, however, can sometimes be understood retrospectively as having been somewhat portentous. For example, Mr Earnshaw's coming downstairs 'one fine summer morning [...] dressed for a journey' (*WH*, p. 30) may be said to foreshadow the discovery of the foundling Heathcliff in Liverpool, just as Cathy's coming downstairs 'on a beautiful spring day', namely, her sixteenth birthday, 'dressed for going out' (*WH*, p. 187) may be said to prefigure her own first encounter with Heathcliff on the moors. Accordingly, it is perhaps not without significance that certain articles of clothing used entirely or partly as outdoor wear should have similarly negative associations. Consider, for example, the cloak, which is worn for outings, particularly as protection from cold or bad weather. Thus mention may be made of Joseph's ordering Nelly in the immediate wake of Mr Earnshaw's death, to 'put on [her] cloak and run to Gimmerton for the doctor and the parson', which she reluctantly does 'through wind and rain' (*WH*, p. 38); of Catherine and Heathcliff's appropriating 'the dairy woman's cloak' (*WH*, p. 17) to shield them from the rain on the night of their ominous visit to the Grange, and which Heathcliff will notice Mrs Linton removing from Catherine while 'shaking her head, and expostulating with [the latter]' (*WH*, p. 44); of the cloak which, worn by Isabella on the night of her elopement with Heathcliff, 'fell back' while she was drinking 'a sup of water', thereby enabling the blacksmith's daughter to see her 'very plain' and hence the following morning to inform people 'all over Gimmerton' (*WH*, p. 117); and, finally, of the cloak which, because she has correctly forecast rain, Nelly 'unwillingly donned' (*WH*, p. 202) in order to accompany Cathy on a walk on the moors that will lead to the latter's ill-fated chance encounter with Heathcliff. Footwear, too, is mentioned in a number of negative contexts, affected as it tends to be in one way or other by the elements. Thus reference has already been made to Nelly's bad cold being caused by her sitting too long in 'soaked shoes and stockings', and may also be made to the shoe which Catherine loses while racing in the rain with Heathcliff towards the Grange on the fateful Sunday evening. It is also noteworthy that at Cathy's first reunion with her cousin Linton at the Heights, he is overheard 'calling to Joseph to bring him dry shoes' (*WH*, p. 190) and then, soon afterwards, being told by Heathcliff to take Cathy into the garden 'before you change your shoes' (*WH*, p. 192). As it happens, Linton will remain indoors, but uneasily so because it is Hareton, not himself, who has subsequently been asked to show Cathy round the Heights grounds.

If the realism of Emily's narrative is partly borne out by references made to attire in various states or as worn for sundry purposes, there can be no question that it is added to by the fact that, far from being always used merely for the comfort or beautification of the human body, clothes are sometimes resorted to in ways for which they are not specifically designed. In that respect, *Wuthering Heights* is noticeably different from those many novels in which clothes almost always perform a traditional role in character description, principally as objects of decorative or physiognomic interest. Consider, first of all, certain items of clothing and their adjuncts whose unorthodox functions help to sustain the dramatic or ironic significance of particular episodes. Thus Mr Earnshaw's 'great coat', which he is assumed to be wearing on the morning he sets off for Liverpool, is referred to on his return home as a sort of carrier of the foundling (Heathcliff) and, because used as such, may well have contributed to the destruction of Hindley's violin and the loss of Catherine's whip. Consider, too, the pinafores which, in the wake of Joseph's three-hour religious service, Catherine and Heathcliff 'fastened [...] together, and hung [...] up for a curtain' in 'the arch of the dresser' (*WH*, p. 17), and which, because soon afterwards torn down by the old servant, prompt the youngsters to pay their illicit visit to the Grange on the Sunday evening.

Handkerchiefs, too, are sometimes put to unwonted use as, for instance, when Heathcliff avails himself of one in order to suspend Isabella's dog Fanny to a bridle hook; when Nelly ties one round the cut on Isabella's neck; or when she unknots the one containing Linton Heathcliff's love letters to Cathy before dropping them in the fire in the latter's presence.[6] And though handkerchiefs are also mentioned now and again in their traditional role of wiping away tears, that role also happens to be twice assigned to the apron, an article shown to be worn by three women — Nelly, Zillah and Cathy — all of whom perform domestic duties in one or other of the two households. Thus when Lockwood sees Zillah being scolded in 'the house' by Heathcliff, supposedly because she showed the guest into the wrong room, he notices that she 'ever and anon interrupted her labour to pluck up the corner of her apron, and heave an indignant groan' (*WH*, p. 25); a sight for which Lockwood is indirectly responsible through having sneaked on her earlier that morning. That an apron is indeed considered a kind of handkerchief for a similar reason is suggested when, having asked Nelly who she thinks has 'given [them] the slip', Mr Kenneth waggishly advises her to 'nip up the corner of [her] apron' just before apprising her of Hindley's death (*WH*, p. 163).

Sometimes women's clothes are utilized as means of comfort or moral support. For example, there is a moment in her consultation with Nelly Dean about whether or not to marry Edgar Linton when, having paused amid the metaphorical comparisons she has uttered in order to distinguish between her love for Edgar and her love for Heathcliff, Catherine 'hid her face in the folds of [Nelly's] gown', which she (Nelly) 'jerked [...] forcibly away', being 'out of patience with her folly!' (*WH*, p. 73). This incident somewhat reminds us of a similar recourse to clothing on Linton Heathcliff's part in Chapter 27 when, disappointed at his self-abasing talk at their second official meeting, Cathy reacts as follows: 'Let go my frock — if I pitied you for crying, and looking so very frightened, you should spurn such pity!' (*WH*, p. 235), little aware as she is that Linton's strange behaviour is almost certainly part of Heathcliff's ruse by which she will be lured into the Heights for her fateful marriage to her cousin. A rather more unconventional, not to say ironic, use of a frock may be said of the black frock which Cathy is wearing as a token of mourning over Linton's recent death and which, shortly after her descent to 'the house', Hareton 'filled' (*WH*, p. 262) with books he has passed down to her from the dresser — a deed that may be considered a poetic foreshadowing of their teacher/pupil relationship.

Another article of clothing worn by women is the shawl, whose protectiveness is first alluded to when Nelly realizes that, on the mistaken assumption that both Catherine and Heathcliff have just returned from their illicit Sunday evening excursion in the rain, she 'threw a shawl over [her] head and ran to prevent them from waking Mr Earnshaw by knocking' (*WH*, p. 41). This reference to a shawl may seem gratuitous by comparison with Nelly's reference to the 'light shawl' covering a moribund Catherine as she sits 'in the recess of the open window' (*WH*, p. 137) of her bedroom, quite unaware that she is about to be visited by Heathcliff for the last time in her life. It is probably with the same shawl that Nelly has some months earlier covered Catherine's bedroom mirror in order to prevent her delirious mistress from continuing to confuse it with the black press, an object whose existence is ominously foreshadowed by Lockwood when he refers to it as part of the furniture he notices in the room he has been shown into by Zillah at the beginning of Chapter 3.

Interesting, too, are the ways in which certain articles of clothing are used inappropriately. One striking example is furnished by the fact that, on Isabella's sudden appearance in the Grange parlour after her snowbound flight from the Heights, Nelly notices that 'her feet were protected merely by thin slippers' (*WH*, p. 150), a detail that realistically evokes the very urgency of Isabella's escape from Heathcliff. Again, the waistcoats worn by Heathcliff, Hindley and Hareton are notable, not for their decorative quality, as they commonly are in many a description of dress in nineteenth-century fiction, but for the usefulness of their pockets, as is evident when, for example, Isabella notices Hindley pulling from his waistcoat 'a curiously constructed pistol, having a double-edged spring knife attached to the barrel' (*WH*, p. 123); or when Hareton 'seized and put [...] in his waistcoat' the note brought by Lockwood to Cathy from Nelly, saying that 'Mr Heathcliff should look at it first', only to be presently moved by the girl's tears enough to fling it 'on the floor beside her as ungraciously as he could' (*WH*, p. 266). In this connection, it is noteworthy how often these and other references to pockets have more or less negative connotations. Take, for instance, the pockets belonging to Mr Earnshaw which, on his return from Liverpool, Catherine and Hindley search through in vain for the presents he has promised to bring them; or the fact that Nelly's having put a stop to the milk lad's practice of bringing Linton Heathcliff's letters to Cathy results in that youngster's henceforth coming to the Grange 'with vacant pockets' (*WH*, p. 201); or the occasion when, suspected by Heathcliff of trying to get out of paying his rent because he has just given notice to terminate his tenancy of the Grange, Lockwood angrily deigns to assure him of the contrary as he 'drew [his] notebook from [his] pocket' (*WH*, p. 269).

Pockets may, of course, also be used to shelter one's hands, as happens from time to time in the narrative, especially in moments of psychological tension. A notable example of this occurs when, as Lockwood observes, Heathcliff suspends his conflict with Cathy in 'the house' towards the end of Chapter 3 by placing 'his fists, out of temptation, in his pockets' (*WH*, p. 25). A similar example is furnished during Isabella's awkward meeting with Hindley in Chapter 13, when, amid his puzzling talk and behaviour he declines to answer her request to be shown to her bedroom by a maid, and, instead, merely 'walked up and down, with his hands in his pockets, apparently quite forgetting [her] presence' (*WH*, p. 122). That Hareton himself might have picked up this curious habit from his father, or even from Heathcliff, is suggested when, during the time Nelly is pleading in vain with Cathy to return with her to Grange immediately after having found her at the Heights in Hareton's company, she notices that the latter 'stood with his hands in his pockets, too awkward to speak' (*WH*, p. 171). It is likely that Heathcliff himself has seen Hareton doing much the same thing when, having told him to show Cathy round the Heights grounds, he includes among his instructions as to appropriate behaviour in her presence that he should 'keep [his] hands out of [his] pockets' (*WH*, p. 192), a piece of advice which he will by no means later apply to himself when, in the throes of a gloomy mood, he receives his tenant Lockwood at the Heights for the first time.[7]

Of all types of clothing referred to in *Wuthering Heights*, however, none is more often mentioned or thematically more interesting than the hat. References to headgear, which include such matters as the tying and untying of women's hats, serve to underpin the realism of the narrative.[8] Headgear sometimes also plays a useful part in the plot, as may be especially noted in Chapter 22 when, having scrambled down the outside of the Thrushcross park wall bordering a highway in order to retrieve the hat that has fallen off her head while she was trying to reach some rose hips, Cathy meets Heathcliff for the second time; an encounter that will lead to a resumption of her fateful relations with her cousin Linton the following day. But hats also contribute to moments of extreme tension in the action. Thus, dismayed by Catherine's violence and deceit during his rendezvous with her at the Heights in Chapter 8, Edgar is described by Nelly as follows: 'The insulted visiter [sic] moved to the spot where he had laid his hat, pale and with a quivering lip' (*WH*, p. 63). Although this detail plainly indicates Edgar's intention to leave forthwith, in the event he fails to do so, just as Nelly herself does when, despite 'hastening to resume [her] bonnet' (*WH*, p. 134) in order to return to the Grange because she has been upset by Heathcliff's verbal cruelty to Isabella, she, too, will stay on much longer than she ought to have done. In both episodes, the failure to pick up a hat and depart will have nefarious consequences, whether, as in Edgar's case, in the form of his ill-fated betrothal to Catherine, or, as in Nelly's case, being browbeaten into making a promise to arrange for Heathcliff an equally ill-fated tryst between himself and Catherine. Again, when in Chapter 19 Joseph arrives at the Grange to take the newly-arrived Linton Heathcliff back with him to the Heights, he is described by Nelly as 'donned in his Sunday garments', whereby, 'holding his hat in one hand, and his stick in the other, he proceeded to clean his shoes on the mat' (*WH*, p. 178). Yet dressed to kill as he is, probably on Heathcliff's instructions and hence seemingly confident of succeeding in his mission, Joseph nevertheless finds himself, despite his initial aggressiveness towards both Nelly and Edgar, ultimately worsted and obliged to return to the Heights, his mission unaccomplished.

The most significant part of this rather comic description of Joseph for our purposes, however, is the reference to his hat, an article of clothing which, worn purportedly for protection against the elements, seems also to be associated with respectability. This may be said to be true even of the occasional references to Linton Heathcliff's cap.[9] The idea of the respectability of the hat is, however, perhaps best conveyed by Nelly's somewhat gratuitous references to her bonnet. Consider, for instance, that moment when, anxious over the recently returned Heathcliff's influence on the two households, she says this at the beginning of Chapter 25: 'Sometimes, while meditating on these things in solitude, I've got up in a sudden terror, and put on my bonnet to go see how all was at the farm' (*WH*, p. 96). And though Nelly's respectability turns partly on her quest to 'warn [Hindley] how people talked regarding his ways' (*WH*, p. 96), such respectability will be shown up rather comically when, shortly before arriving at the Heights for what will in the end prove to have been an abortive visit, she encounters the child Hareton, who, notwithstanding her blandly introducing herself to him as 'thy nurse' and telling him she has come to see his father, has meanwhile picked up a flint that 'struck [her] bonnet' (*WH*, p. 97).

It is perhaps the same bonnet that Nelly will refer to after she has come to the Heights in answer to Isabella's letter of distress. Thus in spite of her apparent refusal to accept Nelly's hint that she has not brought with her 'the expected letter' from Edgar, Isabella, as Nelly recalls, 'followed me to a sideboard, where I went to lay my bonnet, and importuned me in a whisper to give her directly what I had brought' (*WH*, p. 130). Soon afterwards Nelly's respectability will be again manifested when, as we saw above, she describes herself 'hastening to resume [her] bonnet' (*WH*, p. 134) in reaction to the vicious language with which Heathcliff has been addressing Isabella. Nelly's final reference to a bonnet occurs when, just released from her incarceration at the Heights by the sudden appearance of Zillah, she notices that the latter is 'donned in her scarlet shawl, with a black silk bonnet on her head, and a willow basket swung to her arm' (*WH*, p. 246). What is interesting about this detail is the reference to the 'black silk bonnet', which, like the 'scarlet shawl', somehow seems physiognomically appropriate to Zillah's presentation as a person whose arrant respectability is but an expression of the vanity and stupidity she exhibits not only in this context but, more particularly, in Chapter 30.[10]

Just as the hat is a sort of symbol of respectability in Emily's novel, so hatlessness, it would appear, denotes a certain loss or absence of social dignity. One example of this is shown when, having snatched Joseph's lantern in order to return to the Grange, Lockwood finds himself presently floored by the house dogs and ending up 'hatless and trembling with wrath' (*WH*, p. 14); a state of affairs that patently marks a comedown for a man who, in his diary, makes a point of now and then referring to the donning or doffing of his hat when leaving or arriving somewhere, as if to remind himself of his genteel respectability.[11] On the other hand, far from necessarily bespeaking social inadequacy, hatlessness seems virtually a badge of honour for Catherine, at least until her first encounter with the Lintons at the Grange. As Nelly herself makes plain, Catherine's 'feathered beaver' as worn by the latter on her return to the Heights five weeks later, indicates how radically different she now is from the 'wild, hatless little savage' (*WH*, p. 46) she used to be. That this latter image attests the essential Catherine is somewhat corroborated on the night she waits in the rain for Heathcliff to return to the Heights, 'refusing', as Nelly wryly observes, to 'take shelter, and standing bonnetless and shawl-less to catch as much water as she could with her hair and clothes' (*WH*, p. 75). This detail seems thematically linked with Nelly's description of Heathcliff in the Grange grounds on the morning after Catherine's death, 'leant against an old ash tree, his hat off, and his hair soaked with the dew that had gathered on the budded branches, and fell pattering round him' (*WH*, p. 146). Heathcliff's hatlessness here is very probably a kind of homage on his part to the memory of the 'hatless' childhood he spent with Catherine.

Still, hatlessness sometimes assumes a rather more constructive dimension, especially on the day Cathy sets off on her illicit ride to Penistone Craggs, 'sheltered by her wide-brimmed hat and gauze veil from the July sun' (*WH*, p. 169); an excursion which will, however, end in the Heights, where Nelly, finding her in Hareton's company after a long and frantic search for her, almost immediately addresses her thus: 'Put that hat on, and home at once', adding that she will 'tie the riband' (*WH*, p. 171). What follows constitutes one of the most humorous episodes in the narrative, for Cathy not only knocks her hat off her head but avoids Nelly's endeavours to reinstate it, encouraged as she is in her resistance by the amusement shown by Hareton and the Heights housekeeper. And though Cathy's antics are soon abruptly brought to an end when she learns to her incredulous astonishment that Hareton is her cousin, the reader may nevertheless recall that, on arriving at the Heights not long beforehand, Nelly not only noticed that Cathy was 'rocking herself in a little chair that had been her mother's, when a child' but that her hat was 'hung against the wall' and that she 'seemed perfectly at home' (*WH*, p. 170f.) — a detail which, evoking as it does the well-known idiom about becoming part of a family, poetically prefigures the young heroine's eventual betrothal to Hareton.

It is by the time this betrothal has taken place that Lockwood notices on his final visit to the Heights, probably to his dismay, that Hareton is 'respectably dressed' (*WH*, p. 273) during his reading lesson with Cathy; an observation which, while clearly hinting at the young man's rise in social status, is interesting not so much for what it tells us about the person observed as for reminding us of Lockwood's inveterate snobbery as an observer. And though it is true that certain descriptions of clothes in Emily Brontë's novel can tell us something about a character's change of status, as in the case of Catherine and Heathcliff, or, as in the case of Nelly Dean, Joseph and Zillah, underline their essential respectability, it would appear that, where clothes in general are concerned, Emily can scarcely be bracketed with her contemporaries, a good many of whom, including her sister Charlotte, are given to more or less detailed descriptions of clothes, sometimes making references to them in the form of leitmotifs as means of emphasizing the peculiar moral physiognomy of the characters wearing them.[12] On the contrary, attire in *Wuthering Heights* is significant rather for the ways in which individual articles of clothing are used for various thematic or structural purposes, often with negative symbolic intent, but sometimes, as we have seen with respect to headgear, with delightful humour and irony; in a word, in ways seldom to be found in other works of fiction of the period, or, for that matter, in any period. And if in our absorption in the main events of the novel, we readers may be unmindful of the uses of attire in the narrative, it is nevertheless by noting the very economy of Emily Brontë's recourse to all kinds of clothes that we may be confirmed in our awareness of the brilliant artistry with which she has assembled all the elements that make up her masterpiece.

Brontë Studies, 41/3 (2016)

Notes

1   Although no monograph has to my knowledge been hitherto
entirely devoted to this subject, some useful references to clothes
in *Wuthering Heights* may be found in Allan R. Brick, '*Wuthering
Heights*: Narrators, Audience, Message', *College English*, 21
(1959), 80-86; Elliot B. Gose, Jr, '*Wuthering Heights*: The Heath
and the Hearth', *Nineteenth-Century Fiction*, 21 (1966), 1-19; John
Beversluis, 'Love and Self-Knowledge: A Study of *Wuthering
Heights*', *English*, 24 (1975), 77-82; Terence McCarthy, 'The
Incompetent Narrator of *Wuthering Heights*', *Modern Language
Quarterly*, 42 (1981), 48-64; Ian Jack, 'Novels and Those
"Necessary Evils": Annotating the Brontës', *Essays in Criticism*,
32 (1982), 321-37; John Allen Stevenson, '"Heathcliff is Me!":
Wuthering Heights and the Question of Likeness', *Nineteenth-
Century Literature*, 43 (1988), 60-81; Ingrid Geerken, '"The Dead
are not annihilated": Mortal Regret in *Wuthering Heights*', *Journal
of Narrative Theory*, 34 (2004), 373-406. For quotations from
the novel, see Emily Brontë, *Wuthering Heights*, ed. by Ian Jack
and Patsy Stoneman (Oxford: Oxford University Press, 1998);
hereafter *WH*. For the sake of convenience, the first Catherine
will be referred to as 'Catherine', the second as 'Cathy'.

2   See, for example, Albert Genevray, 'Le Portrait au XVIIe siècle',
Bulletin de la Faculté des Lettres de Poitiers, 3 (1885), 72-131; Arthur
Franz, *Das literarische Porträt in Frankreich im Zeitalter Richelieus und
Mazarins* (Leipzig: University of Leipzig, 1906); Edward Chauncy
Baldwin, 'Marivaux's Place in the Development of Character
Portrayal', *Publications of the Modern Language Association of America*,
27 (1912), 168-87; Blanchard W. Bates, *Literary Portraiture in the
Historical Narrative of the French Renaissance* (New York: G. E.
Stechen, 1945); Ruth P. Thomas, 'The Art of the Portrait in the

Novels of Marivaux', *French Review*, 42 (1968), 23-31; D. van der Cruysse, *Le Portrait littéraire en France au XVIIe siècle* (Paris: A. G. Nizet, 1971); R. Nunn, 'Mademoiselle de Scudéry and the Development of the Literary Portrait: Some Unusual Portraits in *Clélie*', *Romance Notes*, 17 (1976), 180-84; Erica Harth, 'The Ideological Value of the Portrait in Seventeenth-Century France', *L'Esprit Créateur*, 21 (1981), 15-25; Hendrik Kars, *Le Portrait chez Marivaux, Étude d'un Type de Segment Textuel* (Amsterdam: Editions Rodopi, 1981); Graeme Tytler, '"Faith in the Hand of Nature": Physiognomy in Sir Walter Scott's Fiction', *Studies in Scottish Literature*, 33 (2004), 223-46.

3   See *Wuthering Heights*, pp. 39, 49, 60.

4   See *Wuthering Heights*, pp. 121, 124.

5   One thinks of the indoor attire of Heathcliff, Lockwood and Isabella as affected by rain or snow. See *Wuthering Heights*, pp. 8, 26, 41, 150.

6   See *Wuthering Heights*, pp. 114, 152, 200.

7   See *Wuthering Heights*, p. 1.

8   For references to the tying and untying women's hats, see *Wuthering Heights*, pp. 46, 171, 217.

9   See *Wuthering Heights*, pp. 177, 183, 190, 194.

10   See especially *Wuthering Heights*, pp. 259-64.

11   See *Wuthering Heights*, pp. 6, 275.

12 This is especially true of some of the characters in *Villette*, notably
Paul Emanuel. See Graeme Tytler, 'Physiognomy and Identity in
Villette', *Brontë Studies*, 38.1 (2013), 43, 45, 50.

Books in *Wuthering Heights*

R eaders who have enjoyed and esteemed *Wuthering Heights* primarily for its principal love story might be intrigued to be made aware of the important role played by books in the narrative.[1] Indeed, quite apart from their function in underlining the social differences between the two households depicted, books prove to be useful means of casting light on some of the major and minor characters portrayed therein. At the same time, it would appear that the author is implicitly intent on raising the question as to the role of books in everyday life. Thus, whereas books certainly form a normal part of everyday life in the civilized societies of eighteenth-century England, it might be just as readily asked not only how far books are necessary, but whether literacy itself is as important as it is assumed to be. Let us, then, consider the two main narrators, Lockwood and Nelly Dean, both of whom are notable for their generally respectful references to books.[2]

First of all, Lockwood is presented at the outset as something of a man of books, as may be gathered from his apparent familiarity, not only with Shakespeare, but with the Bible.[3] Further, his elaborate description of that part of the interior of the Heights known as 'the house' in Chapter 1 already betokens a certain literary bent on his part. It is, however, when he is resting in the bed of the oak-panelled closet in Chapter 3 that he confirms his interest in books while leafing through a collection of some piled on the ledge nearby. Lockwood says nothing about the content of the books, though they are most probably theological texts, as is suggested by the 'Testament' in which he reads 'Catherine Earnshaw, her book' and 'a date some quarter of a century back' (Brontë 1998, 16), that is to say, when Catherine was about eleven years old. That the Testament might have originally belonged to Joseph is suggested when, having been 'hurled' with Heathcliff by Hindley into the back-kitchen, namely, the servants' quarters, for misdemeanours one Sunday, Catherine writes this in the said text: 'I reached this book, and a pot of ink from a shelf, and pushed the house-door ajar to give me light, and I have got the time on with writing for twenty minutes' (Brontë 1998, 17). The fact that the Testament is now lodged in the oak-panelled room would therefore suggest that Catherine somehow kept or retrieved it illicitly in order to prevent Joseph not only from reading her rude comments about him, but also from seeing what Lockwood describes as 'an excellent caricature of my friend Joseph, rudely yet powerfully sketched' (Brontë 1998, 16). And though Lockwood goes on to examine what he refers to as Catherine's 'select' library, he is distracted from their content by the commentaries and diary she has written, 'covering every morsel of blank that the printer had left' (Brontë 1998, 16). That Lockwood may have hardly, if at all, read any of those books is quite likely, for he almost instantly falls asleep after reading only the title of the Reverend Jabes Branderham's sermon, which, together with Catherine's diaries as well as his own memories of the unpleasant experiences he has undergone in the first two chapters, form the bases of his two nightmares.

One has the impression from later references that books are

for Lockwood a means of passing the time rather than a means of spiritual fulfilment. Further, when, in his second nightmare, he 'hurriedly piled the books up in a pyramid' (Brontë 1998, 21) against the window he has broken in a desperate attempt to prevent the wailing waif child from entering the bedroom, we may interpret this gesture as symbolic of his recourse to books as instruments by which to shut himself against the realities of life. At the same time, his carelessly letting his candle burn part of the calf-skin cover of the 'Testament' is enough to indicate his lack of concern for books as material objects. And though Lockwood will later be admirably supportive of Hareton Earnshaw's quest to teach himself to read, he is at best a desultory reader, especially when, on his third visit to the Heights, he responds to Cathy's having informed him that she has no books to read by exclaiming: 'No books! [...] How do you contrive to live here without them? [...] Though provided with a large library, I'm frequently very dull at the Grange — take my books away, and I should be desperate!' (Brontë 1998, 266). Such words are an ironic reminder that, like the girl with whom he fell in love at the sea-coast, what loses its charm for Lockwood is what is all too easily available.

It is in that very library that Nelly has already informed Lockwood in Chapter 7 thus: '[Y]ou could not open a book in this library that I have not looked into, and got something out of also; unless it be that range of Greek and Latin, and that of French — and those I know one from another: it is as much as you can expect of a poor man's daughter' — an utterance made in reply to Lockwood's having assured her that she has 'thought a great deal more than the generality of servants think' (Brontë 1998, 55). And though we might wonder how with her humble background Nelly should have become as literate as she seems to have become by then, it is not implausible that as housekeeper at the Grange, and notwithstanding her educational limitations, she should have turned to books in order to pass some of the time when she is not working. Yet her reading of books appears to have been scarcely discriminative enough to bespeak a genuine love of books for their own sake. Moreover, although before referring to the books in the Grange library, she answers Lockwood's commendation of her mentality by saying that she has 'undergone sharp discipline which has taught [her] wisdom' (Brontë 1998, 55), we may nevertheless suspect that the 'wisdom' she implicitly claims to have partly obtained from books has, however, been scarcely enough to deter her from the moral shortcomings she is later to reveal in her narrative. Practically all references to her reading of books are somewhat perfunctory,[4] thereby indirectly reminding us perhaps that books at the Heights lack the appeal she is subsequently to find in the more or less secular books at the Grange. That Nelly's taste in books seems indeed mundane, not to say mediocre, is implied in Chapter 24 when, convalescing one evening after three weeks of a bad cold, she notices Cathy's reluctance to read to her in the Grange library, unaware as she is that this reluctance is due to her young mistress's anxiety at being delayed in paying an illicit visit to Linton Heathcliff at the Heights that very evening. Imagining, therefore, that Cathy's unwillingness has to do with the fact that '[her] sort of books did not suit her', Nelly then bids her 'please herself in the choice of what she perused' (Brontë 1998, 216). This Cathy does by selecting one of her favourites, thereby adumbrating the idea that, for all her limitations and shortcomings as an early teenager, she is of all the characters second to none for her love of books.

As may be gathered from the foregoing, books in the Heights appear to be mainly of religious content. Certainly Catherine's books referred to in Chapter 3 do not seem to be of secular interest, even though one wonders how far any 'pen-and-ink commentary' of hers, which, according to Lockwood, 'scarcely one chapter had escaped' (Brontë 1998, 16), has to do with the actual content of the printed texts. That such commentaries might have been quite negative is, at any rate, possible in so far as Catherine relates in the diary she writes in the blank spaces of one such book that, in the wake of a three-hour service held in an attic one Sunday, she and Heathcliff are distracted from their private activities in 'the house' by Joseph's foisting upon them what he calls 'good books eneugh if ye'll read 'em' (Brontë 1998, 17). The two books are theological texts, as is evident from their titles; and, having each kicked them into the dog-kennel, the youngsters are reported by Joseph to Hindley, who then hurls them both into the back-kitchen; an incident that soon afterwards induces them to escape from the Heights that same evening and pay their historic first visit to the Grange. In this connection, we may also surmise why Catherine and Heathcliff appear to have no particular interest in books of any kind. Most references to books at the Heights centre on those possessed by Joseph, chief among them being the Bible, by and from which he readily quotes whenever there is a crisis, as, for example, during the storm on the night of Heathcliff's disappearance. Even after Heathcliff's death, and amid a now benign atmosphere at the Heights, as Lockwood himself senses on his fourth and final visit there, Joseph complains about Nelly's light-hearted singing of songs by saying this: 'It's a blazing shaime, ut Aw cannut oppen t' Blessed Book, bud yah set up them glories tuh Sattan, un' all t' flaysome wickednesses ut iver wer born intuh t' warld!' — a sentiment to which Nelly blithely replies: 'But wisht, old man, and read your Bible, like a Christian, and never mind me' (Brontë 1998, 274).

It is partly against this background that we come to understand why Catherine and Heathcliff, capable of reading adult texts as they both appear to be, are nowhere remarked on for, or confess to, a love of books. As has been said above, the books owned by Catherine have probably been given to her for religious reasons, and are more than likely to be of little interest to her at the age of eleven. But even at that age, and living as she does in the late eighteenth century, when children are known to have been remarkably literate, Catherine may be supposed perfectly capable of understanding the content of books meant primarily for adults. This is partly indicated by the fact that she is made by the local curate to 'get by heart' several (presumably) biblical 'chapters' (Brontë 1998, 40) as punishment for her misdemeanours. That Heathcliff has, thanks to the same curate, learnt how to read and write well enough to become remarkably literary in his use of language is suggested by his quite sophisticated account to Nelly in Chapter 6 of his and Catherine's illicit Sunday evening visit to the Grange. Still, by this time deprived of the curate's lessons by Hindley, and despite Catherine's teaching him 'what she learnt' (Brontë 1998, 40), Heathcliff would appear to have lost all interest in books. It is, of course, possible that such an interest has been revived during the three years of his absence from Gimmerton, at least to judge by the extraordinary rhetorical skills he displays after his return to the neighbourhood, most notably in Chapters 14 and 21. Nevertheless, Heathcliff's overt dislike of books is amply confirmed in Chapter 31, when Cathy informs Lockwood that the reason why he (Heathcliff) 'took it into his head to destroy [her] books' is that he 'never reads' (Brontë 1998, 266).

If Catherine's own rhetorical skills, as manifest especially in the striking figurative language with which she expounds her philosophy of life as well as differentiating between her love for Edgar and her love for Heathcliff to Nelly Dean in Chapter 8, may have been partly acquired from some of the books she has read, it is nevertheless clear, particularly after her marriage to Edgar, that she has little interest in books, let alone any love of them, and that notwithstanding that the Grange library contains several books of secular content. The library is quite often occupied by Edgar; and though we are never told of the nature of his interest in books,[5] it is assumed that he is usually reading books there. This is especially implicit during the time Catherine has been sequestered in her bedroom for three nights as a consequence of the showdown between Edgar and Heathcliff in the Grange kitchen. During this period Nelly recalls that Edgar 'spent his time in the library, and did not inquire concerning his wife's occupations' (Brontë 1998, 105) and that he 'shut himself up among books that he never opened' (Brontë 1998, 106). It is during this episode that we once again sense something of the animosity that Catherine harboured against books in her childhood at the Heights. This is quite parent in her following reaction to Nelly's assertion: 'Among his books! [...] And I dying! I on the brink of the grave!' (Brontë 1998, 107). Such is Catherine's disdain and contempt for Edgar at that time that, picturing as she does his solemn behaviour at her deathbed in Chapter 12, she imagines him 'offering prayers of thanks to God for restoring peace to his house, and going back to his *books!*' (Brontë 1998, 107). And when Edgar later comes to Catherine to ask her if she loves 'that wretch, Heath—' (Brontë 1998, 113), as he puts it, she continues to show her resentment of his recent neglect of her by addressing him thus: 'I don't want you, Edgar; I'm past wanting you... Return to your books... I'm glad you possess a consolation, for all you had in me is gone' (Brontë 1998, 113). Nelly's assumption that Edgar has been spending his time reading is doubtless quite unfair to him, all the more as she cannot have exactly known what he was doing there during Catherine's sequestration. If Catherine's hostility towards Edgar's apparent bibliophily somewhat underlines their incompatibility as a married couple, it is none the less a sign of her heavy dependence on him for his loving attentions. Still, even though she is clearly appreciative of those attentions during her convalescence after her 'brain fever' (Brontë 1998, 118), we note that, just before her last tryst with Heathcliff in Chapter 18, Catherine is described sitting in her bedroom where '[a] book lay spread on the sill before her', namely, a book which, as Nelly believes, Edgar had 'laid [...] there, for she never endeavoured to divert herself with reading, or occupation of any kind' (Brontë 1998, 138). Certainly, as far as books are concerned, as we see later in the narrative, Catherine may be said to have been to the very end of her life the antithesis of her daughter Cathy.

Cathy's interest in books is already evident during Lockwood's second visit to the Heights in Chapter 2. The earliest reference to her reading a book occurs when, having been reproved by Joseph for her idleness, she reacts by taking 'a long, dark book from a shelf' and telling him 'how far [she has] progressed in the Black Art' (Brontë 1998, 12), thereby mockingly giving him to understand that his recent mishaps have been due to her recourse to that book. No doubt, the book is some religious text by means of which she is probably making up her spiteful comments in order to tease the old servant into a superstitious frenzy. The book is referred to again when, after advising Lockwood to 'take the road [he] came' in order to get back to the Grange, Cathy is described 'ensconcing herself in a chair, with a candle, and the long book open before her' (Brontë 1998, 12), perhaps as if, irrespective of its content, any book were better than none with which to pass her dreary time at the Heights. But it is when, on the morning after his night spent in the oak-panelled closet, Lockwood sees Cathy trying to read a book in 'the house' by the light of the fire being bellowed by Zillah that she first manifests the importance of books for her, and particularly so since becoming Heathcliff's prisoner at the Heights. That the book itself is quite likely to be one of those she gave to her late husband Linton Heathcliff rather than some theological tome, may explain her continual attempts to read it. This endeavour on her part is quite enough to confirm the chronic hatred that Heathcliff seems to have had for books since childhood, as may be gathered when he scolds Cathy thus: 'There you are at your idle tricks again! The rest of them do earn their bread — you live on my charity! Put your trash away, and find something to do' — words to which Cathy retorts: 'I'll put my trash away, because you can make me, if I refuse', doing so, as Lockwood further observes, by 'closing her book, and throwing it on a chair' and then refusing to do anything except, as she says, 'what I please' (Brontë 1998, 25). Thus through a book we see for the first time a symbolic instance of the open defiance with which Cathy has already resisted, and will later resist, Heathcliff's tyranny over her.

When Lockwood meets Cathy again on his third visit to the Heights and delivers Nelly Dean's note to her, she says this to him: 'You must tell her [...] that I would answer her letter, but I have no materials for writing, not even a book from which I might tear a leaf' (Brontë 1998, 266), the last of which words are an ironic reminder of her mother's illicit use of books. And here Cathy is surely referring to her own books, all of which, as she tells Lockwood, Heathcliff has destroyed. Nevertheless, we note in Chapter 23 that, having come down to 'the house' one Sunday morning several days after Linton Heathcliff's death, Cathy will, despite her standoffishness, presently accept Hareton Earnshaw's offer to hand down to her some books placed high up on the dresser. These are books which Lockwood has not mentioned in his elaborate description of the contents of that same dresser in Chapter 1, but which may have included those that Cathy has given to her late husband, rather than the theological books referred to above. This is suggested when Zillah tells Nelly of Hareton's being bold enough to 'stoop and point out what struck his fancy in certain old pictures which they contained' (Brontë 1998, 262-263). Further, the fact that, as Zillah also observes, Cathy 'continued reading, or seeking for something to read' (Brontë 1998, 263) indicates that those books are of aesthetic interest. Such illustrated books, together with his strong physical attraction to Cathy, will almost certainly have first aroused Hareton's own interest in books and, as we see later, enough so for him to make his bumbling efforts to teach himself to read.

It is, however, not until Cathy's reunion with Linton Heathcliff in Chapter 21 that we first come across references to the books she possesses. Thus, shortly after she has been forbidden by her father to visit the Heights, the injunction proves to have been harsh enough to cause her to weep profusely at her bedside that evening. And though her tearful distress is pooh-poohed by Nelly, Cathy nevertheless asks, albeit in vain, to send Linton not only a note saying that she is unable to visit him at the Heights next day, but also 'those books I promised to lend him', adding: 'his books are not as nice as mine, and he wanted to have them extremely, when I told him how interesting they were' (Brontë 1998, 197). And though refused permission by Nelly to fulfil these requests, Cathy still succeeds in having the books as well as the note secretly delivered to Linton. That books have already played some part in Linton's life by the time of his arrival at the Grange may be gathered from his happy memories of his mother Isabella, herself familiar enough with books at the Grange since her childhood. But apart from one reference by Nelly to Isabella being 'absorbed in her meditations, or a book' (Brontë 1998, 92) during a period of tension following the latter's having told Catherine about her love for Heathcliff, the only other reference to her reading of books has to do with 'some old books' (Brontë 1998, 154) she peruses as a means of passing the time during her cheerless sojourn at the Heights as Heathcliff's bride. While Linton's relations with Cathy are consolidated by the books which she brings him and which he apparently enjoys for their content, Linton eventually turns out to have been ultimately interested in books for their value as material objects. This is made quite apparent when, barely a few days after he has been married to Cathy, he tells Nelly that his father has assured him that 'everything [Cathy] has is mine', including '[a]ll her nice books', before going on to say that, in spite of Cathy's having offered to give him those books, together with all her other possessions, he told her 'she had nothing to give, they were all, all mine' (Brontë 1998, 248).

We can hardly help sensing from such grotesque utterances that, amid his intrinsically possessive attitude towards books, Linton shows how much he differs from Cathy in her regard for books for their content, much of which she values enough to commit certain passages of prose and poetry to memory.[6] Nevertheless, there can be no question that Cathy and Linton are both all too proud of their literacy. This is quite manifest in their childishly snobbish reactions to Hareton's illiteracy in Chapter 21 and, more particularly in Chapter 24, when Cathy herself humiliates the latter for his inability to read 'the figures' (Brontë 1998, 220) above the Heights front door. This very humiliation shortly afterwards induces Hareton to burst into 'the house' at the very moment when Cathy, who happens to have 'brought some of her nicest books' for Linton on one of her illicit visits to the Heights, is about to read a little from one of them. Such is Cathy's fear of Hareton's violent mood at this point that she 'let one volume fall', which, just before shutting the cousins out, he 'kicked' after her (Brontë 1998, 221), thereby ironically reminding us, and perhaps pleasantly so, of the Sunday evening when Catherine and Heathcliff kicked into the dog-kennel the theological books imposed on them by Joseph in Chapter 6. Hareton's rage may be said to derive partly from his apparent awareness that Cathy and Linton's affectionate friendship is bound by their joint love of books. Such a bond is somewhat underlined when, despite having delayed going to the Heights for several days after being turned out of 'the house' by an angry Hareton, Cathy on her return finds Linton 'to [her] inexpressible joy', lying on a sofa in his apartment, 'reading one of [her] books' (Brontë 1998, 223).

Yet noble as is Cathy's lending Linton some books of her own as well as her offering to give them to him after they have been married, we nevertheless sense in these generous gestures on her part something of the snobbery she has already exhibited, and will exhibit quite arrantly, while Heathcliff's prisoner at the Heights. Such snobbery, which is at its most blatant when she refuses to accept that Hareton is her cousin is, of course, the expression of a young girl conscious of her privileged social background and still too immature to accept the realities of life. All this is quite evident when Lockwood, on his third visit to the Heights, hears her mocking Hareton's reading aloud from books he has deprived her of and expressing her annoyance that he happens to have chosen some favourite passages of her own. Nowhere in the narrative does Cathy make herself a more unsympathetic figure than she does in this context, or better justify the negative remarks that have been made about her by some Brontë scholars over the years.[7]

It is, however, easy to forget that Cathy's contemptuous remarks about Hareton's interest in books occur at a time when she is in a state of chronic depression as Heathcliff's prisoner at the Heights, compelled as she is to put up with the company of those whom she, albeit unfairly, considers too inferior to associate with and from whom there appears to be no chance of escaping. Yet Cathy is also intelligent enough to know that the only way out of her impasse, at least while Heathcliff remains alive, is to be reconciled with Hareton, aware as she doubtless is by now of his commendable qualities of character and mindful as she is, too, of his by no means displeasing personal appearance.[8] And this she manages to do both by offering Hareton a book and by offering to teach him to read therewith, even though we might rightly surmise that, had Heathcliff died while she was still at loggerheads with her cousin, there is unlikely to have been any reconciliation between them. All the same, adversely affected as we may sometimes be by Cathy's seemingly excessive attachment to books, we should not forget that, for all her outrageously nonsensical talk and behaviour as an early teenager, she eventually comes across as a person of intrinsically admirable character.[9] Thus, quite apart from her extraordinary devotion to Linton Heathcliff, even when he is at his most tyrannical towards her, not to mention her love for her father and for Nelly Dean, Cathy almost invariably displays an essential honesty and truthfulness not only in what she says but also in what she does. A good example of this may be noted when the Grange groom Michael, having, in return for his willingness to prepare her pony for her illicit evening rides to the Heights, asked Cathy to 'lend him books out of the library', has his request declined because, as she tells Nelly, 'I preferred giving him my own, and that satisfied him better' (Brontë 1998, 218). This act of generosity, linked as it may be with her giving or lending books to Linton Heathcliff, may be said to foreshadow that moment when she will also give Hareton a book of her own, and one by which they will once more become the good friends they appear to have been at their very first meeting at the Heights in Chapter 18.

There can be little doubt, however, that Cathy has been a comparatively unpopular figure for readers of *Wuthering Heights*, perhaps because, after the dramatic love story between Catherine and Heathcliff, she has been remembered chiefly, albeit rather mistakenly, for little more than the inveterate snobbery she exhibits from her earliest years as a sort of spoilt brat until her eventual reconciliation with Hareton. Yet even this reconciliation has not deterred some scholars from somewhat condemning Cathy's teaching Hareton to read as but a way of clipping his wings, not to say emasculating him.[10] This interpretation may have to do with the fact that Heathcliff and Catherine have by then come across to many a reader as characters whose attractiveness as heroic figures is not a little buttressed by their marked lack of interest in, or affection for, books. Something of this attitude is alluded to when Joseph, in his jealousy of Hareton's reconciliation with Cathy in the Heights kitchen through their mutual affection as well as their shared love of books, warns the latter, after she has told her cousin that she will 'leave this book' she has given him 'upon the chimney-piece' and that she will 'bring [him] some more to-morrow', by saying this to her: 'Ony books ut yah leave, Aw shall tak intuh th' hahse [...] un' it 'ull be mitch if yah find 'em agean' (Brontë 1998, 280). Reminding us as they do of Heathcliff's dislike of books and of his practice of destroying them, Joseph's words nevertheless fail to deflate the joyous mood of that instant when one unnamed book has brought together two people destined for essentially heroic status by the end of the narrative, at the same time as the author indirectly reassures us that literacy and a love of books are after all practically indispensable for our appreciation and enjoyment of her masterpiece.

Brontë Studies, 48/1-2 (2023)

References

Brontë, Emily. 1998. Wuthering Heights. Edited by Ian Jack and Patsy Stoneman. Oxford: Oxford University Press.

Buckley, Vincent. 1964. "Passion and Control in Wuthering Heights." The Southern Review 1 (2): 23.

Craik, Wendy. 1968. The Brontë Novels, 34. London: Methuen.

Dawson, Terence. 1989. "'An Oppression Past Explaining': The Structures of Wuthering Heights." Orbis Litterarum 44: 64.

Edgar, Pelham. 1932. "Judgments on Appeal-II. The Brontës." Queen's Quarterly 39: 422.

Gardiner, Alan. 1988. "Does the Novel Deteriorate with the Death of Catherine?" In Critical Essays on Wuthering Heights, edited by Linda Cookson and Bryan Loughrey, 90. London: Longman.

Newman, Beth. 1990. "'The Situation of the Looker-On': Gender, Narration and Gaze in Wuthering Heights." PMLA 105 (5): 1036.

Steinitz, Rebecca. 2000. "Diaries and Displacement in Wuthering Heights." Studies in the Novel 32 (4): 407-419.

Tytler, Graeme. 2017. "The Presentation of the Second Catherine in Wuthering Heights." Brontë Studies 42 (1): 26-36.

Notes

1 Although several references have been made to books in various scholarly writings on *Wuthering Heights*, no monograph has to my knowledge been hitherto entirely devoted to this subject. I have, however, found one article discussing diaries, namely, Steinitz (2000).

2 For the sake of convenience, the first Catherine is referred to as 'Catherine', the second as 'Cathy' throughout this paper.

3 See Brontë (1998, 3, 14, 19, 20).

4 For the only example in the text of Nelly's perfunctory reading of a book, see Brontë (1998, 210).

5 For references to Edgar's actually reading a book, see Brontë (1998, 105, 199).

6 See Brontë (1998, 213, 267).

7 See especially Edgar (1932); Buckley (1964); Craik (1968); Gardiner (1988).

8 See Brontë (1998, 192).

9 See Tytler (2017).

10 See especially Dawson (1989); Newman (1990).

Author's Publications
(in chronological order)

(Books)

Physiognomy in the European Novel: Faces and Fortunes (Princeton, NJ: Princeton University Press, 1982).

Physiognomy in Profile: Lavater's Impact on European Culture, co-edited with Melissa Percival (Newark, NJ: University of Delaware Press, 2005).

Facets of Wuthering Heights: Selected Essays (Kibworth Beauchamp: Matador, 2018)

(Articles)

'Letters of Recommendation and False Vizors: Physiognomy in the Novels of Henry Fielding', in *Eighteenth-Century Fiction*, 2/2 (1990), 93-111.

'Mansfield's "The Voyage"', in *The Explicator*, 50/1 (1991), 42-45.

'Martha Lacy Hall, Louisiana Short-Story Writer', in *Regional Dimensions*, 10 (1992), 52-80.

'Heathcliff's Monomania: an Anachronism in *Wuthering Heights*', in *Brontë Society Transactions*, 20/6 (1992), 331-343.

'Lavater and the Nineteenth-Century English Novel', in *The Faces of Physiognomy: Interdisciplinary Approaches to Johann Caspar Lavater*, ed. Ellis Shookman (Columbia, SC: Camden House, 1993), 161-181.

'Physiognomy in *Wuthering Heights*', in *Brontë Society Transactions*, 21/4 (1994), 137-148.

'Dickens's "The Signalman"', in *The Explicator*, 53/1 (1994), 26-29.

'Physiognomy in Stendhal's Novels: "La Science de Lavater" or "Croyez après cela aux physionomies"?', in *Studia Romanica et Anglica Zagrabiensia*, 39 (1994), 59-76.

'Lavater and Physiognomy in English Fiction 1790-1832', in *Eighteenth-Century Fiction*, 7/3 (1995), 293-310.

Book review of *La communication non verbale avant la lettre*, by Anne-Marie Drouin-Hans, in *Isis*, 87/2 (1996), 340-341.

'Charles Dickens's "The Signalman": A Case of Partial Insanity?', in *History of Psychiatry*, 8 (1997), 421-432.

'"Know How to Decipher a Countenance": Physiognomy in Thomas Hardy's Fiction', in *The Thomas Hardy Year Book*, 27 (1998), 43-60.

Book review of *Der exzentrische Blick. Gespräch über Physiognomik*, ed. Claudia Schmölders, in *History of Psychiatry*, 9/2 (1998), 257-259.

'"The Lines and Lights of the Human Countenance": Physiognomy in George Eliot's Fiction', in *George Eliot—George Henry Lewes Studies*, 36 & 37 (1999), 29-58.

Book review of *Der exzentrische Blick. Gespräch über Physiognomik*, ed. Claudia Schmölders, in *Isis*, 91/2 (2000), 328-329.

'The Presentation of Herr von S. in *Die Judenbuche*', in *The German Quarterly*, 73/4 (2000), 337-350.

'Some Reflections on Lavater's Physiognomic Analyses of Two Engravings of David von Orelli', in *Gegen Unwissenheit und Finsternis: Johann Caspar von Orelli (1787-1849) und die Kultur seiner Zeit*, ed. Michele C. Ferrari (Zurich: Chronos, 2000), 57-70.

'Animals in *Wuthering Heights*', in *Brontë Studies*, 27/2 (2002), 121-130.

'"Faith in the Hand of Nature": Physiognomy in Sir Walter Scott's Fiction', in *Studies in Scottish Literature*, 33 & 34 (2004), 223-246.

'Lavater's Influence on Sir Walter Scott: A Tacit Assumption?', in *Physiognomy in Profile*, ibid., 109-120.

'The Parameters of Reason in *Wuthering Heights*', in *Brontë Studies*, 30/3 (2005), 231-242.

'"Nelly, I *am* Heathcliff!": The Problem of "Identification" in *Wuthering Heights*', in *The Midwest Quarterly*, 47/2 (2006), 167-181.

'The Role of Religion in *Wuthering Heights*', in *Brontë Studies*, 32/1 (2007), 41-55.

'Masters and Servants in *Wuthering Heights*', in *Brontë Studies*, 33/1 (2008), 44-53.

'Eating and Drinking in *Wuthering Heights*', in *Brontë Studies*, 34/1 (2009), 57-66.

'*Wuthering Heights*: An Amoral Novel?', in *Brontë Studies*, 35/3 (2010), 194-207.

'Physiognomy and the Treatment of Love in *Shirley*', in *Brontë Studies*, 36/3 (2011), 263-276.

'The Workings of Memory in *Wuthering Heights*', in *Brontë Studies*, 37/1 (2012), 10-18.

'Aesthetic Attitudes in *Wuthering Heights*', in *Brontë Studies*, 37/1 (2012), 63-74.

'Physiognomy in Anne Brontë's Fiction', in *Brontë Studies*, 37/3 (2012), 227-237.

'Physiognomy and Identity in *Villette*', in *Brontë Studies*, 38/1 (2013), 42-53.

'Thematic Functions of Fire in *Wuthering Heights*', in *Brontë Studies*, 38/2 (2013), 126-136.

'The Power of the Spoken Word in *Wuthering Heights*', in *Brontë Studies*, 39/1 (2014), 58-70.

'The Presentation of Hareton Earnshaw in *Wuthering Heights*', in *Brontë Studies*, 39/2 (2014), 118-129.

'The Presentation of Isabella in *Wuthering Heights*', in *Brontë Studies*, 39/3 (2014), 191-201.

'Facets of Time Consciousness in *Wuthering Heights*', in *Brontë Studies*, 40/1 (2015), 11-21.

'House and Home in *Wuthering Heights*', in *Brontë Studies*, 40/3 (2015), 229-239.

'Weather in *Wuthering Heights*', in *Brontë Studies*, 41/1 (2016), 39-47.

'Clothes in *Wuthering Heights*', in *Brontë Studies*, 41/3 (2016), 239-248.

'Physiognomy and the Treatment of Beauty in *Jane Eyre*', in *Brontë Studies*, 41/4 (2016), 300-311.

'The Presentation of the Second Catherine in *Wuthering Heights*', in *Brontë Studies*, 42/1 (2017), 26-36.

'"He's more myself than I am": The Problem of Comparisons in *Wuthering Heights*', in *Brontë Studies*, 42/2 (2017), 109-117.

'The Presentation of Edgar Linton in *Wuthering Heights*', in *Brontë Studies*, 42/4 (2017), 312-320.

'The Presentation of Mr Kenneth in *Wuthering Heights*', in *Brontë Studies*, 43/2 (2018), 147-155.

'The Presentation of Joseph in *Wuthering Heights*', in *Brontë Studies*, 43/3 (2018), 188-197.

'Rooms in *Wuthering Heights*', in *Brontë Studies*, 43/4 (2018), 300-310.

'The Presentation of Two Housekeepers in *Wuthering Heights*', in *Brontë Studies*, 45/3 (2020), 272-281.

'Violence in *Wuthering Heights*', in *Brontë Studies*, 46/3 (2021), 262-273.

'Weeping and Wailing in *Wuthering Heights*', in *Brontë Studies*, 47/3 (2022), 174-185.

'An Appraisal of Catherine and Heathcliff's Love Relationship', in *Brontë Studies*, 47/3 (2022), 202-213.

'The Presentation of Nelly Dean as a Servant in *Wuthering Heights*', in *Brontë Studies*, 48/1-2 (2023), 23-32.

'Gimmerton in *Wuthering Heights*', in *Brontë Studies*, 48/1-2 (2023), 5-13.

'Books in *Wuthering Heights*', in *Brontë Studies*, 48/1-2 (2023), 14-22.

'The Presentation of the First Catherine in *Wuthering Heights*', in *Brontë Studies*, 48/3 (2023), 261-270.

(Articles reprinted)

'Heathcliff's Monomania', in *Readings on Wuthering Heights*, ed. Hayley R. Mitchell (San Diego, CA: Greenhaven Press, 1999), 102-110.

'Physiognomical Awareness in the Nineteenth-Century European Novel' (excerpted from *Physiognomy in the European Novel*), in *Nineteenth-Century Literature Criticism*, vol. 212, ed. Kathy D. Darrow (Detroit: Gale, Cengage Learning, 2009), 284-301.

'Physiognomy in *Wuthering Heights*', in *Nineteenth-Century Literature Criticism*, ibid., 329-334.

'Eating and Drinking in *Wuthering Heights*', in *Wuthering Heights*, ed. Sunita Mishra (Hyderabad: Orient Blackswan, 2011), 324-337.

'Masters and Servants in *Wuthering Heights*', in *Brontë Studies* (Special Issue) 38/4 (2013), "Signs of the Times: The Brontës and Contemporary Society, A Retrospective Collection of Essays from *Brontë Society Transactions* and *Brontë Studies*", 320-329.